MIDDLE POWER, MIDDLE KINGDOM

DAVID MULRONEY

MIDDLE POWER, MIDDLE KINGDOM

WHAT CANADIANS NEED TO KNOW ABOUT CHINA IN THE 21ST CENTURY

ALLEN
LANE

ALLEN LANE
an imprint of Penguin Canada Books Inc., a Penguin Random House Company

Published by the Penguin Group
Penguin Canada Books Inc., 90 Eglinton Avenue East, Suite 700,
Toronto, Ontario, Canada M4P 2Y3

Penguin Group (USA) LLC, 375 Hudson Street, New York, New York 10014, U.S.A.
Penguin Books Ltd, 80 Strand, London WC2R 0RL, England
Penguin Ireland, 25 St Stephen's Green, Dublin 2, Ireland (a division of Penguin Books Ltd)
Penguin Group (Australia), 707 Collins Street, Melbourne, Victoria 3008, Australia
(a division of Pearson Australia Group Pty Ltd)
Penguin Books India Pvt Ltd, 11 Community Centre, Panchsheel Park,
New Delhi – 110 017, India
Penguin Group (NZ), 67 Apollo Drive, Rosedale, Auckland 0632, New Zealand
(a division of Pearson New Zealand Ltd)
Penguin Books (South Africa) (Pty) Ltd, 24 Sturdee Avenue, Rosebank,
Johannesburg 2196, South Africa

Penguin Books Ltd, Registered Offices: 80 Strand, London WC2R 0RL, England

First published 2015

1 2 3 4 5 6 7 8 9 10 (RRD)

Copyright © David Mulroney, 2015

Manufactured in the U.S.A.

LIBRARY AND ARCHIVES CANADA CATALOGUING IN PUBLICATION

Mulroney, David, author
Middle power, middle kingdom : What Canadians need to know
about China in the 21st century / David Mulroney.

Includes bibliographical references and index.
ISBN 978-0-670-06818-0 (bound)

1. Canada—Foreign relations—China. 2. China—Foreign
relations—Canada. I. Title.

FC251.C5M84 2015   327.71051   C2014-907747-5

eBook ISBN 978-0-14-319439-2

Visit the Penguin Canada website at **www.penguin.ca**

Special and corporate bulk purchase rates available;
please see **www.penguin.ca/corporatesales** or call 1-800-810-3104.

For Janet, the ultimate traveller.

Contents

Preface

This book represents my best effort at facing up to an unpleasant possibility. It began to take shape in my mind about ten years ago, after I was thoroughly rattled by a passage in the opening pages of *Whitehall*, Peter Hennessy's classic account of how government works in Britain. Hennessy explains how the pace of change in society can exceed the ambitions and abilities of well-intentioned public servants. He writes, "It is not much fun in your Indian Summer to have to endure well publicised claims ... that you have presided over thirty years of failure and that nothing short of a transfusion of new blood and new methods will suffice if your country is to survive the result of your life's work."[1]

I retired after more than thirty years feeling profoundly discouraged by what I saw as a steady drift in Canadian foreign policy, most manifest in an inclination to elevate rhetoric and image over strategy and substance, and in a marked preference for seeing the world—and Canada as an actor within it—as we want it to be rather than how it is. I could have stayed on, taken another assignment or two after Beijing, and continued to try to make a contribution from within the system. But I felt the need to step out, to find a space where I could think and read and talk to people as I tried to make sense of the direction we've taken and why.

Although I am not about to take sole responsibility for our predicament, I can't entirely absolve myself of all the blame. I was a part of the system, a senior official, developer and implementer of policy, and a briefer of ministers and prime ministers. But as I progressed in my career, gaining experience and expertise, I found that the possibility of shaping policy was actually diminishing as the gulf between the professional, non-partisan public service and our political masters widened, and as the welcome for the public servant's contribution of fearless advice and loyal implementation was steadily reduced to just the second half of that pairing. Although much of the blame for this serious systemic failure falls on the master, the servant is also left thinking of opportunities lost, challenges unmet and conflicts avoided. Retirement and reflection don't always contribute to tranquility. The best I can do is offer my own, personal assessment of what's going wrong and what we might do to correct it.

My sense of accountability prompted me to depart from the usual course for public servants in retirement: either remaining faithful to the code of *omertà*, taking not just their secrets but just about everything else they know to the grave, or waiting for twenty-five or thirty years, until what they have to say is solely of historical interest. I wanted to make my case while there is still a chance to change our course. But in doing so, I have done my best to remain faithful to the promises I made when I entered the Canadian Foreign Service in 1981. What were shared with me as official secrets remain secret. I have also protected the private conversations and confidences that are the connecting links between public servants and their political masters.

But I have noticed that, out of a commendable faithfulness to these strictures, and influenced by the tendency to classify everything that happens in government as secret, public servants are increasingly reluctant to share anything about their work. That's unhealthy and ultimately undermines public awareness and support for the sophisticated balance in government, between those who are elected by Canadians and those who serve as non-partisan professionals, providing both continuity and dispassionate, expert advice. Instead, politicians, regardless of their political persuasion, are now much less squeamish about breaking old conventions relating to where ultimate accountability lies. So public servants, while obligingly silent, are increasingly held responsible for any and all problems. In fact, public service, equated in partisan discourse with lethargy, risk avoidance and self-seeking, is increasingly perceived *as* the problem.

This silence is having an impact on broader awareness among Canadians about how government functions and just what public servants do. Almost inevitably, at some point during the many talks I have given since retirement about Canada's work in China, an audience member has made the comment that he or she was unaware of all the things foreign service officers do for their fellow citizens. If nothing else, this book gives me a chance to share the story of the Canadian Foreign Service more broadly, to introduce colleagues who are, to borrow the words of Joseph Conrad, "worthy of my undying regard."[2]

My own views about China and how to manage our relationship with it have changed over time. While my affection and respect for China and its people remain undiminished, my thinking about the nature of its political system has hardened and darkened over the years. My great fear is that my generally dim view of the latter will be taken as my judgment of the former, too. In this, I subscribe fully to the wise words of that brilliant sinologist Pierre Ryckmans, who, working under his pen name of Simon Leys, wrote, "As always, in China, individual thoughtfulness and subtlety victoriously counterbalance the stupidity and obscurantism of the system."[3]

Prologue

It took only about five minutes for me to walk east from my office at the University of Toronto to that fashionable stretch of Bloor Street where the Montblanc outlet and other high-end stores are located. My mission was simple: I was going to replace a wallet I had given to my wife as a birthday present. Although her tastes are very modest, she prized the wallet for being both elegant and functional, an exotic amid the workaday contents of her purse.

She hadn't had much time to enjoy it. It was stolen from our backpack while we were travelling a few months later. I was the custodian of the backpack and was embarrassed and annoyed. Janet simply wanted her wallet back. The original had been purchased while we were still living in Beijing. I had gone to the Montblanc outlet located in Oriental Plaza, a vast shopping mall that runs along the north side of Chang'an, the Avenue of Eternal Peace. The mall takes up an entire block, ending at the Wangfujing shopping street just east of Tiananmen Square.

Many people who have visited China are struck by the sheer amount of retail space under construction. Although it is typically assumed that everything in China needs to be built on a bigger scale than anywhere else, the sight of multiple malls going up in the same neighbourhood seems to defy common sense. That suspicion is quickly confirmed by walking through vast complexes housing an array of similarly deserted stores.

What distinguishes Oriental Plaza from many other Beijing malls is the fact that it is usually very busy. In addition to the retail space, it houses office towers and a luxury hotel. Pedestrians often choose its climate-controlled walkways over Chang'an, which, despite its soothing name, is vast and impersonal at foot level, a traffic-clogged canyon feeding cars into the square that is the very heart of the capital and the country.

I am a terrible shopper and try to get in, make my purchase and get out as quickly as possible. This Beijing Montblanc outlet was ominously busy, but I was served quickly and efficiently, steered through an almost bewildering array of choices to the wallet I thought Janet would like best. My most vivid memory is that the salesperson put on white gloves to show me the wallets. I had never before bought anything that required the donning of white gloves, and I was deeply impressed. It was a done deal.

Months later, in the Montblanc store half a world away on Bloor Street, I again walked past the counters displaying pens and cufflinks and began inspecting the wallets. It was a wintry weekday in Toronto but the season of New Year in the Chinese world. As I looked, I was lulled by a familiar murmur, something that caused my present to merge subtly with my past. I gradually lost track of where I was. Everyone else in the Toronto store was speaking in the standard Mandarin of Beijing. The sense of déjà vu carried on to the cash register. The salesperson completed the transaction by offering me candies in shiny wrappers and a red envelope containing an invitation to enter a lucky draw for small prizes, things that retailers commonly present at Chinese New Year in Beijing.

As I walked back along Bloor Street I heard more Chinese than English, and watched as Mandarin-speaking shoppers surged in and out of the very expensive stores. I later made it a habit to drop in to luxury stores on Bloor Street and in Toronto's high-end malls to ask salespeople about the importance of Chinese customers to their business. I learned to reframe my question slightly to focus on the number of customers who speak Chinese, many of whom, it turns out, charge products to credit cards with Toronto addresses. Sales staff typically reported that Chinese-speaking shoppers represent at least 50 percent, and often far more, of their customer base. Such shoppers, they added, tend to be the only people snapping up the $3000 shoes and the $5000 handbags, often purchasing several items at a time. The people at Toronto's tourism promotion agency told me that virtually all Chinese tour buses make a shopping stop on trendy Yorkville Avenue, home to even more luxury outlets.

In the late winter of 2013, Torontonians were eagerly anticipating the arrival of a pair of giant pandas from China. But they were paying less attention to a far more important, more transformative flow of visitors from the People's Republic. Canada's stock was rising in China. It was rising among those who had the money and freedom to travel, and among those who wanted a safe and highly respected destination for the education of their children. And it was rising among those who wanted a second address in a healthy and politically stable location, a place far removed from the pollution and congestion of Beijing and Shanghai.

That same year, describing China's appetite for luxury products, the *Financial Times* would comment dryly, "China has vast potential for producing large numbers of aspirational consumers."[1] The ability of its citizens to satisfy such aspirations in places like Toronto, New York, London or Tokyo isn't the only manifestation of China's lengthening reach. Almost everything emanating from China—from its economic power to its growing impact on global security, the environment, health and food safety—is happening on a scale and at a pace that is unprecedented. The reverberations are being felt around the world.

FOR CANADIANS, exposure to China's unbridled exuberance and seemingly limitless appetite, to its dreams and ambitions, and to its long-nurtured fears and resentments is an entirely new phenomenon. It is so new that we are still not paying attention to the sweep and significance of what is happening, much less thinking clearly and carefully about how to respond.

I've spent the months since my return from China reflecting on this development, and talking to a cross-section of Canadians—teachers, tour operators and real estate agents; people who sell lobsters, market milk and purvey fancy purses; bankers, traders and investors; doctors, lawyers and architects; federal, provincial and municipal officials; China boosters and China bashers—all of whom are experiencing the transformative impact of China's long, global reach.

I have distilled from their comments and observations, and from my own professional experience, some ideas about how we might do a better job—a more thoughtfully self-interested job—of managing our side of the relationship with China. This is something that I will come back to. But I want to begin by exploring the phenomenon that struck me most forcefully in the course of my travels and conversations: the extent to which the energy generated by China's dramatic rise is rippling across our daily Canadian life.

FACING OUR FUTURE

ONE

A Middle Power in Middle Age

Canada's Department of Foreign Affairs, Trade and Development has its headquarters in the Lester B. Pearson Building in Ottawa. The structure's distinctive design is a testament to those who believe that public buildings should be something more than mere office space. Although it fits neatly within an Ottawa skyline designed to give pride of place to the Peace Tower, the Pearson Building manages to create an impression. Viewed from the Quebec side, it seems a natural feature of the site it occupies above the Ottawa River, like slabs of rock that have been stacked by the rise and fall of the water.

My attachment to the Pearson Building is probably due to the fact that I more or less grew up with it. Although I was raised in Toronto, I spent part of each summer in Ottawa. My great-grandmother still lived in the house an even earlier generation of the family had built in Lower Town, home to Ottawa's working-class Irish and French. I was in my teens when they broke ground for the Pearson Building, and I watched it come to tower over the crowded streets of Lower Town. Not surprisingly, it loomed large in my career hopes and dreams.

Getting into the Canadian Foreign Service involved writing an exam and surviving an interview with representatives from what were then its three branches: Foreign Policy (what most people have in mind when they think of what diplomats do), Trade and Immigration. It took me a couple of tries writing the exam before I got to the interview stage. On the big day I awoke suffering from a headache and flu-like symptoms. I soldiered on as best I could, then amazed the interview board by fainting in mid-sentence, cracking my head on the board-room table.

The interviewers were good sports, and offered me a second chance a week later. The key question they asked me dealt with the still-grim situation in Cambodia—this was the late fall of 1980. Cambodia's descent into the killing fields had been the subject of a lengthy piece in *The New York Times* earlier in the year, something that I had read with great interest. I answered confidently and made it through the interview.

I was offered jobs in both the foreign policy stream and the trade stream. All along I had been interested in foreign policy, but I found the pitch from the trade people much more lively and welcoming. So, with a few misgivings, I changed my plans and opted to become a trade commissioner, meaning that my work abroad would involve helping Canadian companies win business overseas.

As it turned out, I benefitted from one of the reforms of the Trudeau era. The prime minister had been worried that too many Canadian ambassadors he met on his travels seemed unfamiliar with trade promotion and uncomfortable in the presence of Canadian business people, so he insisted that all young diplomats get at least some trade experience. As a quid pro quo, trade commissioners were encouraged to take on at least some foreign policy work as a prepara-tion for their own ambassadorial ambitions. I welcomed this chance to broaden my professional horizons and made sure that I got experience in foreign policy as my career progressed.

In those days junior officers were expected to do whatever they were told. So, on my first assignment, to Seoul, South Korea, although I was mainly involved in helping Canadian lumber companies and coal exporters win contracts in Korea, I was also expected to cover consular work—meaning assistance to travelling Canadians—whenever an extra hand was needed. I remember visiting a prison in Seoul to check in with a young Canadian man who had been incarcerated for smuggling gold into the country. After listening to his compelling protestations of innocence, I dutifully checked on his treatment, health, diet and general well-being. As I was leaving, I asked him if there was anything special he wanted. He asked for a recent copy of *The Globe and Mail*, adding "and make sure you send the whole paper." When I gave him a quizzical look, he curtly shot back, "Gold prices."

My first ambassador was a remote and forbidding figure. While he did agree to invite the new officers to a welcoming lunch at his residence, the meal concluded with him advising us that there was no need to return the invitation. Although there were only nine Canadian diplomats on the staff (I was the ninth and the lowliest in terms of seniority), I spoke to him no more than three or four times during the course of that first year. These were not lengthy conversations and invariably ended with a "Yes, sir" from me. He was the absolute authority in the embassy and was, like many heads of mission in those days, a forceful and concise writer. He enjoyed the ambassadorial prerogative of adding his last name to the close of the telegrams carrying his observations back to Ottawa, a lingering reminder of the very personal role and responsibility of the envoy. He was trusted as a professional, non-partisan and deeply experienced advisor to the government.

I was lucky enough to spend the majority of my career working in or on Asia. It's a region that has captured my imagination and affections since my arrival at the port of Singapore as a backpacker setting out on a cross-Asia adventure in early 1975. After my posting in Seoul, I served in Shanghai, Kuala Lumpur, Taipei and Beijing. I also spent three years on leave from government to serve as executive director of the Canada China Business Council. My postings alternated with assignments back in Ottawa. Over time, I got to run the Asia Pacific branch of Foreign Affairs, then to serve as the foreign policy advisor to the prime minister, and later to help run Foreign Affairs as its associate deputy minister, a period that mainly saw me focused on our mission in Afghanistan.

Foreign service, with its itinerant lifestyle, is very much a family affair. My oldest son started preschool in a room in the British consulate in Shanghai, hiked through the jungles of Malaysia with his Scout troop, and still hangs out with his Taiwanese high school pals.

I am very proud of my association with Canada's foreign service, and grateful for the rich experiences it provided. I would like to be able to say that I left government service confident that the country is on the right track in terms of its approach to foreign policy, that we have a clear vision for Canada in the world, and the will and expertise to pursue it. But over the thirty-plus years of my career I have witnessed a national loss of focus, a lack of seriousness and ambition when it comes to making our way in the world. What makes this even more troubling is that this growing national ambivalence is particularly evident in our relationship with China, a country that is becoming an increasingly important shaper of our own future. Indeed, one of the reasons I retired was to take the time to think more carefully about this phenomenon, and to secure the freedom to speak and write about it.

Three factors contribute to what I see as our declining performance in steering an international course for Canada. The first is persistent confusion about our role as a middle power. Because our core economic and security interests have been safely embedded in a stable and largely comfortable relationship with the United States, we have felt free to choose where and how we engage elsewhere on the international scene. This has enabled us to play and, indeed, to help invent the role of middle power. The vocation has been well defined by Gareth Evans, former foreign minister of Australia, another country that has aspired to middle-power status. According to Evans, "Middle Power diplomacy is, in short, the kind of diplomacy which can, and should, be practised by states which are not big or strong enough, either in their own region or the wider world, to impose their policy preferences on anyone else, but who do recognize that there are international policy tasks that need to be accomplished if the world around them is to be safer, saner, more just and more prosperous (with all the potential this has, in turn, to affect their own interests); and who have sufficient capacity and credibility to be able to advance those tasks."[1]

Canada's middle-power vocation has mainly been pursued through a network of international organizations, with the United Nations at its heart. And just as Evans delicately places in parentheses the possibility that making the world a better place may pay dividends at home, we have been similarly circumspect about making a direct connection between the global good and our own interests. That may be because of our natural generosity, but it could also be because we've been so confident that our core interests are already safely protected in our North American cocoon. At times, we have seemed unaware of the connection between our global activism and our national interest, even in its long-term sense. As former Canadian diplomat Arthur Andrew, writing about Canadian diplomacy in the years after World War II, admitted, "It was almost as if Canada had no national interests that were uniquely its own, that all this country wanted was a world at peace and it would take it from there."[2] Of course, we actually *did* have national interests, such as growing our economy and warding off any threats posed to Canada by a belligerent and ideologically inimical Soviet Union. But all of that was largely advanced through our relationship with the United States.

Many came to see participation in the UN as a uniquely Canadian vocation, an end in itself. We began to lose track of the essential connection between Canadian foreign policy and our own long-term interests. This could be forgiven as a delightful eccentricity as long as the United States maintained its role as the engine of global economic growth and the enforcer of global order. But things are changing quickly. As important as the U.S. continues to be, this long-reigning superpower is increasingly required to share power with others. The days of free-riding in an American-dominated world are over. How well we manage our foreign policy has a direct impact on our own ambitions for the future. The road to prosperity, security and well-being—for us and the world around us—increasingly runs through the effective engagement of major new powers such as India, South Africa, Brazil and, most important of all, China.

But we seem unconvinced of the need to engage any of these countries consistently, seriously and with specific Canadian objectives in view, and are particularly ambivalent when it comes to China. While that national hesitation is perhaps understandable given how unlike us China is, it represents an increasingly costly and worrisome failure on our part. And even if we were convinced of the need for a more thoughtful engagement, I'm not confident that we have the ability to craft and deliver a foreign policy capable of addressing these new priorities.

This brings us to the second problem undermining our ability to steer a course for Canada in the world: the increasingly chaotic and uncoordinated way in which we attempt to "manage" international relations. The price we pay for our inability to bring coordination and purpose to our international activities was brought home to me most forcefully during my work on Afghanistan, when it was my job to bring about much-needed cooperation among the various Canadian players. But it was also a daily challenge for me when I lived in Beijing.

I played several roles as Canada's ambassador. I represented the Canadian government in meetings with Chinese officials. I also helped introduce Canada to Chinese people through my travels, public speaking, media interviews and outreach via social media. And each week I met and briefed many of the Canadian business people, journalists, artists, teachers, athletes and human rights advocates whose visits make up the human dimension of the relationship.

But what I saw as my most important job was helping to build consensus in the Canadian government about the key objectives that we absolutely need to achieve in the relationship with China. This meant thinking hard about how China can contribute to Canadian prosperity through trade and investment; how we can work with China to promote global health, food safety and environmental protection; what we can do to encourage China to play a peaceful and constructive role in the world; and how we should engage China on fundamental questions about human rights.

I came to see my job as that of "connector of last resort," and spent most of my time getting people at the embassy to share information, work together, and stay focused on a very few big, long-term objectives for Canada. Getting these priorities right invariably required the talents, energy and experience of multiple departments working closely together. But that was already something of an alien concept in Ottawa.

Government, like just about every other part of Canadian life, has become more international. When I worked in the embassy in South Korea in the early 1980s, the ambassador was the boss of a small team of Foreign Service officers, who reported directly to him, and a military attaché, who was expected to be a team player. By the time I became ambassador in Beijing, more than twenty-five years later, I was the nominal head of a group of more than sixty Canadians drawn from more than ten federal departments and three provinces. Such broad representation should actually be a good thing, and would have been but for the fact that it has emerged without any planning about how to manage it, and without any inclination by anyone in Ottawa to show real, coordinating leadership. As a result, the bureaucracy has reverted to its natural preference for turf protection, with each department going it alone. Even among the Foreign Affairs contingent at the embassy in Beijing, officers were micromanaged by individual sections operating in isolation in distant Ottawa.

Fortunately, by the time I became ambassador, I already held the rank of deputy minister, and could insist on a higher degree of collegiality. But even with that seniority, getting even a modest degree of coordination was a full-time job. More junior ambassadors simply get shunted aside. Nor was there anyone senior back in Ottawa who spent much time thinking about the priorities for Canada in its relationship with China, much less coordinating our assets and resources to achieve them. That left it to me to fill that vacuum in leadership from afar via late-night phone calls and return visits to Canada, elbowing my way into issues and projects that departments normally managed in isolation.

Think of what happens when part of Ottawa decides that it wants a major increase in the flow of students or tourists from China, while another part of Ottawa, unconsulted and unconcerned, determines that we need to make it more difficult to obtain a visa to come to Canada. Once, in Taiwan, I had to recall two officers who were heading to the airport at the same time in separate cars. One, from the immigration department, was eager to help Taiwanese officials prosecute a Canadian who was accused of being part of a fake passport ring. The other, from our consular team, was hurrying to meet that same Canadian, whom he saw as a client needing our assistance. I made it clear that assistance, notably helping the Canadian obtain basic legal advice, came first.

But at least when I ran things in Taiwan I was asked to comment on the performance of the various Canadian staff working in our Taipei office, regardless of which departments they came from in Ottawa. By the time I got to Beijing, this practice had been abandoned. I sent in my views to various parts of Ottawa anyway, because I thought such oversight important when it came to the many senior people working at the embassy, at a hefty cost to the Canadian taxpayer. I never heard back, nor did I ever get the sense that my views were appreciated.

This can be dismissed as bureaucratic trivia, but to me it pointed to a larger issue. The federal public service has a problem with leadership. Attempting to exert it is increasingly seen as intrusive and undemocratic. Broad consensus, no matter how unambitious and tenuously achieved, is always preferred. That's a recipe for mediocrity and muddle in foreign policy and in just about every other dimension of government. My great worry is that on those rare occasions when Ottawa does think of foreign policy, it is seen as the sum total of what every department and agency has on its international wish list.

Unlike the professional public service, politicians don't have a problem identifying and pursuing specific goals when they venture outside of Canada. The problem is that these don't always have much to do with foreign policy. What I see as the third impediment to advancing our international interests more effectively is the steady encroachment of domestic political considerations into our foreign policy calculations.

It would be naive and undemocratic to argue that domestic politics has no place in our foreign policy. But political leaders need to rely on something more than the most recent polling data in navigating international issues. Consider the growing obsession with photo-ops, the tendency to see foreign leaders as mere props on a set designed wholly for Canadian audiences. There is also our increasing preference for rhetoric—the more extreme the better—over more careful behind-the-scenes engagement. The resulting "megaphone diplomacy" is gratifying to some audiences at home, but it erodes and undercuts whatever real influence Canada might have had.

The most obvious manifestation of our lack of seriousness is the tendency to use regional travel as a form of outreach to politically important ethnic communities in Canada. Our diversity is an undeniable Canadian advantage, and should form part of the briefing we use to promote investment, tourism and education to foreign audiences, particularly when we want to make a point about how welcoming Canada is. But this shouldn't be among the main topics on our agenda when leaders meet, nor should the accompanying delegations from Canada be so relentlessly tailored to the ethnicity of the country being visited. The prime minister of India is aware of the fact that there are many people of Indian origin in Canada. And the premier of China is similarly well briefed about the presence of Chinese diaspora communities across our country. Indeed, given China's experience of waves of emigration over the centuries, its leadership is distinctly unsentimental about the vast Chinese diaspora around the world. Canadian politicians have encountered this ho-hum response from foreign leaders. But they're far more interested in the coverage on the 6 P.M. news back home and, most important, in Canada's ethnic media.

Part of the problem is that we have lost track of the necessary division of labour between partisan political staffers, who, with an eye to the next election, keep politicians focused on their immediate political agendas, and public servants, who take the long view, providing professional, non-partisan advice to the minister or prime minister of the day. Both perspectives are important, but we're losing the necessary balance between them. Short-term political advice is winning out over seasoned long-term viewpoints.

I have had to discourage political staffers from using Canadian members of Parliament of Chinese origin as interpreters at events in China. Although it makes for a touching video clip back home, it is much less effective in China. For one thing, despite being of Chinese ethnicity, such MPs often struggle to speak the standard Mandarin used by their audiences. For another, people in China are likely to be far more impressed by the very *absence* of hoopla, by how normal and unexceptional it is for Canadians of Chinese origin to be elected to Parliament. Positive impressions are reinforced by seeing them act like MPs, not interpreters.

As proud as we are of our diversity, we need to remember that leaders in powerful and important countries such as India and China are focused on serious international issues. They expect our leaders to be similarly focused. In fact, we have an interest in ensuring that the Indians and the Chinese think of us as something more than a home

to large, politically sensitive diaspora communities, especially since neither government is shy about wading into those same communities in
Canada when they want to snoop on or admonish their former citizens. This tendency also leads to some bizarre incidents that can hijack
agendas. I accompanied Prime Minister Paul Martin on a visit to Asia
in early 2005. He was joined by a number of Indo-Canadian MPs who
happened to be Sikhs. At the outset of the visit, the MPs were embarrassed by an article written by a Sikh religious leader in India deplor-
ing the trend toward accepting same-sex marriage, which at that time
happened to be the subject of a bill working its way through Canada's
Parliament. This in turn became a major issue when the prime minister came to face the press with his Indian counterpart.

I can appreciate that Canadian politics can't be left completely
behind when a prime minister travels, but a flurry of questions to the
Canadian PM about how same-sex marriage legislation would affect
religious groups in Canada ate up much of the press availability, leaving the Indian prime minister watching in confused silence. Finally, a
Canadian reporter put a question to the Indian PM: what did *he* think
of same-sex marriage for India? After a lengthy pause, the Indian
leader politely suggested that it wasn't an issue for which there would
be much "appreciation" in his country.

Despite the onrush of globalization and the transformation of
Canadian society through immigration, it's as if we've become less
curious about our place in the world, and steadily more focused on
our own affairs. This is our collective failure, but one that has been
exacerbated by a lack of political will and leadership.

WE HAVE NOT ALWAYS lacked visionary leaders capable of
helping us to understand our place in the world. Pierre Trudeau was
famous for his energetic if eclectic internationalism. My only chance
to meet him came long after his retirement. He was visiting China

as a distinguished advisor at a special Beijing meeting of the Bank of Montreal's board. I was struck by the way Chinese guests, not expecting to encounter Trudeau, were almost overwhelmed in his presence. In their enthusiasm, they made it clear they were meeting someone whose leadership had produced the formula that made possible China's diplomatic relations not just with Canada but also with the many countries that followed our lead.

At the time of Trudeau's death in 2000, I was running the office that looks after Canada's interests in Taiwan in the absence of official diplomatic relations. That we still had interests in Taiwan, and that we had been able to preserve and advance them even after recognizing China, was largely due to the elegant and simple formula for recognition that Trudeau had championed. (We simply took note of China's claim that Taiwan is an inalienable part of China's territory.) Canadian government offices around the world set out a book of condolences to mark Mr. Trudeau's death. In a special gesture of respect and affection, Trudeau's book was accompanied by a single rose in a vase. I stayed in the lobby of the Taiwan office to greet visitors. Throughout the afternoon, I heard a steady stream of very personal testimonials about how Trudeau's vision and style had influenced them and shaped their appreciation of Canada.

Under Trudeau, Canada launched two initiatives aimed at animating our broader diplomacy. One of them, his controversial "Third Option," would have seen Canada reinforce its links with important partners other than the United States, meaning Europe and Japan. But it languished and faded without much serious effort having been expended to advance it. For many pragmatic Canadians, the Third Option was not about securing our future, but instead represented, at least insofar as Europe was concerned, a dubious move in the direction of a vanishing past. Trudeau's other great foreign policy initiative was, of course, the establishment of diplomatic relations with China. Here, as we will see, the challenge was reversed, with Trudeau looking far into the future, farther indeed than most Canadians have yet been able to see.

Another internationally minded prime minister, Brian Mulroney, possessed legendary diplomatic skills, something I had the chance to discover first-hand. Despite the shared last name, there is no close family connection, though we are both part of the Irish diaspora that settled along the Saint Lawrence Valley in Quebec (his family) before moving into Ontario (mine). I never had the chance to speak with him until I was well on in my career. In 2006 I was assigned to the Privy Council Office (PCO) to serve as foreign and defence policy advisor to Prime Minister Harper. On Boxing Day of that year, former U.S. president Gerald Ford died. I was asked to phone former prime minister Mulroney to see whether he could attend the funeral on behalf of Canada. I reached him in the midst of his Christmas getaway with his family. But he was unperturbed and readily agreed to attend.

Just after New Year's, my assistant at the PCO stuck her head in my office to tell me that Brian Mulroney was on the phone. Assuming that it was my brother, Brian, I asked her to tell him I would phone him back. She hesitated, and then said, it's *the* Brian Mulroney. I took the call. What followed was a twenty-minute tour-de-force briefing, a concise and highly relevant report on what the key international guests who gathered for the funeral had said about topics that were of current interest to Canada. It was so complete that I had no need to ask questions when it was finished. I remember that my note-taking hand was stiff and sore when the call ended.

THE LAST PART OF MY CAREER was spent during the Harper years, a period that has featured instances of bracing and much-needed realism in the management of international relations. But it is also a period that has been undermined by partisanship and complicated by strange and sudden bouts of silence in the face of controversial issues and difficult decisions.

Although, as his foreign policy advisor in 2006, I was privileged to have frequent, direct access to Prime Minister Harper when he travelled, the nature of the job had clearly changed under the new government. Previously, the role of foreign policy advisor had been the sole preserve of a highly experienced diplomat whose job was to provide disinterested professional advice to the prime minister of the day, uncoloured by the needs and agendas of the Department of Foreign Affairs. While I played that role to a certain extent, my identity as a public servant meant that I operated at a much greater arm's length. The PM typically introduced me to foreign leaders as his "bureaucratic" foreign policy advisor, a portfolio I shared with a highly partisan Conservative Party staffer who was introduced as his "political" foreign policy advisor. Indeed, one of my main tasks was fending off the more ideologically extreme agendas of my "political" counterpart. I wasn't overly fond of my dreary "bureaucratic" title, which pointed to much greater shifts in thinking about how foreign policy gets done.

Following his 2006 victory over Paul Martin, Stephen Harper immediately challenged the foreign policy status quo. His was, at least in its earliest manifestations, a government of the suburbs and small towns, of small business and small communities. Going or gone were the internationally inclined Red Tories such as Joe Clark, Flora MacDonald and Barbara McDougall. There was to be a new agenda, aimed at returning the country to what were seen as its traditional values and partnerships. We would be guided by core beliefs, would support our true friends, and would speak out against hypocrisy in the international system.

More than once, the prime minister condemned the tendency of "going along to get along." But that, unfortunately, had come to represent at least a part of the daily reality facing those whose job it was to navigate the United Nations. There were fireworks when our ambassador to the UN Conference on Disarmament warmly welcomed the

North Korean diplomat who had, almost unbelievably, been made chair of the conference. The ambassador's welcome, which probably passed unnoticed within the clubby context of the UN system, undermined the condemnation of the appointment that his boss, Foreign Affairs Minister John Baird, had uttered only days before.

A disconnect also existed between the prime minister and his diplomats in relation to our ultimately futile campaign to win a seat as a non-permanent member of the UN Security Council. The prime minister was not originally inclined to pursue this goal. When he did come around, he was frustrated by persistent efforts by Foreign Affairs to discourage him from taking firm measures in support of Israel, an orientation that was at the heart of his and his party's convictions, a core interest. He was told that this would jeopardize our chances of being elected. It didn't help that when he asked why we wanted to win a seat, he would be told, "So that we can advance our core interests." The PM went against his best judgment and agreed to launch a campaign to win the seat. Despite going into the vote with a comfortable margin of "confirmed support," we experienced what a disgruntled Australian ambassador to the UN has called the "rotten lying bastards" phenomenon[3] and went down to an embarrassing defeat.

Perhaps the most prominent example of what the new government saw as a conflict between Canada's reflexive desire to be a good international citizen and the pursuit of our core national interests was our participation in the Kyoto Protocol to the United Nations Framework Convention on Climate Change, which Jean Chrétien's Liberal government had signed, to great acclaim, in 1997. Harper saw this commitment, in which Canada agreed to reduce greenhouse gas emissions from 1990 levels by 2012, as wrong-headed on two counts. First, we had clearly taken on a commitment that was beyond our willingness, if not our ability, to implement. By the time Harper arrived on the scene, we had done almost nothing to meet our target. In fact, our emissions had increased significantly. Second, the protocol failed to include the world's two largest carbon emitters, the U.S. and China, thus putting us at a disadvantage, particularly in terms of our closest neighbour and major economic partner. After much acrimonious internal debate, and after absorbing much criticism from a range of observers, foreign governments among them, we withdrew from the protocol in 2011.

Insisting on paying greater attention to national interest is an obvious and essential part of any successful foreign policy. But unless a country wields unlimited power, it needs to balance ambition with a degree of accommodation. This isn't a case of going along to get along, but it does involve a willingness to listen, build trust, find allies and show some ability to compromise. Instead, we came to take pride in being among the first to close embassies, cut off dialogue and impose sanctions in the face of clearly unacceptable international behaviour. And while our new-found toughness made us the first to pack up and leave, our relatively small size made us among the last to be welcomed back. We seemed in danger of replacing international activism with mere rhetoric. This was risky because, even at the end of the first decade of the twenty-first century, we were still very much a middle power as Gareth Evans would define one: still unable to impose our policy preferences on others, still obliged to work with others to achieve at least some of our objectives.

THE WORLD WAS CHANGING in other ways that called into question the comfortable status quo of Canadian foreign policy. Anyone who was paying even the slightest degree of attention to international affairs could see that powerful new players were coming to prominence, meaning that we were ignoring certain relationships, above and beyond our privileged partnership with the United States, at our peril.

Pressure was building to consider new directions for Canadian diplomacy. This was described by media commentators, business leaders and academics in different ways. Sometimes the target was described as

Asia, sometimes as Northeast Asia (meaning China, Japan and Korea), and sometimes as China and India. Another variant was a call for a BRICS strategy, using the acronym that captures the very diverse but formidable grouping of Brazil, Russia, India, China and South Africa.

The common denominator and energizing force in all these groupings is China. While the United States was almost completely absorbed with costly wars in Iraq and Afghanistan, China was surging to a position of influence and, in some cases, dominance over broad swaths of the global economy. Betting on a super-charged variation of the traditional, export-led development model favoured by Asian Tigers such as Korea, Hong Kong and Taiwan, China's economy had been growing at roughly 10 percent a year for decades. But, unlike the others, its far larger economy was continuing to grow at this pace into the twenty-first century. China's economic and political model enabled it to drive resources to the manufacturing sector and to the infrastructure needed to support it. Entire mountains of Australian iron ore were transformed into steel for airports, bridges, train lines and skyscrapers. Long a dominant force in the manufacture of inexpensive toys, tools and gadgets, China was moving up the technology ladder. It became the world's number one producer of automobiles in 2008. Two years later, China overtook Japan as the world's second-largest economy.

But China's dynamism was more than economic. Leaders in the People's Republic of China (PRC) used America's almost decade-long distraction in Iraq and Afghanistan, and its resulting absence from East Asia, to reinforce China's diplomatic and military power. By the time of the Beijing 2008 Olympic Summer Games, the international press was full of articles about a China that could do no wrong. It was *de rigueur* for foreign visitors to China to sound this same note, often adding a plaintive query about why we weren't able to achieve such wonders in the West. This was a particularly popular refrain as the global economic crisis deepened and China was seen as a lone and very welcome generator of global growth.

While the world was coming to China, China was increasingly coming to the world. Buyers, sellers, investors, tourists, students and immigrants from China pumped life and optimism into battered economies everywhere. Canada was no exception.

THE FIRST DECADE of the twenty-first century represented something of a Chinese rediscovery of Canada as an investment opportunity, an education provider, a vacation destination and a place to shop for property as a hedge against possible unwelcome developments back home. This was happening so quickly that Canadians were essentially playing catch-up, belatedly trying to understand one phase of this process as it was overtaken by another.

Canada's national mood was characterized by what might best be described as ambivalence in the face of these changes. Indeed, in the early years of his time in office, it seemed as if Harper were departing from the generally friendly approach to China that had prevailed, more or less, since the establishment of diplomatic relations in 1970. While Harper was predictably criticized for his lack of enthusiasm, much of the national debate operated on the assumption that the nature and shape of our relationship with China was entirely up to us. But that wasn't at all the case. Chinese investors, traders, students and tourists were eagerly reaching out to us. So, too, was China's government, sometimes in the form of official diplomatic overtures, but also via clandestine methods, including traditional espionage, extensive cyber-attacks, and aggressive efforts to influence or intimidate people in Canada. We couldn't count on the U.S. to shield us from the more problematic and messier aspects of China's rise. America was embroiled in its own larger and far more consequential realignment with China.

The hard truth is that we need to step up our foreign policy game to engage a rising China. We need to invest the kind of time and

attention in the relationship that we have rarely devoted to any relationship beyond our engagement with the United States. And while
our relationship with the U.S. is far more extensive and still much more
important, it is a partnership with a country that is very much like
us. Engaging China intelligently means facing up to a country that is
not only unlike us but also one that sometimes acts in ways that run
counter to our own values and interests.

Of course, there is even more to the issue than that. China is an
increasingly influential, if selective, player within important international organizations, and an all too often disruptive presence outside of them. Working constructively with China one-on-one, and as
a partner in the United Nations and other organizations, is central
to our middle-power agenda for making the world, in the words of
Gareth Evans, "safer, saner, more just and more prosperous."

Managing our relationship with China will require us to think more
carefully about our interests and our assets. And we will need to do a
much better job when it comes to the actual *delivery* of foreign policy.
Instead of simply assuming that the various departments and agencies will organize themselves, we need to ensure that the leadership
is in place to hold people accountable for achieving clearly defined
national objectives. It would be a big help, of course, if we could grow
up and see foreign relations as something more than an extension of
Canadian domestic politics.

We need to grow up in other ways, too. At our worst moments, we
infantilize foreign policy, thinking that we should form relationships
with countries because we like them. There are some aspects of modern China—starting with the nation's record on human rights—that
are undeniably *unlikeable*. These and other differences will generate real
tensions in the Canada–China relationship, and dealing with them will
almost certainly be an increasing challenge for us. But not engaging
China just isn't an option.

CHINA AND
CANADIAN PROSPERITY

TWO

Blue Lobster Tweets

L ittle more than a decade ago, the China Fisheries & Seafood Expo was a relatively modest event in what was still something of a backwater, far removed from the main centres of the international industry. But China Fisheries is now a necessary part of the international circuit for companies seeking to carve out a foothold in the most promising seafood market anywhere. By the summer of 2013, demand from China, coupled with low catches around the world, meant that global fish prices had reached all-time highs.[1]

I visited the show at its setting in the northeastern port city of Qingdao in 2011. That year, the Canadian government was sponsoring a large national stand, with booths for exporters from Atlantic Canada and British Columbia selling products such as lobster, salmon, herring, snow crab, shrimp and prawns. The reason was simple: while traditional markets for Canadian seafood were being flattened by the global economic crisis, demand from China was growing. China's appetite for Canadian seafood was less than half of the demand from the traditional markets of the European Union in 2007. But by 2012, we were selling significantly more to China than we were to *all* of the then twenty-seven countries of the E.U. combined.[2] Better still, Chinese consumers, attracted by Canada's reputation for quality, were open to trying new products, meaning that species that the Canadian industry had previously ignored as having no commercial value were now in demand.

I travelled to the show as part of a delegation led by Canada's then fisheries minister, Keith Ashfield. The group also included embassy chef Rosalyn Ediger, who had become a star on the embassy's increasingly popular weibo account. Weibo is a Twitter-like form of microblog followed by hundreds of millions of people in China. Although we were relative latecomers among the Beijing-based embassies active in social media, we were quick to gain a following. Among other good things, it was clear that our followers in China liked Rosalyn's tweets about Canadian food and recipes. They also appreciated her enthusiasm for Chinese culture, cuisine included, and commented frequently about her warmth and friendliness. China's weibo followers have well-developed sensors for the insincere, bureaucratic or simply boring, none of which applies to Chef Rosalyn.

During my regular speaking engagements on college campuses in China, I would ask for a show of hands from those students in the audience who followed us on weibo. I noticed a gratifying increase month by month.[3] I would then ask if they followed anybody from the embassy in particular, having already dropped the broad hint that I was a regular contributor. No matter how shamelessly I lobbied, Chef Rosalyn always topped these informal polls.

I was eager to explore the application of social media to traditional trade promotion. I wanted our embassy communications efforts to get beyond mind-numbing press releases with their inevitable photos of touring delegations, official handshakes and ribbon-cuttings. I was attracted by the lively, unscripted and real-time interaction that weibo offered. Even more important was the promise of access to hundreds of millions of followers in parts of China well beyond our network of offices.

We launched the project quietly. I knew that if we sought formal approval from Ottawa, our proposed postings would be subject to intense and very slow review at headquarters. Anything lively or spon-taneous would almost inevitably be scrubbed out. The likelihood of being able to get back to our followers with answers to their questions in a reasonable amount of time would be reduced to zero.

Early on we had accepted that part of the price of operating a microblog was living with some negative comments, such as inevitable complaints about the seal hunt or Canada's lack of support for the Kyoto Protocol. We would, of course, respond to these according to Canada's official position, but we left the negative material up on the site. We weren't about to censor or delete the criticism. Our willingness to address difficult issues was key to our credibility—and it offered our Chinese followers an important lesson about how Canada works.

Or how it should work. Official Ottawa is risk-averse at the best of times. Sadly, the communications sections of most government depart-ments have evolved into something that brings to mind Newspeak as practised in the creepy totalitarian state envisioned in George Orwell's novel *Nineteen Eighty-Four*. But instead of claiming, like the apparatchiks around Orwell's Big Brother, that "Freedom Is Slavery," our depart-mental communications gurus seem to believe that "Communication Is Silence." They are perversely dedicated to *not* communicating. This inclination has its origins in political pressure from the top, something that has worsened in the last decade. But it has become so automatic, so ingrained, that public servants have adopted it as a standard oper-ating procedure, self-censoring with almost as much zeal as the most partisan of the political types.

I justified our autonomy according to a razor-fine reading of the rules. Officially any communications in English and French need to be cleared with headquarters. Since our weibo communications were conducted only in Chinese, I could (somewhat uneasily) exempt us from the requirement to run everything by Ottawa. That said, I also accepted ultimate responsibility, and knew that it was my neck on the block should things go wrong.

I wasn't particularly worried. I kept a careful eye on the site and on the young team who managed it and acted as editors for all submissions, my own included. I accepted the fact that a Canadian male in his mid-fifties was not necessarily in sync with the young and hip Chinese demographic group we were cultivating. And although I can get by in conversational Chinese, I would compose my tweets with a young Chinese colleague, someone who would help me with my characters and lead me safely through the minefield of slang, in-jokes and double entendres that, intentionally or otherwise, liven up weibo postings. I enjoyed learning to embrace a haiku-like brevity in my tweets, grateful for the fact that you can say a lot more in 140 Chinese characters than in 140 Latin letters. I normally tried to convey my Canadian perspective on a China that I was still, a quarter century after my first visit, happily discovering.

I answered questions about myself, my work, and the nuts and bolts of running the embassy, including how much I spent on travel and hospitality. Ultimately, I was able to create a conversation about how our diplomats, myself included, are held accountable by the Canadians they work for. This is a subject of keen interest in China, where the abuse of power by officials generates huge popular resentment.

My answer to a question about what kind of car I drove went viral. That's a very sensitive topic in China, where the perks for vast numbers of officials include an expensive limo. I tweeted a picture of the embassy's Camry hybrid. Some users were impressed by Canada's frugality. Others thought we were just cheap. I explained that the choice wasn't mine, that Canadians actually have rules about these things, and that public officials are expected to follow them. I came to see weibo as a way of letting Canada speak for itself.

I had entrusted leadership of the weibo project to its instigator, Mark McDowell, someone who had worked with me years earlier in Taiwan. I had come to know him as an outspoken, irreverent and absolutely brilliant foreign service officer, among the most original of thinkers when it comes to using social media to energize our communications with new audiences. At the time of the Qingdao trip, the weibo project was still seen as the exclusive property of Mark's public diplomacy group. For almost everybody else in the embassy, it was still seen as a burden being inflicted on people who had other, real things to do. Worse, it was also seen as the ambassador's pet project, which fed a general sense of skepticism among colleagues, and had embassy managers worrying about how to pay lip service to it without actually changing how they worked. This was entirely understandable. I had been around long enough to know that the project wouldn't succeed until a broader range of senior people in the embassy came to believe that it would help them. It was my job to create opportunities for finding out how, where and indeed whether social media could extend our reach.

Our simple, although somewhat unscientific, measure was to track and assess responses by our followers. Tweets about Canadian food in general, and Chef Rosalyn's approach to cooking it in particular, generated real enthusiasm. One of our all-time most popular tweets was a quirky story about the appearance of a blue lobster in a haul off Atlantic Canada. Enthusiastic Chinese followers had two questions: What makes a lobster turn blue? And, what does a blue lobster taste like?

Weibo became a key tool in that rapidly growing part of our work that we conduct with real people rather than governments. It allowed us to introduce followers throughout China, far beyond the reach of our offices, to Canadian food, wine and consumer products, and to highlight opportunities for travel and study in Canada. Weibo also helped us to demystify the process of obtaining a Canadian visa and it enabled us to get messages out, quickly and informally, to Canadians who are resident in distant Chinese provinces.

So, the trip to the Qingdao expo had a subtext. I wanted to use Chef Rosalyn's active presence to bring the Trade section onside when it came to using social media. She spent her time tweeting about Canadian seafood, sharing recipe ideas and taking questions from

Chinese followers directly to the participating Canadian companies. It was a compelling example of how social media is changing the way we work.

That's not to suggest weibo will forever be the embassy's social media vehicle of choice. Indeed, Chinese officials began to crack down on weibo in 2013, and by 2014 growth had slowed, suggesting an uncertain future. It was also alleged that an increasing number of Canada's followers were fake, or were, as they are known in China, "zombies."[4] But having seen first-hand how powerful a communications platform social media can be, I remain an optimist. My sense is that, if weibo can't recover, Chinese netizens will simply use another medium. My main worry is that people in Foreign Affairs will use any such growing pains as an excuse to give up on social media in China. The department is full of very bright people, but sometimes they turn that energy into finding creative reasons *not* to do things.

While part of my time at the expo was spent checking in with Rosalyn, my main job was to introduce our fisheries minister to local officials, brief him in advance of meetings and media events, and ensure that he had the opportunity to keep up with business from home. But I also took the time to have my own private words with each Canadian exhibitor. I was doing what Mao called "seeking truth from facts." Talking with the visiting Canadian exporters was my opportunity to confirm that what I thought I knew about the market for Canadian seafood in China was actually true.

I have been interested in the fisheries sector since my days as a junior trade commissioner on a training assignment in Newfoundland in 1981. In those days I would meet foreign seafood buyers in St. John's, and then drive them to meet exporters in the processing plants that dotted the bays and inlets of the island. Each visit would start with our local host at the plant delivering a rant against government in general and the federal government in particular. (That would be the same government that was at that very moment bringing foreign buyers to the plant.) These traditional formalities out of the way, coffee would be served and we would get down to business.

Those plant visits were my introduction to the marketing of squid and snow crab, capelin and cod. It was a good time to be involved in the fish business. The northern cod stock was considered an almost unlimited resource. The U.S. market was booming, Europe was developing nicely and Asia was an interesting gleam on the horizon.

On one occasion during that year in St. John's, I was asked to welcome two visiting officials, pioneer trade commissioners from a China in the earliest stages of Deng Xiaoping's daring program of reform and opening to the outside world. It was hoped that they could learn the ropes from their Canadian counterparts. It is hard to believe now, but that effort was a tiny part of a much larger and highly uncertain experiment. China was just emerging from the wreckage of the Cultural Revolution. The infamous Gang of Four had just been put on trial, and Deng himself was recovering from having been purged and persecuted. He was desperately trying to reanimate China's economy, to put the country back to work.

The visit to St. John's by these proto–trade commissioners was my professional introduction to China. The trouble was that they spoke little English, and I was a few years away from my own study of Mandarin. I improvised, threw out the official agenda, and simply took them out of St. John's and down along the southern shore of the Avalon Peninsula to see its fishing villages along with its lovely coves and rocks, birds and seascapes. And over the course of the day, although I can't explain how, I did manage to convey a basic sense of what I did for a living, about how I went about the business of helping Newfoundlanders sell their products overseas.

My two guests were clearly delighted by what they had seen. And although they had almost certainly been instructed to keep foreigners at a distance, they graciously asked if they could take me out for a Chinese meal at the end of the day. This tested my ingenuity further, and, in the end, all I could find was a place offering that ominous combo of "Chinese and Canadian food." After we had picked our way through several courses, alternating between gooey and formidably deep-fried, I was thanked for giving my visitors the chance to sample local cuisine.

Almost thirty years later, in the booths at Qingdao, I was meeting battered survivors from the Canadian fisheries sector. The U.S. market was flat, and Europe and Japan were in decline. China, long an exotic add-on to marketing trips to Japan and Hong Kong, was opening up at the most opportune time. What I heard, in booth after booth, was a sense of bewildered gratitude, with more than one exporter asserting that he would have been out of business if it hadn't been for China. There was real conviction behind these testimonials and with it a willingness to do the hard work to build a new China-oriented business.

Clearwater Seafoods of Nova Scotia had a major presence at the show. It was then in the midst of a patient effort to shift from supplying lobster as a generic commodity to Chinese brokers and importers to selling clearly identified Canadian lobster as a brand of choice for Chinese consumers. Part of the challenge involved overcoming the market dominance of Australian rock lobster. This is a staple at Chinese banquets, with the tail, the best part of the Australian lobster, being carefully presented to the guest of honour. Canadian lobsters have the additional benefit of sporting two meaty claws. But that creates a protocol problem. How do you present two delicacies to one guest of honour? Clearwater's solution was to extract and artfully plate the meat from the claws, and present the dish with the right amount of panache to the VIP guest. This worked well and testified to much careful prep work by Clearwater with chefs, servers and restaurants in China.[5]

During the Chinese New Year season of 2011, Clearwater had begun selling its live lobsters with a special sleeve on the claw, marking each distinctively as a Clearwater product.[6] The next step for the company involves entering the China market at the retail level, selling its product directly to Chinese shoppers. The company's China sales have grown from less than $20 million in 2009 to more than $70 million in 2014. Thanks to some hard work by the company's sales team in China, retail sales now represent a small but promising part of the total. By the end of 2014, Clearwater had managed to get its products into roughly 150 outlets in China, recording more than $1 million in sales directly to Chinese consumers.[7] Ian Smith, Clearwater CEO, is passionate about China, and also dedicated to "seeking truth from facts." The company's success, and its growing confidence, is based on more than a decade of hard-earned experience and meticulous research on the ground. Clearwater is reinforcing the growing Chinese perception that Canadian seafood comes from a special place known for its cold, clean water. That's the key step in moving from selling lobster as an undifferentiated commodity to marketing it as a high-quality dining experience, a taste of Canada.

On the plane back to Beijing from Qingdao, I kept thinking about China having "saved" the Canadian fisheries industry. What struck me was how I had heard almost the same message from other Canadian business people. At the China Mining Congress and Expo in the fall of 2010, for example, the Canadian booth was literally rocking. Exhibitors from every region of Canada were there introducing mining projects to potential investors. The interest from Chinese visitors was electric, and with good reason. China was by this time dominating the global trade in minerals, accounting for more than half of the worldwide trade in iron ore; more than 40 percent of trade in copper, coal, lead and zinc; and more than 35 percent of the trade in nickel.[8] This dominance was partly due to the requirements of China's explosive growth, with highways, airports, rail lines, power plants and entire new cities being constructed at a dizzying pace. Don Lindsay, CEO of Canada's Teck, a major supplier of copper, frequently made the point that those who scratch their heads wondering at China's appetite for minerals might simply consider how much copper is required for the installation of 200,000 kilometres of power transmission lines over a five-year span.[9] The impact on resource-rich nations was powerful.

Canada and, to an even larger extent, Australia powered through the economic crisis thanks to surging demand from China.

While the minerals sector represented the most dramatic example of what China's rising tide could do, Canada's forest products exporters were also benefitting from the surge in new construction. And it was due again to a phenomenon that had its origins in the upheaval of the global financial crisis. China's dramatic growth from 2009 onward was generated by stimulus spending designed to carry its economy over and above the turbulence that had engulfed almost everyone else. Meanwhile, ground zero for the global crisis was the U.S. housing market, which traditionally drives demand for Canadian lumber sales. As the U.S. and other lumber markets were falling, China was experiencing a spectacular real estate boom that saw lumber imports surge. During May 2011, Canada actually sold more lumber to China than it did to the United States. That year, it was estimated that ten thousand people in British Columbia were employed thanks to China's demand for lumber.[10]

This surge in demand was the vindication for a long and arduous process of building the market in China for Canadian lumber. One of my first projects as a young trade commissioner working out of our newly opened consulate general in Shanghai in 1986 was to keep tabs on a model farmhouse that was being constructed on the edge of the city. The materials had been donated by the Council of Forest Industries (COFI) of British Columbia. COFI also provided a project manager who would fly in from Vancouver from time to time to monitor the process. I was asked to keep an eye on the project between visits.

COFI and the B.C. lumber industry were responding to another outgrowth of Deng Xiaoping's reforms. Farmers were now being given permission to sell a portion of their produce on a commercial basis. The effect was electrifying. Rural incomes were rising quickly, and particularly in the traditionally rich communities of the Yangtze

Delta, between Shanghai on the coast and the old capital of Nanjing 300 kilometres up the river. The first thing that newly rich farmers spent their money on was housing.

On his regular visits, the Canadian project supervisor oversaw the most important parts of the project, such as ensuring that a plastic vapour barrier was correctly installed in the wood frame so as to prevent the dampness of the Yangtze Delta from seeping through the walls. But he left the finishing touches to a local crew. While the end result was in places slapdash (on opening day, an overturned pail of whitewash left its legacy along one wall), it was impressive compared to its neighbours. Yet the house still looked like something local, and not as if it had been transplanted from one of Vancouver's wealthier suburbs.

Years and millions of dollars in promotional work would follow, patiently building the case for Canadian-style wood-based construction. The process probably would have moved faster if Canadian suppliers had not had the distraction of the large and readily accessible U.S. market right next door. But even with a more consistent promotional effort, gaining the support of architects and builders and turning around the Chinese bureaucracy, so that building codes would allow for the use of lumber, was not going to happen overnight. We were still hard at it when I returned to China almost twenty-five years later.

A key to success in any such effort requires you to be able to see the big picture and make creative connections. That's a challenge for Foreign Affairs as a department, and for the government in general. A big part of my job as ambassador was acting as a promoter for Canadian products. An equally important part was, as I mentioned in the previous chapter, acting as what I came to call "connector of last resort," catching disconnects from an unfocused Ottawa before harm was done or opportunities missed in China.

At one of the embassy's morning meetings, my interest was piqued by a quick reference from the person in charge of administration.

Headquarters in Ottawa intended to upgrade the entrances to the main embassy building and to the official residence, where I lived. In the new Ottawa, the people who plan these things have their own team at the embassy who report directly back to them. That reality inspired my morning meetings, giving me a chance to ask questions and hunt for looming disconnects. As I enquired further, I discovered that the main part of the job involved replacing the big cedar beams that grace both entrances. After twenty years of absorbing Beijing pollution, it was time for something new. The schedule was pretty much complete, but it hadn't occurred to anybody in Ottawa that installing beautiful new cedar beams at the entrance to the major showcase for Canada in China might be of more than administrative significance.

I succeeded in getting the project timed to coincide with the long-planned visit of a B.C. forestry delegation and minister. We organized an unveiling for local architects, builders and the construction media. It came with a lion dance, confetti, streamers and lots of food. Chef Rosalyn managed to find some unused pieces of cedar, and on these she grilled B.C. salmon for our key contacts. High-quality Canadian products, Canadian design, food and culture connect wonderfully in people's imaginations. But we need to be able to make those connections in the first place.

In the wake of the deadly Sichuan earthquake of 2008, Chinese officials took particular interest in the advantage of using wood-frame construction for public buildings. A portion of the assistance from Canada in response to the tragedy was channelled into the construction of wood-frame facilities, including a school and a home for the elderly. This was managed with sensitivity, the main message being that building with wood is safer than the local alternatives. One of the worst and most incomprehensible aspects of the tragedy was the number of children who had died in shoddily constructed concrete schools. (The artist Ai Weiwei was courageous enough to make this public, something that led to his later mistreatment by vindictive

Chinese authorities.) The Canadian buildings were not just safer, they were faster to erect, which saved money and allowed communities to get on with rebuilding and recovery.

In early 2010, I visited a Canadian-built school in a district that had been heavily damaged by the quake. I was deeply impressed by what I saw and made the case for Governor General Michaëlle Jean to spend time in the town during her official visit to China that summer. By then, the community was regrouping with obvious pride around their attractive new school. As it turned out, messages about the benefits of using wood in construction came up even earlier during the governor general's visit. I acted as the emcee for a lively discussion she held with Chinese and Canadian architects at the B.C. pavilion at Expo 2010 in Shanghai. The theme of the expo was "Better City, Better Life." It was something that the governor general wanted to explore in more detail with such an experienced and opinionated group. More than one of our Chinese guests said that China's fast-paced urbanization, and the resulting spread of forests of identical high-rise towers, was *not* translating into better cities or a better life. Sitting there, in a stylish boardroom beautifully framed, panelled and outfitted in Canadian wood, and gazing at posters of a green and vibrant Vancouver fresh from the triumph of its Olympic Winter Games, it was hard not to be interested in potential Canadian solutions.

Nobody doubted that it would often be difficult to transfer Canadian practices to the vast, overflowing and hugely complicated canvas of modern China. But as demand for private homes grows, and as people explore new approaches to the design of public buildings, wood-frame construction is an increasingly interesting option.

EARLY IN THE SECOND DECADE of the twenty-first century, and almost without our noticing it, China emerged to become Canada's second-most-important economic partner. It was still far from the U.S.

in terms of importance to us, but it was increasingly pulling away from everybody else.

Canadians are used to the fact that we buy a lot of our goods from China, something that visitors to Home Depot, Walmart or Canadian Tire learn pretty quickly. What they are probably less aware of is that we now sell more to China than to any country other than the United States. Between 2003 and 2013, our exports to Japan grew by a little more than $2 billion to reach $10.5 billion. Exports to China in that same period grew five-fold to more than $20 billion. We tend to lump China in with other developing countries. But if we drill down to examine Canada's trade with the collectivity known as the BRICS— Brazil, Russia, India, China and South Africa—we find that two-way trade with China, the total of our exports and our imports, was by 2013 closing in on $73 billion. The total of our trade with the rest of the BRICS *combined* stood at a little over $15 billion.[11]

Most of our export success with China is concentrated in agricultural products, minerals and forest products, including lumber and wood pulp. Some of our export numbers are hidden, masked by the difficulty in tracking what Chinese people pay us for services, such as banking and insurance. Canada's banks and insurance companies represent major success stories in China. Much of that is due to their patience and persistence in the market, something measured not in years but in decades. These institutions have worked hard at building their relationship with China, becoming good corporate citizens through investment and the support of charitable activities in China, and by generously funding training for Chinese officials in Canada. The training part is particularly important. It not only generates gratitude and loyalty but also helps to build awareness of the stability, sound management and careful stewardship of resources that Canadian banks and insurance companies are known for. These virtues took on a new lustre as the global financial crisis deepened and financial institutions from the U.S. and other countries began to look less imposing and reliable.

On my arrival in Beijing in the late summer of 2009, I learned that I would have a visit from the then finance minister, Jim Flaherty, just a few weeks later. An early visit is a mixed blessing because it means that you have to get up to speed even faster than normal. But it also means that you hit your full stride that much earlier. Flaherty was accompanied by Mark Carney, then the governor of the Bank of Canada, and Julie Dickson, then the superintendent of financial institutions—in other words, the regulator of Canada's banks.

I have sat in on hundreds of meetings between senior Canadians and their foreign counterparts. While I listen carefully to what's said (and how it's translated) I try hard to get a sense of intangibles such as mood and tone, and I look for the non-verbal cues of body language.

The Chinese are exquisite hosts. This is partly because they have been at it for several millennia, but also because Beijing is one of the busiest stops on the international circuit. Senior officials there juggle multiple delegations daily. What I picked up on from the Chinese in the meetings with Flaherty and his delegation was something more than diplomatic courtesy. Our hosts—the minister of finance, the central bank governor and the heads of the major Chinese banks—listened intently and showed that they liked what they were hearing. Although they had met Canadians before, we have traditionally been burdened with a reputation for stodginess and excessive caution. On the plus side, unlike others, we aren't given to lecturing the Chinese about how to manage their economy.

But now, boring was good. From the finance minister on down, officials seemed genuinely (and positively) surprised by the strength and resilience of Canada's financial sector. They were also impressed that Flaherty had brought the bank governor and the chief regulator. They appeared to understand and appreciate the effective and very real division of labour among the top Canadian officials. The visit underlined a key message about Canada as a rare Western economy that had found the right balance between appropriate regulation to protect consumers and respect for free-market operations.

This positive impression extended to our banks and insurance companies at just the right time. Economic reforms have smashed China's iron rice bowl, the cradle-to-grave support provided by a Chinese state that was landlord, educator, doctor and employer. This painful but necessary measure revitalized the Chinese economy by exposing it to the energy and discipline of the market, but it also forced Chinese households to confront a daunting new world. They were now "free" to secure their basic necessities for themselves, but had few vehicles for doing so. There was a growing need for new financial products and services that could generate sufficient returns but reliably, predictably and safely. Here again, well-governed, carefully regulated and prosperous Canada offered a compelling example.

IT WASN'T HARD to be enthusiastic about Canada–China trade relations as the first decade of the new century came to a close. We were generating big export numbers in commodities such as minerals and forest products. We were also building on our strong foundation as a supplier of agricultural products, such as wheat and barley, and were now winning market share for Canadian beef, pork and seafood, and for processed items such as snack foods, juices and wine. The services side looked equally promising, with the success of Canadian banks and insurance companies in China and the welcome spending by growing numbers of Chinese students and tourists in Canada.

A big part of my job as ambassador involved worrying. One of the things I worried most about was our failure to make similar progress in manufactured goods and high-technology sectors. We currently hold about 1 percent of China's market for imports. In recent years, we have actually outperformed many of our developed-world competitors, growing our admittedly much smaller share of the China market while theirs has diminished. This difference is largely due to surging sales of Canadian minerals, wood pulp and agricultural products.[12]

When I worked in China in the 1980s, Canadian factories were equipping China's newest power plants. Nortel was bringing telecom service to vast populations previously without modern communications. And Bombardier's trains and aircraft were linking China's far-flung cities. By 2012, only Bombardier was still active in China. The others had either scaled back and refocused or, like Nortel, disappeared entirely. While foreign competition was a factor in this evolution, in many industrial sectors survival now depends on being able to compete with China's own manufacturers, which are themselves intent on capturing global market share.

Bombardier, like other major foreign firms supplying China's transportation sector, has transferred significant amounts of technology as a precondition for staying in business. This has led to the emergence of Chinese manufacturers who are both partners and competitors. By the time you subtract the components that Bombardier's Chinese partners now provide, and what is coming from other parts of Bombardier's global manufacturing chain, the Canadian content of what the company sells in China is now much less. That said, it does tend to be concentrated at the high-technology end of the spectrum. You can debate the wisdom of transferring large amounts of technology to a country that aims not just to replace you domestically but also to compete with you internationally. But the very fact that Bombardier is still in business offers a compelling rationale for its strategy. The idea is to use every cost advantage that an increasingly global presence provides, and to be sufficiently innovative to stay a step or two ahead of the competition, which is increasingly Chinese.

And given the way China is changing, we can't afford to ignore opportunities for selling higher-technology goods and services there.

For one thing, we are almost certainly reaching the end of the great commodities boom generated by China's stimulus program. While that's a sobering development for Canada, whose exports to China are dominated by commodities, it's an even bigger challenge for Australia, whose exports are dominated by a *single* commodity. In 2001, Australian exports to China were $9 billion. By 2011, they had increased to $77 billion. That's largely a story of iron ore shipments. Iron ore represented 16 percent of Australian exports to China in 2001, and an astounding 57 percent of exports in 2011.[13] Exports to China account for almost one quarter of the gross state product of resource-rich Western Australia, where most of the iron ore originates.[14]

By contrast, Canadian exports have enjoyed a significant, but much less spectacular, rise, growing from $4 billion to $16 billion in that same 2001–2011 period. In 2011, exports of minerals, pulp and paper, and other forest products represented $8 billion, or half of our total exports.[15] While we are less exposed to a decline in a single commodity than Australia is, we are not out of the woods entirely.

We need to think carefully about possible new directions for the Chinese economy. The leaders of China have made it clear that they want to move from the current heavy dependence on government-driven investment in infrastructure to a more sustainable pattern of consumer-led growth. That suggests rising consumer demand for goods such as higher-quality processed foods, improved housing and building materials, and advanced automotive parts. We will see even more Chinese tourists and students exploring the wider world, Canada included. Back home in China, governments will be forced to deliver higher-quality health care, better environmental protection and a more innovative and student-friendly approach to education.

Nor will China stop importing commodities. The mix will likely change, with demand remaining strong for energy inputs such as uranium and liquid natural gas (LNG), and for the potash-based fertilizer required to coax more production from China's farms. But it's not as if any of these goods will simply sell themselves. Almost everything that people have said about the difficulty of doing business in China is true and is likely to remain true for a long time.

Intimidating differences in terms of language, culture and business practice are just the start. China's economy is continental in terms of its vast geographic expanse and huge population. It is remarkably diverse: home to amazingly prosperous coastal cities and internal provinces and territories where poverty is still common. It is a modern nation-state that uneasily incorporates imperial possessions acquired centuries ago. Although China is increasingly open to the wider world, many of its people harbour a deep sense of grievance for the unfair treatment meted out by rapacious foreigners when the country was weak. Add to this the perils of systemic corruption abetted by a Communist Party that has a very selective interpretation of the concept of rule of law, and it is clear that the playing field is tilted to a dizzying degree against the foreigner.

China is, of course, changing in impressive ways: Courageous officials are experimenting with fairer and more transparent regulations. Consumers are demanding that their rights be respected. Visionary entrepreneurs are embracing the highest standards of business ethics for themselves and their companies. But the process is still piecemeal and unpredictable. On good days, it is of the "two steps forward, one step back" variety. On not-so-good days, it is the reverse. So the hard truth is that the single market that will contribute most significantly to global and Canadian growth is likely to remain difficult, frustrating and often infuriatingly unfair. We are going to have to get used to that.

A second challenge flows from the fact that we are probably coming to the end of that phase of China's development marked by an unbroken run of spectacular growth. The country has been growing at roughly 10 percent annually since 1980. This growth continued in the face of the global economic crisis. Indeed, the years 2009 and 2010 represented a period of triumph for those most bullish on China, people who believed that it could do no wrong and that growth would never end. But by 2014 the strains wrought by growth that was as unbalanced as it was unprecedented were beginning to show.

As the Chinese economy slows, the China bears will have their day. Many will argue that this marks the end of China's re-emergence as a global power. Some will predict that China will quietly return to being the underperforming slumbering giant that it was up until 1980. Others, of a more apocalyptic inclination, will assure us that China will descend into chaos sufficiently violent to cause the country to fragment. These outcomes are indeed possible. But if China's recent history is anything to go by, it is clear that economic management is the nation's strong suit. China has faced seemingly insurmountable economic challenges before, and readily overcome them. Betting against China's ability to adapt and innovate its way out of trouble is usually a losing proposition.

It is more likely that China will simply adjust to a lower, but still significant, level of growth. If this is managed correctly, it will enable China to make the difficult transition to a more stable and more prosperous middle-income status, as Korea and Taiwan have done. If it isn't managed correctly, China will be a powerful but unpredictable global player, one characterized by boom-and-bust economic cycles, dangerously uneven income distribution and higher levels of political instability. Under this scenario, it will be a bit like Russia under Vladimir Putin, but a lot more prosperous, capable and influential.

The challenge for Canada is that slowing growth in China will be felt differently in different parts of our economy. Demand for some commodities, such as copper, iron ore, lead and zinc, will slow. But even at lower levels of growth, China will still remain a formidable consumer of these products. And China will still have an appetite for quality Canadian food products, for technologies that can make its cities more livable and for services that provide better care for a rapidly aging population. Whatever the scenario in China, Canada will almost certainly continue to welcome large numbers of high-net-worth Chinese visitors looking for their place in the Canadian dream. In other words,

Chinese demand for what Canada has to offer will continue to grow, but we will have to adapt as demand patterns change.

Signs of slower growth in China will provide an easy excuse for some business people in Canada to avoid the real difficulties, frustrations and unpredictability that are part of doing business there. But this would mean passing up one of the best available opportunities to grow our own economy.

FOR MANY CANADIAN EXPORTERS, the challenge of doing business in Mandarin is daunting enough, particularly when traditional markets in places such as New York State and California still beckon. But as formidable as the language barrier is, China's opaque business culture represents an even bigger impediment to progress. Although we are not unfamiliar with old boy networks in Canada, in China, who you know means virtually everything.

Almost every exchange in Chinese life adds to or subtracts from your indebtedness to someone else. Favours, gifts and good deeds are quantified and monitored as carefully as any other tradable commodity. Establishing *guanxi*, a connection that represents a call on someone for something, can mean the difference between being in the information loop or on the outside, between loyalty and capricious betrayal, between success and failure. This comes at a huge cost. At its mildest, *guanxi* leads to expectations about hiring someone's relative or providing privileged access to somebody instead of making him line up like everybody else. (The Chinese talk about going through the *hou men* or back door.) These things aren't unheard of in Canada. But *guanxi* is so pervasive in China that it distorts almost every transaction, leading to rigged and opaque insider arrangements that disadvantage less fortunate customers, shareholders and foreign partners.

The role of the Communist Party in commercial affairs complicates things even further. Closeness between your Chinese partner and Party officials is a given and means overwhelming home-court advantage on any issue about which you might disagree. It sometimes turns out that, given the interconnections between the Communist Party and business at all levels, your local partner actually *is* the Party.

Lack of respect for the rule of law leads to some other mind-boggling situations, including a number of outrageous examples of intellectual property theft in which the Chinese partner not only steals his foreign partner's idea but then successfully sues him in local court for having the temerity to continue using the technology he (the foreign partner) developed in the first place.

There are many accounts of trusted Chinese employees taking valuable production secrets to the local competition or even siphoning money from the joint venture to build a competing factory down the road. And although Chinese entrepreneurs are themselves the victims of such piracy, there seems to be a special dispensation in place, a will-ingness to look the other way, when the target of predation is a foreigner. Foreigners begin with the disadvantage of being viewed as outsiders. But they are also burdened with the accumulated baggage of Chinese history. The Party regularly reminds the Chinese people of the coun-try's century of humiliation at the hands of foreigners. Striking back by appropriating technology for the motherland can seem downright patriotic. In July 2014, Canada's IMAX won a $7 million judgment against an employee who took the company's technology for trans-forming 2-D films into 3-D films to China, where he set up a rival com-pany. What made the case challenging is the fact that the employee's new venture was being supported by the Chinese government.[16]

China is also adept at marshalling the massive research capability built into its universities and its bureaucracy, most formidably within the vast network of the People's Liberation Army, to promote entire indus-tries in support of national objectives. In many cases, China's indus-trialization has also received a boost from overseas, partly through legal means such as licensing and technology transfer, partly through a concerted effort to welcome home brilliant scientists who have been working abroad, and partly through information obtained through industrial espionage. Back home, national champions are further cultivated through such traditional techniques as suppression of foreign competition and access to abundant cheap loans.

This can have far-reaching consequences. Thanks to massive subsidies to local manufacturers, China has quickly come to dominate the solar panel industry worldwide. This triggered bitter trade disputes with the U.S. and the E.U., which argued that China has been dumping panels—in other words, selling at less than the cost of production. The knock-on effect is that prices have been forced down so aggressively that many firms in China and abroad have been put out of business. Others have had to pare costs to the bone, a consequence that has unfortunately led many in the industry to abandon commitments to recycling and other green initiatives.[17]

The playing field in China is anything but level, and foreign technologies that are the product of years of research and significant investment are under constant threat. But with traditional markets weakened to the point of anemia, this represents the new normal for Canadian firms, and for everybody else.

But while China abounds with business horror stories, there are also many positive narratives. We should start by remembering that China is neither static nor monolithic. American writer and China watcher James Fallows describes this very well: "What is true in one province is false in the next. What was the exception last week is the rule today. A policy that is applied strictly in Beijing may be ignored or completely unknown in Kunming or Changsha. Millions of Chinese people are now very rich, and hundreds of millions are still very poor. Their country is a success and a failure, an opportunity and a threat, an inspiring model to the world and a nightmarish cautionary example."[18] In other words, be careful when making broad generalizations about China, and don't get too comfortable with what you thought you knew about the place.

This is partly explained by China's history and geography. Although China has been more or less unified since the days of Emperor Qin Shi Huang more than two thousand years ago, China's regions, separated by deserts, mountains and great rivers, have developed very differently. While these differences have been lessened by advances in telecommunications and transportation technology, by the huge migration of people from the countryside into the cities, and by the orthodoxy imposed under Communist rule, they haven't disappeared entirely. It is also true that the spirit of regional autonomy often combines with entrepreneurial savvy, meaning that Beijing's edicts are obeyed only so long as they don't interfere with local business opportunities. The maxim "the mountains are high, and the emperor is far away" captures this opportunistic spirit nicely.

And then there is the fact that China changes over time. Although it can appear resolute, united and almost defiant to the outside world, China's often anarchic entrepreneurial energy creates many openings for new ideas and experiments. China's pragmatic leaders wisely tolerate this creativity. Interesting but potentially uncomfortable new ideas that emerge in the regions—such as experiments in local governance or innovations in financial services—are fenced off and allowed to run for a while. Those that have merit are adopted more widely.

Nor is China completely immune to outside pressure. The country was welcomed into the World Trade Organization (WTO) in 2001 because its trading partners saw it as being in their collective interest to bind China ever more closely to a rules-based international system. Supporting China's WTO bid was also seen as a means of assisting those leaders, led by the determined Premier Zhu Rongji, who were nudging, cajoling and dragging China further along the path of economic reform and opening. Zhu and his reformers could point to outside pressure and expectations to bolster their campaign for market-based reforms.

While it is undeniably true that China's WTO membership has brought wide benefits at home and abroad, it is also true that China's adherence to a rules-based system has been partial at best. This is partly because of the diversity described above. While a committed core of technocrats in Beijing is convinced of the benefits of having everybody play by the rules, officials at the local level often do their best to ensure that the rules don't apply to them. China has been described as struggling with a somewhat toxic mix of authoritarian and inadequate governance.[19] This works against the consistent embrace of international rules and regulations.

Support in China for a rules-based international system took another knock with the global financial crisis. Critics pointed to the fact that the system's strongest proponents, the U.S. and Europe, were in disarray, while China was doing just fine, despite its incomplete and selective embrace of the rules. To the iconoclasts in China, the WTO represents not a rules-based system, but a Western system, one designed to hobble and constrain China at the very moment of its return to global economic power. As the economic crisis deepened, and as the United States in particular appeared to stumble, voices emerged to challenge the adoption of what were described as Western theories designed to frustrate China's long-awaited return to greatness.

The good news is that China's exposure to the international system, and the undeniable prosperity this has engendered, has helped to create enclaves of reform. We are witnessing the slow emergence of an ecosystem in China's coastal cities in which the stability and predictability of a rules-based system is seen as advantageous. This has in turn encouraged the development of a basic infrastructure of legal and financial services, and has allowed for greater tolerance of the free flow of information on which fully functioning markets depend.

This cautious opening to a more rules-based business environment, starting with China's big coastal cities, has allowed more space for occasionally discordant voices, such as the admirably outspoken American and E.U. chambers of commerce, which can apply collective pressure against particularly egregious efforts to restrict opportunities for foreign firms. So, despite the many difficulties that foreigners face in doing business in China, there is a growing portion of the country where traditional legal protections are taking hold and where business advocacy groups such as chambers of commerce can be of real help. But these reformist gains are tenuous. While China's leaders commit to allowing greater scope for the market to operate, the fact that the Party sees itself as being above the law means that these reforms are always subject to the whims of those in power.

Another traditional tool that foreigners rely on in the China market is support from their own governments. In many ways, China represents a last bastion for the role of government in business. This is largely because China remains a place in which many aspects of life are controlled by government, and in which bureaucrats still wield decisive authority. Governments traditionally provide three main types of support for their companies in China. The first and most common form is in raising awareness of foreign products and services. Being part of a well-publicized, high-profile visit to China is a powerful advantage for a company, especially for Canadian firms, which tend to be lesser known than their U.S., European or Japanese competitors. Getting to see senior decision makers in China is very hard to do. High-level Chinese officials don't accept cold calls.

But they will happily meet with visiting foreign officials. And any meeting with a Chinese minister, mayor or provincial governor typically includes all the key officials who work for them. The effect is to gain access to people you might otherwise spend years, and thousands of dollars in travel costs, trying to see. This door-opening is something that Canadian mayors, provincial premiers and federal ministers do to good effect. I am less convinced that this is something that visiting prime ministers should do. This turns them into supplicants and almost automatically concedes an advantage to the Chinese leadership in discussions of their far broader agenda of political, security and human rights issues.

The second form of support from government is in negotiating the infrastructure of trade treaties and bilateral agreements on which a sophisticated, rules-based partnership rests. Although we have made progress with China in recent years, much work remains to be done here. Indeed, I am concerned that we have actually lost momentum in China.

The third form of support involves senior Canadian officials helping to secure fair treatment for Canadian firms who have been unfairly disadvantaged in their efforts to enter the market or are being held back by some impediment that arose after they got in. Depending on what's at stake, this is a job for senior people, including the prime minister in the most serious cases. This isn't about seeking favours (which have to be repaid). Instead, it is about levelling the playing field so that foreign firms have the chance to compete fairly, according to their merits and according to the rules. But it takes real skill to keep this in perspective.

China all too often succeeds in creating the impression that its partners need to behave in ways that China defines as "friendly" if they are to enjoy a successful economic relationship. Friends, in China's view, don't rock the boat. And they are suitably grateful when China generously agrees to play by the rules. Just as in centuries past, China seeks to bind other countries to good behaviour by impressing them with access to the leadership and seducing them with gifts, or what appear to be gifts. A meeting with one of China's leaders at Zhongnanhai, that oasis of trees, water and tranquility in the very heart of Beijing, involves impressive showmanship. Anticipation builds thanks to the fussy nervousness of officials as they line up the foreigners by rank, waiting for the signal to send them into the meeting room. Then comes the big moment when the calm and well-groomed Chinese leader greets the delegates, who are invariably dazed by the camera lights, the crush of unfamiliar people and the grandeur of the meeting room. Finally, the meeting begins with the Chinese leader—someone who must be unimaginably busy, pre-occupied with great affairs of state—rattling off a series of statistics about Canada, leaving the delegation almost breathless with disbelief, and immensely touched by his intimate knowledge of their affairs.

The objective of this exercise is to personalize the relationship in the eyes of the visitor (much less so in those of the Chinese), creating something like an obligation to behave in ways that China considers (that word again) "friendly." The reason why this has remained in the Chinese playbook for more than a thousand years is because it works. Access to leaders is seen as crucial to securing business. The withholding of access, because of some problem in the relationship attributed to the foreigner, is seen as a serious and potentially costly penalty.

When British prime minister David Cameron visited Beijing in late 2013, the event was widely portrayed in the Chinese media as an attempt to make up for what they considered to have been a serious indiscretion, namely Cameron's earlier meeting with the Dalai Lama. Cameron arrived with more than a hundred business people, and he interrupted the British parliamentary calendar in his eagerness to show up on time. The visit was a clear commercial success. Chinese banks increased their presence in London, and China expressed interest in investment in high-speed rail and nuclear power in the U.K. But it was humiliating for Cameron and for the British organizers of the visit, who were otherwise treated with disdain by the Chinese. The visit was a coup for China because many will simply choose to believe that the price for coveted Chinese investment is cooperation on sensitive issues like Tibet.

Lost in this perception is the notion that Chinese firms might see it in their long-term interest to invest in Britain purely on the basis of the business case, or that it is in fact China that should be offering to change its behaviour if it is to compete in a rules-based global economy. The idea that the only way to succeed in China is by kowtowing to the powers that be in Beijing is of dubious validity. China does indeed mete out punishment from time to time, but mainly when the costs are judged to be limited and the target is unlikely to strike back. When imprisoned

Chinese dissident Liu Xiaobo was awarded the Nobel Peace Prize, China vented its fury on Norway, where the prize is awarded. There has since been a sharp fall in imports to China of Norwegian salmon.[20]

The idea here is to intimidate at least some partners (and the smaller the partner the better) to distract China's larger partners from the reality that, in an increasing number of sectors, price and quality matter more than politics. As the *Financial Times* pointed out, Germany's strong economic partnership with China does not flow from Chancellor Merkel's assiduous courtship of China's leaders: "German business does well in China because it makes lots of things that the Chinese want to buy."[21]

Canada essentially invented high-level, high-profile trade promotion with the massive Team Canada trade missions of the 1990s. They were innovative and effective in their day, but that day has long passed. National leaders ultimately pay a price for playing the role of trade promoters, as it immediately puts them at a disadvantage with their Chinese counterparts, who know how to work a now-tired formula to advantage. Leaders should stick to the big picture, which includes frank talk about fair treatment for their companies. But they should leave the promotion to others.

Although we can point to good work done by all levels of government in Canada when it comes to levelling the playing field with China, it's also true that our efforts have been heavily focused on natural resources and agricultural commodities. The single most ambitious example of government support during my tenure was our effort to reopen the Chinese market for canola, a plant derived from rapeseed, that, when crushed, can be transformed into a high-quality cooking oil and a very effective cattle feed. By the time I arrived in Beijing as ambassador, we were selling more than $1 billion worth of canola to China annually. At roughly the same time, we also began to note increased rumblings from Chinese producers of rapeseed, a product that competes with canola. Local producers weren't happy about the competition from a high-quality, competitively priced Canadian import. Within weeks,

Chinese quarantine officials began raising concerns about something called blackleg, a fungus. It's not a particularly nice name or condition, but it doesn't pose a risk for the people who buy canola seeds from us.

Wily officials often use plant and animal health issues to solve more mundane trade problems. The negative impact on canola exports was immediate: China suddenly blocked all canola shipments from Canada, citing the risk to its own rapeseed crop. I immediately raised our concerns, not only with Chinese quarantine officials but also with the senior people at the Foreign Ministry in Beijing, with whom we were then planning Prime Minister Harper's first visit. I told them that the ban was having an impact on farmers across western Canada, and that the issue was certain to be raised by the prime minister when he came to town. The Chinese tried to play this down, suggesting that it was a quarantine issue, and that it was too technical for such a high-level conversation. I replied that we went to the trouble of setting up such high-level conversations precisely to address real issues like this.

And the prime minister did raise the issue, as did Agriculture Minister Gerry Ritz, who accompanied him. While in China, Ritz also helped build interest in expanding imports of canola oil from Canada. This had the benefit of being a higher-value export than canola seed and free of any blackleg concerns. Ritz made multiple follow-up visits to China, with reopening the canola market a central objective. The Canola Council of Canada was also fully engaged, as was our embassy team. Back in Canada, significant testing was done to illustrate how the effects of blackleg fungus could be mitigated. Trade missions visited regions far from China's rapeseed-producing areas to open up new markets. And a major trial was done with farmers in China to make the case for using canola meal as a feed for cattle. By 2012, sales of the broader range of canola products to China topped $3 billion and represented more than half of our agricultural exports to the PRC.[22]

We're used to mounting a full-court press to help secure fair access for Canadian agricultural products, lumber, fish, and even seal meat.

This is important for our economy, vital for the regions concerned, and actually works. But we rarely rise to anything like that sustained and coordinated effort to win support for higher-technology products. We'll mount a thoughtful and sustained high-level effort to win access for Canadian blueberries. But for BlackBerry, not so much.

Part of the problem is that the federal government is largely organized along resource lines. The federal departments of Agriculture, Fisheries and Oceans, and Natural Resources have important international roles. There is no equally clear mandate for promoting higher-technology goods and services, beyond the broad, comprehensive responsibility that belongs to Canada's trade commissioners.

It is also true that the resource-focused Western provinces are far more active in China than are Ontario and Quebec, where our manufacturers and technology firms are concentrated. I accompanied Premier Brad Wall (Saskatchewan) and his then counterparts Gordon Campbell (British Columbia) and Ed Stelmach (Alberta) when they led a three-province mission to China in 2010. They delivered an effective and carefully coordinated pitch promoting the resource wealth of western Canada. They wisely steered clear of anything beyond a general investment pitch (they are, after all, competitors when it comes to investment). The only weak part of the campaign came when one of the three would earnestly remind his audience that together, the three jurisdictions "represent a combined population of 9 million people." Chinese guests would look puzzled and murmur, "Did he say 90 million?" not quite understanding why we Canadians were so impressed by such a modest number.

I did see Jean Charest in China when he was premier of Quebec, but here, too, his focus, which was well conceived and delivered, was to explain *Plan Nord*, his blueprint for the development of the province's resource-rich north. Ontario premier Dalton McGuinty visited China during my posting, and although I made a pitch to him about the necessity of coming to Beijing, the ultimate destination for all serious

China players, he focused his visit on East China, where Ontario has a low-profile twinning relationship with the province of Jiangsu. The result did little to change Ontario's near invisibility on Chinese radar screens.

Visiting premiers can be great connectors. Helping the Chinese understand that Ontario is home to leading universities makes it easier for them to believe that Ontario is also an incubator of innovative companies. Talking about the Toronto International Film Festival helps potential investors to think of the city as being home to creative and globally engaged people. The premier of Ontario, a province that on its own imports more than $25 billion from China annually, could make a bigger splash in Beijing than the leaders of many countries. But he or she would have to visit consistently to do that.

Fortunately, there is good reason to believe that engaging China may indeed be back on the province's agenda. Having won a majority, Ontario's current premier, Kathleen Wynne, appears much more willing to invest time in the personal dimension of the relationship. I had the chance to speak with her in advance of a trip she made to China in late October 2014. I was impressed by her keen interest, but also by her calm, unflappable manner. The trip was announced at a time when demonstrators were in the streets of Hong Kong, protesting a decision by Beijing to restrict upcoming elections to only those candidates acceptable to China. Wynne was immediately asked about this by the media, with one columnist even suggesting that she cancel the trip.

Wynne was courteous but very clear in response, pointing out that respect for basic human rights is simply part of the Ontario conversation: "We support freedom of speech, we support people's right to express themselves in a peaceful setting and so I will continue to reinforce that message wherever I am."[23] Interestingly, Philippe Couillard, the premier of Quebec, who joined Wynne and the premier of Prince Edward Island in China, took a different approach to a similar question about raising human rights in China. Couillard seemed on the defensive, reassuring his audience that he wouldn't lecture his hosts, and adding, "You have to see it also in the context of Chinese civilization, which is a very ancient civilization, where things are moving, but they move at their own pace,"[24] effectively echoing China's own preferred talking points.

In my view, Wynne, who was leading a delegation featuring sophisticated companies in health care and environmental technologies, did the better job, among other things describing the context necessary for success in modern business, one in which information flows freely, contracts are respected and knowledge workers thrive.

And then there is municipal diplomacy, meaning exchanges between Canadian mayors and their Chinese counterparts. China still largely adheres to a system of strict reciprocity, meaning that if a foreign mayor visits, the local mayor acts as host. This is true even if the Chinese city is many times larger than the foreign one, which is always the case when Canadians come to call. In China, mayors have a significant degree of authority in making decisions about the goods and services, technologies and infrastructure systems the city requires.

This means that having access to Chinese mayors is important for firms doing business in areas such as environmental technologies, urban transportation, architecture, health care (with a growing emphasis on eldercare), education and financial services. Such access is a huge advantage to Canadian firms that would otherwise face the daunting task of trying to figure out how and where to penetrate an imposing bureaucracy. A well-planned municipal visit can save a company half a dozen expensive trips to China.

Western mayors, such as those of Victoria, Calgary and Edmonton, do this well. Vancouver mayor Gregor Robertson starts with the advantage of having Norman Bethune, still a great hero to the Chinese, as a distant relative. But I was also impressed by his skill in using his access to build awareness of Vancouver's capabilities in green technologies and in creative industries such as animation. There is more to it than that, however. As cities become more active globally, mayors play a big role in creating an international narrative, helping citizens at home under-stand how and where their city connects with key partners around the world. That is happening in cities like Vancouver and Calgary.

But it hasn't been happening in Toronto, which has a sorry rec-ord of starts and stops when it comes to building relationships with China. Toronto's official sister city is Chongqing, the massive slice of urban sprawl and surrounding farmland that was carved out of Sichuan province in 1997. It became one of four Chinese cities (the others are Beijing, Shanghai and Tianjin) that report directly to the central government. Population statistics for cities in China are con-tentious, because most municipalities include a significant surrounding region of rural towns and villages. By most estimates, Chongqing's total population is thirty million. The central city represents about a quarter of that. Although it has recently become notorious because of a vast scandal that led to the downfall of one of its leaders, for-mer Party secretary Bo Xilai, it remains the platform from which the development of China's west is being launched.

The mayor's office in Chongqing is decorated with photos of its sister cities, including Toronto. But its relationship with the Canadian city has been moribund, at least at the highest level, for years. This is probably because Toronto taxpayers take a dim view of travelling mayors. While frugality is not a bad thing, it comes at a cost in such a diverse city whose economy is increasingly dependent on what hap-pens beyond North America. That saved Torontonians considerable embarrassment during the Rob Ford years, but over the longer term it represents a costly missed opportunity, a failure to make the most of Toronto's China connections.

When I served as executive director of the Canada China Business Council in the mid-1990s, people often asked me why my office was in Toronto rather than Vancouver. I explained that it was because I could walk from my office to the headquarters of almost all of the major Canadian companies that provided our core funding. If you think about the size and dynamism of the Chinese cultural community in Toronto (and when it comes to promoting tourism or education, it *does* make sense to talk about the diaspora), and the many links to China forged by institutions such as the University of Toronto and the Royal Ontario Museum, it becomes easier to think of Toronto as an Asia Pacific city. Except that we don't. Ignoring this aspect is certainly bad for Toronto. But it's bad for Canada, too. We can't engage China successfully if we leave our major city on the bench. During the course of her China visit, Premier Wynne paused to offer up a "hallelujah" on learning of John Tory's election victory in the Toronto mayoral race. While he will have his hands full dealing with the dysfunction left over from the Ford era, he would do well to work closely with the premier in linking the province and its major city more closely with China.

Bringing more of Canada into the economic relationship with China, broadening and diversifying what we sell there, is of critical importance. But it won't happen on its own. Competition will be fierce, and we will need to use every tool in the tool box to crack open the market for Canadian firms. We're at a crossroads in our trade relationship with China. Its dynamic rise has been the salvation of our resource sector and is sustaining many of our farming and fishing communities. China's next phase of development will be led by consumers and by political leaders who are struggling to deal with the needs of an increasingly urban and rapidly aging population. Meeting these new opportunities will require much greater effort from us. We will need to be savvy enough to spot new trends and use new tools. We will have to be patient when it comes to building awareness for Canadian products and the Canadian brand, using to good effect the door-opening potential of expanded provincial and municipal diplomacy. And we will need to be confident enough to remember that our long-term success will be based not on favours or even friendship, but on providing the things that China wants to buy.

THREE

Cold Feet and Mixed Signals

B y the end of 2009, the chill in Canada–China relations that had
characterized the early years of the Harper government was
behind us. The prime minister's highly successful visit in early
December of that year signalled that a page had been turned and a
new chapter was beginning. But as is the case with just about everything in China, the explanation for the improvement was more complicated than it appeared, and owed less to our renewed attentions
than it did to the appetites and energies of confident new shapers
of China's international policy. By the time of the prime minister's
visit, we were well into a Chinese discovery of Canada as a destination for investment in resources. This was the latest step in an ambitious effort that saw China's major state-owned enterprises (SOEs)
expanding their global reach, deploying vast and growing reserves of
cash to secure footholds in key markets.

China's small-time traders and restaurateurs have traditionally
been the first into any new market, setting up shop as opportunities
presented themselves throughout Africa and in Latin America, and
moving quickly into the cities of newly liberated Eastern Europe.
On my visits to Afghanistan, I was always amazed to see Chinese
businesses emerging in a Kabul that was still largely hidden behind

sandbags and barbed wire. Over the last two decades, China's biggest players—its large mining firms, shipping companies, banks, hotels
and manufacturers—have joined the rush to go global. For Canada,
the most active players have been China's three major state-owned oil
companies—China National Petroleum Corporation (CNPC), China
National Offshore Oil Corporation (CNOOC), and China Petroleum
and Chemical Corporation (SINOPEC)—and the sovereign wealth
fund China Investment Corporation (CIC). Their pattern of activity
in Canada says much about what China was, what it is now and what
it is becoming.

Depending on where you are in the debate about Chinese investment, SOEs are either admirable free-market offspring born of Deng
Xiaoping's reforms, or Trojan horses, vehicles for bringing the very
worst of the Chinese Communist system into the Canadian economy.
My sense is that neither caricature is true or, perhaps more accurately,
that both are. SOEs are for the most part hybrid entities, creatures in
transition, neither quite as bad nor quite as good as often made out to be.

China's SOEs emerged out of the drive by Mao to create a state-
owned, centrally planned economy. The oldest SOEs began their
existence as branches of vast government departments responsible for
managing important parts of the state's infrastructure. SOEs are now
in a second phase in the evolutionary process, a period during which
day-to-day management has been transferred away from government
and into carefully structured corporations. During this second phase,
steady efforts have been made to improve internal governance, to weed
out weaker players and to separate, to the extent possible, management from all but the broadest forms of government policy direction.[1]

But these laudable efforts should not obscure the fact that the third
phase, which would involve cutting the tether to the state altogether,
remains a distant objective. As far as SOEs are concerned, the tether
may be much longer these days, but it still runs back to the centre of
power in Beijing. In his book *The Party*, Richard McGregor makes the

important point that, although its role and significance are masked by the sheer exuberance of China's economic growth, the Communist Party is a pervasive presence in today's China. "Peek under the hood of the Chinese model," he cautions, "... and China looks much more communist than it does on the open road."[2]

Xi Jinping may be China's president, but he wields real power from his position as Party chairman. Despite its name, the People's Liberation Army is the Party's army, reflecting the enduring truth of Mao's observation that "political power grows out of the barrel of a gun." And virtually every significant organization in China— municipal governments, SOEs and even universities—has its Party committee, which operates alongside, and in some cases with more real authority than, the more visible governance structures headed by mayors, CEOs or presidents.

In the case of SOEs, additional links connect their executive suites back to the Party. Researchers have described the revolving door that brings officials into SOEs and in turn ushers SOE executives back into high office. Technically, people who work at SOEs are not government employees, but in fact in many cases they are still ranked according to a parallel system. Not surprisingly, although the pay is much better in an SOE, many aspire to get back into government so that they can climb the next rung of the ladder.[3]

In my interactions with SOEs over the years, I have seen a steady shift in thinking and in style, particularly among the rising stars in their management ranks. These younger executives often seem more like their counterparts in multinational corporations, and less like officials in one of China's ministries. They stress the fact that their interests, at home and abroad, are driven by financial considerations, that their objective is to make money, not to stockpile strategic resources for China. But change isn't as evident at the highest levels of many SOEs. Before and after the prime minister's 2009 visit, when I called on the top people in those SOEs most interested in Canada, it was not uncommon to hear them delivering the same political talking points about the need to respect China's core interests that were dispensed by officials in the Foreign Ministry.

More often than not, in these high-level sessions, our meeting would open with my host offering a deluge of mind-numbing statistics about the size and scope of the enterprise. I would hear about vast workforces, vertically integrated operations, and other operations that seemed to have absolutely no link, vertical or otherwise, to the core business of the company. On those occasions, seated alongside my host, at the top of a U-shaped array of plush arm chairs, I would get the feeling that I was listening not to the CEO of a Fortune 500 company, but to a minister of old.

The major exception to this pattern of partial transformation is CIC, a sovereign wealth fund and, along with the larger State Administration of Foreign Exchange, one of the principal vehicles through which China seeks to maximize the return on its vast (close to US$4 trillion) holdings of foreign exchange. Just before my arrival in the summer of 2009, CIC had purchased 17 percent of the Canadian mining company Teck. Both CIC and Teck were enthusiastic about the partnership, which opened the China market to Teck at a time when demand for copper was soaring. As a result, CIC was already carefully exploring other Canadian projects.

In a refreshing departure from Chinese meeting protocol, people at CIC got down to business immediately. They were also impressively well prepared, quickly getting down to the outstanding opportunities and problems with exacting precision. I brought a succession of Canadian officials to see them, and would carefully coach people to skip the breezy overviews about Canada or a particular province being "open for business," and to be ready for blunt and highly informed questions about specific issues.

CIC's then chair (and now China's finance minister), Lou Jiwei, and the very engaging Gao Xiqing, who served as president, set the

straight-talking tone. Before my first meeting with Gao, I was ush-
ered into a very plain boardroom. One of the chairs around the table
was fitted with the kind of cushion used by people who have back
problems. The junior person who showed me in made it clear that
this was where Gao would sit. Then he whispered dramatically, "Too
big to fail." At first I thought he was imparting some general insight
about the viability of CIC. But then it occurred to me that he was,
in fact, referencing the title of Andrew Ross Sorkin's book about the
meltdown on Wall Street, a book in which Gao makes a brief but
memorable appearance. When things were at their darkest, John
Mack, CEO of the investment bank Morgan Stanley, was desperately
seeking an investor to save the firm. Although only created the year
earlier, CIC was already sufficiently credible to be on Mack's list of
possible saviours. Gao handled the (ultimately fruitless) negotiations
for CIC. What adds a touch of the bizarre to the account is that Gao
was suffering from a flare-up of recurring back pain, and conducted
things with Mack while lying flat on his back.[4]

Gao's unsparing critique of the excesses he had witnessed on Wall
Street was delivered with a disarming sense of humour. In an interview with James Fallows, he described the challenge of trying to brief
China's leadership about derivatives, the financial instruments whose
tenuous, more-than-once-removed association with the real economy
came to symbolize the precariousness of pre-crisis economic growth.
He used a simple analogy to explain things to the leadership:

> First of all, you have this book to sell. [He picks up a leather-bound
> book.] This is worth something, because of all the labor and so
> on you put in it. But then someone says, "I don't have to sell the
> book itself! I have a mirror, and I can sell the mirror image of the
> book!" Okay. That's a stock certificate. And then someone else says,
> "I have another mirror—I can sell a mirror image of that mirror."
> Derivatives. That's fine too, for a while. Then you have 10,000

mirrors, and the image is almost perfect. People start to believe that these mirrors are almost the real thing. But at some point, the image is interrupted. And all the rest will go.

When I told the State Council about the mirrors, they all started laughing. "How can you sell a mirror image! Won't there be distortion?" But this is what happened with the American economy, and it will be a long and painful process to come down.[5]

Gao and his colleagues were under considerable pressure to succeed. High-flying and free-wheeling, CIC was still seen as an experiment and therefore carefully watched by key observers in Beijing. Some of the corporation's early investments, notably in the investment firm Blackstone, had not initially been successful, and this had generated considerable criticism. The negative commentary was probably more intense in Beijing than it might have been elsewhere. For one thing, the centre of power in China features as much back-biting and poisonous rivalry as the top of any organization. Add to that the ability of CIC's rivals to play the patriotic card, since any losses registered by a manager of China's assets could accurately be described as losses to the nation. There is no more damaging criticism of a Chinese official than that he has given up a national asset to greedy foreigners.

My early discussions with Gao were about CIC's plans for Canada. It was already evident that CIC's stake in Teck was a success for both sides, bringing needed investment to the Canadian firm and opening it up to exciting new possibilities in China. CIC became a welcome public proponent of the benefits of investment in Canada and, in due course, opened its first-ever overseas office in Toronto.[6] CIC was in fact exploring investments in a broad range of sectors and regions and via a diverse assortment of vehicles. But its leaders, like its counterparts in China's three major oil companies, were most intent on the oil sands of northern Alberta, where CIC ultimately invested in two projects.

By 2009, Canada's advantages as a destination for investment in natural resources were readily apparent to Chinese investors. Canada is not alone in being rich in energy and minerals. But unlike most resource-rich destinations, which tend to be concentrated in the developing world, Canada offers a stable and predictable business environment. Costs in Canada are higher than in the developing world when it comes to wages, taxes and an array of inputs. But stability—the confidence that the rules won't suddenly change—means a lot, making Canada more attractive in the long run.

The only comparable destination is Australia, which was already the site of far more extensive Chinese investments. This prompted ambitious Chinese investors to diversify, to look for the next Australia. And in addition to wanting to stay ahead of the crowd, China's most savvy investors were aware of turbulence in the Australia–China relationship, including some unfavourable decisions on Chinese investment proposals and, in the wind, rumours of a major new tax on mining.

CHINA'S THREE MAJOR oil companies were relatively early movers into international markets. They understood, well in advance of China's accession to the WTO in 2001, that they would inevitably be exposed to competition from more nimble foreign firms. They needed to learn quickly, and the best way to learn was by getting into offshore ventures themselves. But they were careful about how much challenge they were willing to accept. Although they had been visiting western Canada since the 1990s, China's major oil companies didn't pursue significant investments there until the middle of the next decade. They were keenly aware of how little they understood about the North American market, and remained most active in the developing world where the business environment was less sophisticated and, as a result, more permissive.

And when they did start to explore opportunities in Canada, it was clear that China's SOEs did indeed have a lot to learn. Investment in major projects in developed countries involves more than securing approvals, by whatever means necessary, from the ruling elite. In open, democratic countries like Canada a diverse array of actors have strong views, which they freely express, about investment in general, and foreign investment in particular. Debate is stoked to even higher levels of intensity when the investor is from China. This Canadian wariness runs headlong into a Chinese mindset that is shaped by insecurity and a deep sense of victimization, something that often renders Chinese investors unable to understand what is happening to them and why.

China's own narrative about itself, as woven by the Communist Party, is that the country has suffered more than a century of humiliation, beginning with the First Opium War in 1839 and continuing right up until the establishment of the People's Republic in 1949. Since then, so the narrative goes, foreign enemies have sought to undermine the "New China," to keep it backward and subservient. SOEs are by definition playing with the nation's cash, and if one of their foreign investments goes sour, they run the risk of being criticized for having been duped by slick foreigners. If that's not enough psychological baggage to carry going in, there is also the widespread belief that something akin to national feelings are on the line.

China seems to be the only country in the world that can have its feelings hurt. Or so its leaders claim when other countries do things like welcoming the Dalai Lama or honouring a courageous Chinese dissident. Of course, China is less squeamish about the feelings of other nations, and readily lashes out when foreigners have the temerity to say or do things displeasing to China. Senior Chinese officials claim to be wounded, deeply and personally, by criticism from the media, local communities or NGO groups. What another foreign investor would consider to be a fairly predictable challenge is often portrayed by Chinese business people as something akin to a national affront. While this is very much part of the theatrics of Chinese negotiations, the people handling the negotiations on the Chinese side often *do* feel hurt and offended when people on the other, the "foreign" side, refuse to offer up concessions. Some SOE managers appear to confuse the SOE and its interests with China itself, allowing any bump in the road of negotiation to be transformed into an insult to the nation. This is another example of the hybrid nature of many SOEs, which have yet to make the transition to becoming truly global multinationals, and of SOE executives, who are often, at some level, still creatures of the Chinese state.

It is also true that, despite having considerable international experience, SOEs tend to be poor at understanding local cultures and conditions. Up until fairly recently, this failing was compounded by the disinclination of most SOEs to take on foreign business advisors. That is an example of the kind of false economy that is still common in China, the notion that you pay for goods but not for services, hardware but not the accompanying software. It is also true that, until recently, even those SOEs that had engaged foreign advisors had a hard time figuring out how to work with them. For their part, the foreign advisors were often equally lost within the complexities of the SOE.

Many Chinese organizations, SOEs included, remain opaque, rigidly hierarchical and wedded to the notion that you get ahead by never giving the boss any bad news. Deference rather than honesty is the path to success. While this is changing over time, the growing pains are real and persistent. That's a tough environment for a foreign consultant whose job includes giving unwelcome advice. As a result, many SOEs were essentially flying blind when it came to Canada. At the very best, they might consult their guidebooks on doing business in the U.S., thereby ignoring the significant differences in terms of how both countries work. Worse, they tended to place the same low value on communications in Canada that they do in respect to communications in China. As a result, SOE executives often failed to explain the advantages their investment would bring and, worse, failed to understand who was criticizing them and why.

When I arrived in China in 2009, feelings were still bruised by the failure of what had been, up to then, China's largest bid to invest in Canada, the effort by the SOE Minmetals to acquire Canada's Noranda. The bid had been launched in 2004. After months of speculation, and considerable public controversy, Minmetals abandoned its bid in March 2005. (After Noranda merged with rival Falconbridge, the new entity was itself taken over by Swiss-based Xstrata.) There was a widespread sense among many of the people I talked to that the failure of the Minmetals bid was due to an inexplicable lack of friendliness on our part. And, although it had happened before Prime Minister Harper came to office, the collapse of the deal tended to get associated with the more general chill that had descended after his election in 2006.

For many in China, the failure of the investment was due to the unwillingness of something called Canada to warmly welcome it. Much less attention was paid to possible misgivings of the Noranda board, the market in general, the media, or various informed and uninformed observers. Few seemed to think that Minmetals was even partly responsible for failing to understand the complexities of a high-profile takeover in a country like Canada, where transactions like this generate lively public debate, and for failing to devise a strategy to address these challenges. Even those Chinese observers who had argued most strenuously, while the deal was under scrutiny in Canada, that SOEs are not mere proxies for the Chinese state, later appeared to see the Minmetals decision as an unfriendly act, a rebuff of China itself.

And China *was* a factor in the debate. Many Canadians were unconvinced that Minmetals was an independent actor, and believed instead that the government of China was actually using the company's bid to somehow lock up valuable Canadian resources. While you may disagree with this view, it is not hard to understand why many people hold it. But this has more to do with the complexity and opacity of the Chinese system than it does with a more general anti-China attitude.

Attempting a large and ambitious investment in an open society such as Canada requires the investor to enter the arena of public debate and make its case. One very good way of addressing public concerns that the investment is only about enriching China is by advancing a compelling argument as to why it is good for Canada.

Only a few years after the failure of the Minmetals bid, the situation had changed. By 2009, Chinese investors, convinced that they had found the next Australia, were taking a second look at Canada. Many in this country were looking back with keen interest. By that time, fewer potential investors were knocking at the door, and almost none were as cash-rich as the Chinese. And, given Chinese growth rates, it was a good bet that, over time, China would only become more important as a partner. By 2013, China was the world's third-largest foreign investor, behind only the U.S. and Japan.

For their part, the major Chinese oil firms had finally begun to avail themselves of good guidance in the form of Canadian banks, law firms, accountants and communications advisors. They tested the water carefully, moving quickly from non-controlling stakes in oil sands projects to steadily larger investments. Announcements of Chinese investment intentions surged from under $5 billion in 2009 to over $20 billion in 2012.[7] The lion's share of the 2012 total was represented by CNOOC's $15-billion bid for outright control of Calgary-based Nexen. Seeking control of a Canadian oil company was a bold step, but CNOOC showed that it had been paying attention to Canadian concerns. Its proposal talked about using Calgary as a base for managing Canadian and wider regional operations, and listing shares on the Toronto Stock Exchange.[8]

The debate in Canada that followed the bid was notable for its cross-currents. Many commentators expressed concerns about an entity very much identified with the Chinese state taking a controlling stake in a Canadian company in such an important sector. These anxieties were only partly assuaged by arguments pointing out that

China's major oil firms tended to behave like other major oil firms, selling their production where they could get the best price rather than slavishly sending it home to China.[9]

As this was playing out, the Obama administration, responding to concerns from U.S. environmentalists, held up approval of the Keystone Pipeline, a north–south system that would add much-needed capacity to deliver Alberta oil to the U.S. Gulf Coast. This issue got tangled up with the Nexen debate in a variety of ways. It led Canadians in general to think seriously about the cost of having only a single buyer, the United States, for our oil, and about the extent to which diversifying our markets is in our national interest. And it led some to think that growing Chinese investment in Canada could be used as a wedge in the Keystone debate. Of course, the reality is that responding to growing interest from China—and from Korea and Japan—does make sense for Canada, as does figuring out how to ship Canadian energy products, safely and sensibly, to the Pacific, Gulf and Atlantic coasts.

This broader turbulence meant that the Nexen takeover was under scrutiny by the federal government for longer than expected. It was ultimately approved, but with approval came new conditions for SOEs investing in the oil sands. In future, controlling stakes would be allowed only on an exceptional basis. The government was steering SOEs back to the much less contentious route of investing as minority shareholders.

There are a number of possible reasons for applying such limits on investment. One has to do with national security. If a resource is determined to be so valuable and so scarce as to be central to our national security, it makes sense to apply investment limits. But after touting Canada as an energy superpower, it would be hard for the government to make the case that CNOOC was threatening our energy security by acquiring a mid-sized Canadian producer.

Another reason for applying restrictions is linked to a more general worry about the gradual disappearance of head offices in Canada as

Canadian companies are bought up. This is a valid concern and worthy of debate. But it has less to do with Chinese investment than it does with foreign investment in general. And any such debate should force us to think about the cost of intervention in terms of our ability to attract the financing and new technologies we need to develop the Canadian economy. Further, if we *are* willing to allow foreign takeovers—and this has been central to the development of Canada's energy industry—it makes little difference whether the investor is a Chinese SOE or a foreign multinational. The key issue is that investors operate in accordance with Canadian law and all of the regulations relevant to that particular sector. In such cases, it is up to us to make full use of the authority that we already have. This means being clear at the outset about what is non-negotiable when it comes to factors such as worker safety, environmental protection and adherence to the rules of a free market. And it means following up consistently to ensure full compliance.

What is it about China and Chinese companies that makes us doubt our ability to apply our own rules and enforce our own laws? Our own eagerness to make a buck, for one thing. In some instances, local levels of government are so keen to woo a Chinese business partner that they appear open to concessions that could undermine existing regulations and policies. I have been in situations where trying to uphold a well-founded policy position in the face of intense pressure from China was made much more difficult because of counter-messaging behind the scenes by another level of government in Canada. This gave hope to the Chinese petitioner that the federal government would ultimately give in, something that made the negotiation much more difficult to conclude. Such situations remind me of the cartoon character Pogo's rueful observation, "We have met the enemy and he is us."

Many praised the Nexen decision as walking a fine line between our commitments to the Chinese and our worst fears about them. If nothing else, it enabled us to live up to our assertions about Canada being open for business but allowed us to put some markers down about the type of clientele we were so open to serve. Had the decision been preceded by greater efforts to share information and build a higher degree of mutual trust, and had it been followed up with messages helping SOEs to better understand the areas that were still open to them, it might have been less discouraging to the Chinese.

But context is everything. Much had changed in the relationship by the time that the Nexen decision was announced late in 2012. The year had begun with much enthusiasm. The prime minister's February visit to China had secured agreement, after more than a decade of negotiations, on the text of a Foreign Investment Promotion and Protection Agreement (FIPA). And during the visit, the Chinese had indicated a willingness to go even further. Uncharacteristically, where normally they would have waited patiently for us to make the first move, they pressed us to consider the launch of free trade negotiations.

But by the end of the year, the situation was different. The FIPA deal that had been celebrated in Beijing in February hadn't been ratified by Parliament, and the question about possible free trade was still hanging in the air, unanswered by us. While other national leaders jostled for opportunities to call on newly appointed President Xi Jinping, Canada was content to let things ride. We simply went silent. In fact, it wasn't until more than two years later, on a Friday afternoon in September 2014, with most Canadians already focused on one of the last weekends of summer, that the FIPA was quietly ratified in Ottawa.

The Nexen debate laid bare significant Canadian ambivalence about the nature and pace of our engagement of China. Far from being willing to consider even more ambitious objectives, Canadians were more interested in taking a pause. Polling conducted by the Asia Pacific Foundation of Canada in 2012 showed that 75 percent of Canadians opposed the idea of Chinese SOEs taking a majority stake in Canadian firms. The same poll showed that only 12 percent of Canadians had warm, positive feelings about China.[10] Whether, at times like this, it is sufficient for governments in Canada to follow public opinion rather than to lead it is, of course, another question.

It is not surprising that Canadians have lingering concerns about SOEs, about their links to the Chinese state and about their possible motivations. Although the Chinese sometimes see such concerns as a personal affront, they are for the most part founded in understandable skepticism on the part of Canadians about the extent to which SOEs meet our own expectations of openness, accessibility and transparency. If SOEs have generally upped their game when it comes to operating in Canada, they still fall short on community engagement and full and transparent communications.[11] Canadians can also be forgiven for wondering whether they should be willing to work with Chinese companies whose track record in places like Africa leaves much to be desired.

But although we have the right to insist that SOEs work harder to become good corporate citizens wherever they invest and that they embrace the rules, discipline and transparency of the market, we can't simply sit back and wait until some distant day of reckoning arrives and we are ready to do business again. When he was serving as vice-chair of the Canadian Imperial Bank of Commerce, Jim Prentice made the point that Canada's energy sector has capital expenditures of $50 billion annually, of which Canadian capital markets raise $14 billion each year.[12] Closing the door to Chinese investment implies a serious decision about our own future. It also underestimates our ability to influence what happens here in Canada. There is no doubt that we are going to have to work harder at understanding what SOEs are now and what they are becoming. As we do this, we will find that they are not identical, that some have evolved more than others, and that while some seem stuck as creatures of the state, others are moving briskly in the direction of the market.

We should also be careful about making fixed and final decisions today about Chinese partners that are likely to be different tomorrow. Today's CNOOC is unlike the entity it was ten years ago. And it will almost certainly be something different ten years from now. We should also be aware that the high-profile activities of SOEs can distract us from the growing importance of private sector firms in China, whose international ambitions and appetite for investment offer exciting new possibilities for Canadian firms.[13] In the meantime, the flow of Chinese investment into the Canadian oil patch has, in the words of the *National Post*, "dropped off a cliff," a precipitous decline that Jim Prentice attributed to factors including the new SOE ownership guidelines, and concerns about our continuing inability to get a pipeline built to the Pacific.[14] Others point to rapid and radical changes in the global energy picture, much of this due to the emergence of plentiful reserves of shale gas as an attractive alternative.

The fact is that the Chinese oil companies and CIC have struggled with their initial investments. Dealing with new technologies and an uncertain market, and learning to work cooperatively with the communities on whose land the developments are taking place, are part of a steep learning curve. This should have provided an opportunity for us to help the Chinese along that curve, with the objective of encouraging further investments in the resource sector and, over time, investment in other parts of our economy. But our ambivalence about China has slowed efforts to build the infrastructure of agreements and official exchanges that underpin a sophisticated relationship. We dragged our feet on implementing the FIPA, and showed no interest in setting up a sophisticated dialogue on energy involving multiple players from both countries, something the Chinese encouraged us to consider. Far from creating new mechanisms through which we can communicate, fully and effectively, we've simply put the conversation on hold. It is no wonder that the Chinese are confused, somewhat suspicious and much less enthusiastic than they used to be.

As a result, unlike Australia, the U.K. and Germany, we aren't benefitting from an evolution in Chinese investment, something that sees Chinese firms progress along a learning curve, displaying growing confidence and sophistication in doing business in developed, Western economies. Elsewhere this has led to Chinese investment in basic infrastructure, food processing, commercial real estate, telecommunications and financial services. Some may think that we dodged a bullet by shutting the door to any new acquisitions with what was essentially a one-off approval of CNOOC's takeover of Nexen. But the reality is that we have shot ourselves in the foot, signalling our suspicion and ambivalence when it comes to Chinese investments that many of our allies see as an increasingly important source of growth.

NO DISCUSSION of Chinese investment is complete without at least some reference to reciprocity, the principle that Canadian investors in China should have the same access and protections that Chinese investors have in Canada. The current reality is that they don't. In the space of my own career, I have watched the rise and fall of the Canadian mining sector in China. Canadian mining firms originally made inroads in China because they have the technology China needs to extract its resources safely and efficiently.

But over time, Canadian firms, like mining companies from the U.S., Australia and South Africa, have been squeezed out of the projects they largely developed. Typically, after spending a lot of their own money to discover a deposit of some mineral, the Canadian firm finds its progress blocked. A crucial next level of approval is held up indefinitely. Often, this coincides with the emergence of a new Chinese partner, a firm closely linked to the local authorities or, this being China, a firm that is actually *owned* by them. The result, in case after case, is that, after being squeezed relentlessly, the Canadian firm is forced to give up. In the best cases, they are awarded some lesser settlement, but nothing like what participation in the commercial phase of the project would have brought to them.

Similarly frustrating impediments arise in many sectors. Often, the flimsy rationale is some variant of what I call the "rule of the comma." It is not uncommon for Chinese counterparts to want to revisit the terms of a contract when it suits them to do so. The ominous precursor to this is the observation that "conditions have changed." Shortly afterward, it will be pointed out to you that there is a problem with the agreement. It is almost invariably minor (symbolized for me by the absence of a comma), but this creates the pretext for revisiting the agreement in ways that favour the Chinese partner. The foreigner will point out, in vain, all of the much more major Chinese errors, lapses and shortcomings that have been indulged. But having been ignored, these Chinese errors and omissions are now sealed off and forgotten. Not so for any infelicities that can be attributed to the foreign partner. Many a contract has been reopened and many a profit margin shaved down to a shadow of its former self through this procedure.

Given the uneven pace of development in China and the almost inevitable disconnects between how laws are interpreted nationally and locally, it is impossible to draft a document that can't be challenged. Not challenging it depends on mutual goodwill, something that is, in all too many cases, only present so long as the Chinese side is beholden to its foreign partner. Once that perception vanishes, conditions have changed and a pretext is found for revisiting the agreement. While this is deeply frustrating to foreign investors, it is also part of the daily reality for many people in China. Given the complexity of the legal system and the tax code, and given the latitude taken by Party functionaries in interpreting both, it is almost impossible, even with the best of intentions, to stay within the limits of the law.

Chinese authorities use this pervasive ambiguity to maintain compliance. People are free to get rich in the new China, but the state retains the ability to take everything away from anyone who crosses it. In the last chapter, I mentioned how the artist Ai Weiwei shamed authorities by speaking out about the shoddy construction that caused so many children to die in the Sichuan earthquake. I had the chance to talk to him about this. I called on him at his compound in the suburbs of Beijing, where he is under house arrest. Official surveillance cameras monitor traffic at the gate. Far from being intimidated, Ai has been inspired by the very heavy-handedness of the police. One response was to go a step further, putting himself under the twenty-four-hour gaze of what he called "weiweicam" and uploading the resulting footage to the internet. He also fashioned small cameras as art objects and positioned some on the wall that fronts his house. The door to the compound bears his company name: Fake Design. In English, this plays on the ambiguities around what is bogus and what is genuine in the world of art. It also brings to mind current Chinese concerns about fakery in the products they buy, even in the food they eat. The word's Chinese pronunciation—"fah keh"—is a play on another four-letter English word.

There wasn't much mischief or levity in our conversation that morning. Instead, I was struck by the quiet intensity with which Ai spoke. He was describing his recent incarceration, a time in which he was held incommunicado, subject to harsh treatment and relentless interrogation. A capable, experienced and confident man, Ai said he was unsettled by the speed with which the authorities "could take me to such a place"—in other words, quickly bring him to a level close to emotional and psychological collapse.

Such treatment was meted out because the artist was attracting international admiration for doing what artists do: calling attention to the absurdity, banality and criminality of the powers that be. It took some time for a rationale for the arrest to emerge, suggesting that the actual reason was to remove a troublesome individual from the public eye. Ultimately, the alleged rationale for detaining Ai was to enable officials to conduct what amounted to a tax audit. Ai was clearly the target of the whole Kafkaesque process, even though the company being investigated was actually controlled by Ai's wife. He was released after more than two months' detention and only then on the condition that he agree to pay what ultimately amounted to millions of yuan in back taxes. Donations from supporters, some simply tossed over the wall of his compound, allowed him to meet the amount required for immediate release. He has refused to pay the remainder. The point that authorities were making was not lost on others: we can always find a pretense for locking you up and taking away everything you have.

A recent survey suggested that roughly half of wealthy people (meaning those with a net worth of more than US$1.5 million) in China are actively considering emigration within five years.[15] Finding better education opportunities for their children is typically cited as the leading reason, and concerns about pollution and tainted food products follow. But there is also uneasiness related to the very real possibility that wealth that was gained quickly could just as quickly be taken away. Concern has been fuelled by online chatter about rising income inequality in China. Might the state, anxious to placate a restive underclass, suddenly decide to rob from the rich?[16] But as Rupert Hoogewerf, whose *Hurun Report* surveys trends among China's richest people, points out, not all would-be emigrants completely cut their ties with China. A foreign passport is seen as something of an insurance policy. Indeed, according to a 2011 *Hurun* survey, some 80 percent of would-be emigrants also intend on retaining their Chinese passports, something that will probably hold true as long as prospects for making money in China are better than they are in emigration destinations like the U.S., Australia and Canada. Although wives and children may take up residence abroad, many husbands continue to spend most of their time in China. Says Hoogewerf of such families, "They still have their businesses in China and most of their assets are in yuan."[17]

Acknowledging that the playing field is uneven for everybody who has to deal with the Chinese state, even Chinese people themselves, is of little consolation for foreign businesses. They watch, with mounting frustration, as Chinese investors win approval to invest in places like

Canada while they are often stymied in China. But trying to enforce reciprocity on investment deals is almost always a bad idea. For one thing, the consequences of reciprocity are also felt by the home side. Any tit-for-tat cancellation of a Chinese project in Canada would hurt Canadians, too. While the Chinese can ignore public opinion, we, fortunately, can't.

We can lift our game by working with allies, both outside and inside China. I have noted the excellent work done by groups such as the American and E.U. chambers of commerce. They represent the U.S. and European business communities in China, and are well resourced, impressively staffed and open to working with a range of like-minded partners, Canadians included. They are adept at identifying protectionist storm clouds on the horizon, and also skilful at devising strategies to counter them. We also need to build a sophisticated infrastructure of agreements, dialogues and official exchanges. We did have reason to celebrate when, after more than a decade of negotiation, Canada secured China's agreement on our bilateral FIPA during Prime Minister Harper's visit of February 2012.

The FIPA is not a panacea. Critics point out that the agreement with China is not as strong as others we have signed. But ours would provide more protection to Canadian investors than they currently enjoy. Among other things, it ensures that investors will not be discriminated against in comparison to their foreign competitors, and it offers protections against arbitrary acts, such as expropriation by host governments. It allows for neutral, third-party arbitration, not to overturn existing laws but as a means of determining fair compensation.

Negotiating a strong FIPA represents a good example of how a bilateral initiative can advance a broader agenda. In the words of Robert Zoellick, former president of the World Bank and, before that, America's top trade official, "Chinese reformers believe that bilateral investment treaties will help them fight favouritism and corruption, remove onerous regulations that choke market competition, improve uneven law enforcement, and shrink the advantages enjoyed by state-owned enterprises."[18] It was discouraging, although not entirely surprising, to see how quickly concerns were raised in Canada about the dangers of signing an investment deal with China. The FIPA was transformed by its critics into a device that would overturn Canadian laws and give Chinese companies the ability to loot our resources, despoil our environment and endanger our workers. The reaction represented a worrying failure of confidence. People somehow felt that we could be made to do things contrary to the laws and regulations that we have established.

There is a hard kernel of truth in this sense of anxiety, something that brings us back to the challenge at the heart of our engagement of China. To the extent that Chinese companies, SOEs in particular, are seen as parts of a secretive, non-transparent and ideologically unfriendly state, they will be subject to suspicion. As one analyst put it, "China's form of state capitalism is particularly opaque, and in the eyes of some foreigners, this taints all Chinese companies, not just SOEs. The reason is so simple and so sensitive that few dare speak of it: the Chinese Communist Party. The Party is powerful and pervasive yet also completely elusive, like a great ethnic masonic lodge backed by the world's largest standing army."[19]

But we also need to remember that this is an unfinished process. Governance of SOEs is continuing to evolve, and reforms appear to be accelerating under President Xi Jinping. We can't wait until every firm in China has reached some distant milestone of development before being willing to allow any to invest in Canada. Indeed, few Western corporations can point to an unblemished track record when it comes to their global investment performance. Nor can we wait until China consistently treats foreign investors fairly. China has the capital we need to develop our economy and is home to a steadily increasing number of competent global investors. At the end of the day, our best protection is our transparent, rules-based business environment, and our feisty and well-informed democracy. Continuing to grow our economy and ensure our long-term prosperity is a matter of self-confidence in our regulations, and in ourselves.

It would help enormously if Canadians could feel confident that our own firms are equally welcome in China. We need to work diligently to level the investment playing field. And we need to hold China accountable through instruments like a FIPA. China's official line is all about mutual respect and long-term friendship. These are wonderful objectives, but we need to be equally emphatic that they are only truly realized when China provides the same welcome to our investors that we do to theirs. In the meantime we should be guided by skill, confidence and enlightened self-interest, tapping into China's growing wealth to further develop our own economy.

THE PEOPLE-TO-PEOPLE
CONNECTION

FOUR

Breaking the Breakfast Barrier

I n the last few hours before Prime Minister Harper's December 2009 meeting with his Chinese counterpart, it looked like a deal to open the door for rapid increases in tourism from China would slip through our fingers. It had seemed to be in the bag on the very eve of the visit. And although I had duly reminded the embassy team to expect at least one last-minute crisis, I hadn't anticipated the threatened unravelling of everything we had patiently negotiated, including the highly prized tourism agreement. I had also expected that, if we were to have any last-minute drama, it would be engineered by the Chinese side as a means of wringing out a few last concessions. Instead, we had a crisis of our own making.

We were more than a decade late in getting to an agreement that would open up Canada to Chinese tourists. By 2009, a steady evolution in Chinese policy had opened up group tourism to just about everywhere. Everywhere but Canada.

CHINA WAS SLOW to allow its citizens to travel internationally. This is a natural impulse for a state that reflexively seeks to control every aspect of daily life. But in the precarious first decades of the People's

Republic, travel controls had the added rationale of preventing the out-flow of precious foreign currency.[1] Over time, foreign travel to a few select places was gradually made easier. Permission was granted to visit Hong Kong and Macau, which were in any event soon to be restored to the motherland. Then states in Southeast Asia that were deemed reliable, such as Thailand, Malaysia and Singapore, were opened up to Chinese tours. In time, other Southeast Asian states were added.[2] In 2011, when I visited Siem Reap, the Cambodian city that is the gateway to the sprawling temple complex of Angkor Wat, I was told that hotel capacity had expanded tenfold in a decade, with much of the demand coming from China.

As permission was extended to additional countries, the process was formalized through agreements that identified each new foreign partner as an approved destination. Specific travel agencies in China were per-mitted to sell package tours to these countries. The partner countries would in turn issue special Approved Destination Status (ADS) visas to Chinese travellers who had registered for the tours. Such visas were gen-erally approved quickly and easily because the Chinese agencies that sold lucrative ADS packages had a strong incentive to ensure that all their travellers returned to China as promised. While many Chinese people did manage to visit Canada in the absence of ADS, they mainly did this as members of official delegations or as an add-on to their business trips or studies in Canada. Without ADS, Canadian destinations could not be advertised and sold for group travel by China's huge tourism agencies.

That China was keen to maintain a strong grip on outbound travel is not surprising. While pressure to meet demand from a newly prosper-ous and footloose population was mounting, the government wanted to prevent corrupt government officials from slipping out of the country with embezzled funds. This is a continuing preoccupation. One way of maintaining control is for the Chinese government to ensure that all travel by high-level officials, a category that includes senior executives of state-owned banks, has to be approved by the Foreign Ministry. I can recall receiving an irate message one evening from an executive at a Canadian bank. He was upset because the embassy had issued only a single-entry visa to an important Chinese business contact, a high-level banker who had requested a multi-entry visa. When I checked with our visa section, I discovered that his application had in fact been revised by China's Foreign Ministry before it ever got to us. A multi-entry visa would have given the banker the ability to travel to Canada whenever he wished, an option his government wanted to exclude.

According to the Washington-based NGO Global Financial Integrity, between 2002 and 2011, more than US$1 trillion in illegal funds flowed out of China.[3] Much of this was accomplished through dodgy invoicing practices designed to park money abroad or to launder it before sneaking it back into China. Part of this flow comprised the ill-gotten gains of at least some of what in China are termed "naked" officials, who park family members in desirable destinations such as the U.S., Australia and Canada. They see foreign property as a sound investment and a convenient bolt-hole should they need to leave China quickly.[4]

IN 1999, AUSTRALIA AND NEW ZEALAND were the first non-Asian destinations to be awarded ADS.[5] That same year, Canada received an unexpected visitor from China. Accused of heading a multi-billion-dollar smuggling empire, Lai Changxing was a key figure in the underworld of China's Fujian province. His corrupt connections extended beyond his hometown and likely included some very senior officials in Beijing. Lai's arrival in Vancouver marked the beginning of his twelve-year struggle to stay in Canada, beyond the reach of Chinese officials who, he claimed, were more concerned about covering up their own misdeeds than seeing justice done.

Lai's presence in Canada was a major irritant to the Chinese, prompting a campaign that involved increasingly intense hectoring, including a tirade from then President Jiang Zemin himself. The

Chinese wanted Canada to send Lai back on the next plane. Period. But by this time, Lai had entered Canada's refugee determination process. The Canadian response, delivered consistently to the Chinese throughout long years of hearings and appeals, was that Lai's fate would be determined by an independent process beyond the reach or influence of any third party, including the Government of Canada.

These wheels move slowly, and the Lai case was still a major sore point when I served in China a decade later. I made it my business to visit a different university campus each month to give a talk about Canada. While relations were generally very friendly, I would inevitably get a question, delivered bluntly and with some passion, about why Canada was "harbouring" Lai. As a follow-up, I would be asked if it was because we wanted to keep his stolen billions ourselves. I could then normally expect some jeers and heckling from the audience.

I would begin my response by observing that, in China, people sometimes regard it as inappropriate for a foreigner to ask a difficult question about a controversial topic, something often described as hurting the feelings of the Chinese people. I would then point out that answering tough questions was actually part of my job, and that they could rest easy that my feelings had not been hurt. That generally got a friendlier laugh. I used such opportunities to talk about the importance of judicial independence. I explained that although the Government of Canada did not believe that Lai was a refugee, we would have to prove our case before a judge, who would assess the case according to Canadian law. I acknowledged that we all wished that things could move faster. But I also noted that, if I were ever before a judge, I would value careful deliberation and fairness more than a speedy verdict.

Ultimately, Lai's final appeal was turned down, and he was returned to China. When that happened, we published the judge's ruling on the embassy's weibo. The first posting was pulled from the site, one of the only times this ever happened to us. Figuring that we had been caught by one of China's notorious internet filters, we simply substituted

"Chinese financial fugitive" for the name Lai Changxing in the tweet. This time it stayed up. While many of our followers still posted cranky responses about Canadian justice, many others wrote to say they were impressed by the transparency of the Canadian legal system.

One of the most notable consequences of the Lai case was China's refusal to consider Canada as a candidate for ADS for much of the time the case was under appeal.[6] Chinese officials explained, somewhat sanctimoniously, that they could hardly expand tourism to a country willing to harbour Chinese fugitives. Missing in the Chinese account was any recognition of the fact that they had failed to alert us to Lai's fugitive status until long after he had slipped into Canada. Nor did they acknowledge that Lai's refugee case was strengthened by the many imperfections in their own legal system.

I was running the Asia Pacific branch at Foreign Affairs when the Lai case emerged as a major irritant in 2001. I can recall telling a nearly apoplectic Chinese ambassador (who actually did have heart surgery in Canada shortly thereafter) that any retribution China exacted would only have the effect of diminishing the relationship between the two countries. I assured him, accurately enough, that nothing China did would have any impact on the progress of the refugee determination process. The damage done by China's withholding of ADS from Canada was indeed self-inflicted, on the one hand hurting the Canadian tourism industry as intended, but on the other, disadvantaging millions of Chinese tourists who dreamed of Niagara Falls and the Rocky Mountains. Over the intervening years, more than a hundred countries, from Myanmar to Mozambique, were awarded ADS while the Canada–China impasse over Lai continued.

ONLY MONTHS after I got to Beijing in the summer of 2009, I was asked by Ottawa to check with the Chinese on possible dates for a visit to China by the prime minister. It would be his first visit since taking office in early 2006. The relationship had, to date, been marked by chilliness and mutual misunderstanding, and both sides were ready to put this behind them. The Chinese quickly agreed to dates in December.

On the Canadian side, we had high expectations, believing that we could use the good feelings generated by the visit to secure ADS. Late in the fall, I had a brief airport meeting with the then foreign minister, Lawrence Cannon, who told me bluntly that the success of the visit would be judged by whether or not we got the tourism deal. "And we are going to get it, right?" he asked as he got up to catch his connecting flight. It wasn't as if the importance of securing ADS had escaped me, but the question was bracing nonetheless. I told Cannon that I thought it was within reach.

By this time, I had met many representatives from Canadian communities that, with tourism from the U.S. still in a post-9/11 decline, desperately needed the revenues from Chinese tourists. I told colleagues at the embassy that our pursuit of ADS was like the campaign to reopen the canola market: an opportunity for us to deliver something that would have a positive impact in communities around the country. This wasn't just the typical hype of a pre-visit pep talk. The age of Chinese mass tourism was already upon us. Indeed, by 2012 the Chinese had passed Americans and Germans to become the biggest spenders globally, laying out more than US$100 billion on international travel.

My first meeting to plan the visit was with a senior official named He Yafei, a rising star in the foreign ministry. A few months later, He would be parachuted into the seat across from President Obama, somewhat awkwardly representing China in the confusing final sessions of the climate change talks in Copenhagen. I would do the detailed planning work with an official one rank below him, but by having a star like He open things up, the Chinese were sending a signal that they wanted the visit to be a success.

Over lunch, I floated the idea of having a joint statement, a document that the prime minister and China's premier, Wen Jiabao, could sign. In addition to being a record of agreements reached during the visit, it would allow us to point the way to a more ambitious bilateral agenda for the months ahead. I saw the statement as a highly useful way of organizing thinking on both sides. Normally, I would have had to wait for an answer from the Chinese. The request itself might even have been turned into a bargaining chip, something that we would have to pay for. But my hunch was that the Chinese wanted to get things on track, and quickly. I was right. Mr. He agreed to the idea before the arrival of the fruit plate that marked the end of the meal.

The lunch had been set up on fairly short notice, so I hadn't had the time to agree on a game plan with my headquarters in Ottawa. Strictly speaking, I should have sought prior approval before floating the idea of a joint statement. But I had taken a gamble because I thought we needed to move quickly to secure agreement. And I didn't want to get held up by a risk-averse Ottawa. Instead, I relied on the white lie that the idea of a joint statement had "come up" over lunch, and that the Chinese side seemed to like it. Ottawa gave me the green light to proceed.

We suggested to the Chinese that the embassy do the first draft of the joint statement, something I handed to Rachael Bedlington, one of the most capable China specialists in Canada's foreign service. Although the Chinese added a few things over weeks of discussion, it was essentially her document that was ultimately presented to the two leaders. In her first draft, we made sure to include a reference to China having granted ADS to Canada. When it came back from the first review by the Chinese, our words were still there. The Chinese had simply put them in brackets. That meant that while the Chinese had yet to sign off, the matter could be considered for negotiation. We had already come a long way.

I knew that we had to find a means of allowing the Chinese to feel that they had secured something in exchange for awarding Canada

ADS. Although they were signalling their general willingness to move forward, Foreign Ministry officials needed to have something to show to their more hard-nosed colleagues in the security agencies. Otherwise they would be criticized for offering a concession to Canada. In our meetings with the Chinese negotiators, I suggested that we take some time to think about the progress we had made in promoting cooperation between police forces in both countries. This was, I pointed out, something that had become necessary as our people-to-people interactions multiplied. The RCMP had, in particular, shown great skill in cultivating contacts among counterpart agencies in China. They were working together on crimes including drug smuggling, human trafficking and even murders.

I suggested that we ask the two leaders to acknowledge this cooperation in the joint statement and announce their intention to push for an agreement on sharing the proceeds of crime. This would create a mechanism for actually returning to the Chinese authorities any funds seized from Chinese criminals in Canada. It would show respect for China as a partner and help to remove the notion that Canada was somehow interested in pocketing funds illegally brought into the country by Chinese fraudsters. The Chinese liked the idea and it was included in the draft text. (An agreement on sharing the proceeds of crime was ultimately negotiated in 2013, making Canada the first country to establish such a mechanism with China.)

After each exchange with the Chinese, we would send the joint statement back to Ottawa to have its relevant paragraphs reviewed by technical experts in all the departments and agencies that would play a role in its implementation—places such as the RCMP, Environment Canada, Agriculture Canada and the Department of Justice. Since it was a document for the PM's signature, it was also sent to the Privy Council Office, whose job it was to run the text by the prime minister's own office. As the weeks went by, the brackets came off one by one. Just days before the PM's arrival, they came off the reference to ADS.

On the morning of the official meeting at the Great Hall of the People that would launch the joint statement, I did my briefing of the PM and his staff. One of the political staffers gleefully pounced on a sentence in one of the later paragraphs. He said that while it was technically correct, it wasn't a good reflection of where the government was "politically." This is exactly the kind of advice that political staffers are expected to give, and it is why draft texts get sent back to Ottawa at each stage in the negotiations. The problem was that the document had been through this vetting, had already been approved by China's State Council, and was to be signed in a matter of hours. The Chinese would be right to expect that we had been as diligent and professional as they had been in securing the required approvals.

As everybody else got up to join the motorcade that would take the PM to a photo opportunity at the Great Wall, I was instructed to "fix" the wording. There wasn't much time. After a quick visit to the Wall, the delegation would race back to Beijing for the meeting with the premier. I braced myself and called my Chinese counterpart. He was enraged and sputtered into the phone that he had already secured the premier's approval of the document. If we tried to change a word of the text we could forget about the joint statement. Then he stopped taking my calls.

I sat down, feeling a bit sick, and began to deconstruct the offending sentence. I tried to do the minimum to it possible, enough to change the tone sufficiently to pass muster with PMO but not so much as to further enrage the Chinese. The trouble was that I couldn't get through to anybody on the Chinese side. In the end, we simply texted the revised wording to them and waited. As the motorcade was returning to the hotel, the Chinese called back to say that we had a deal.

I am hard pressed to explain what happened. I am sure that the Chinese, for their part, saw this as some diabolical, last-minute effort by Canada to gain advantage. Would that we were so clever! It was instead an example of Ottawa's increasingly Canada-centric view of the world. Everything, everywhere becomes an extension of Canadian politics. That's not simply because every initiative, even in foreign policy, is judged by its impact on Canadian voters. This has always been the case, and for good reasons in our democracy. The real problem is that this fixation has led inexorably to the dubious notion that the conduct and tactics of Canadian politics have a universal applicability. In other words, the view seems to be that you can massage a document with the Chinese as readily as you can do a last-minute edit to a press release for an announcement in Kitchener, Ontario.

This wasn't my only experience of this growing tendency. On another visit, I arrived at an event to find young political staffers from Ottawa giving hands-on directions to a collection of confused and increasingly testy high-ranking Chinese officials. They were physically positioning the officials as if they were students lining up for a class photo, conveniently forgetting that we were the visitors and that manhandling senior people in China is not a smart thing to do. We are quickly losing our feel for the "foreign" in foreign policy.

SINCE THE SIGNING of the agreement actually implementing ADS in the summer of 2010, tourist traffic from China to Canada has grown spectacularly. By the end of 2013, we were welcoming close to 350,000 Chinese tourists, more than double the total from 2009.[7] The change was noticeable almost immediately in the immigration section of the embassy; what used to be considered the "summer" busy period was soon arriving as early as March and running until well into October. ADS also encouraged Chinese airlines to move quickly to add Canadian destinations to their schedules. Not all of the increase could be attributed to ADS-qualified travellers. But the rise in awareness that was generated by the big tour companies and their advertising led to increases in other categories, including those wealthier individuals who were travelling to Canada on their own. The high-profile success of the Vancouver 2010 Olympic Winter Games helped enormously, too.

Having acquired ADS, the challenge for the Canadian tourism sector was to use that opening to make Canada a truly preferred destination. I worried from the outset that Canadians put more energy into lobbying for ADS than into thinking what to do once we had it. My sense is that it's a mixed bag. We're doing better in a lot of respects, but so are other attractive international destinations, such as Australia, the U.K. and the U.S. Meanwhile the Chinese market continues to grow and transform.

The two bucket-list, must-see destinations for Chinese travellers to Canada are Niagara Falls and Butchart Gardens, which is just outside Victoria on Vancouver Island. After I left China, I travelled to both places to speak with local tour operators. I was impressed by how much time people in these top destinations are devoting to figuring out just what Chinese tourists want and how to deliver it to them. In Niagara Falls, for example, they were changing traditional opening times to accommodate early-rising Chinese tour groups. As I dug deeper, I discovered that tour operators in the Yukon, at Via Rail (marketing the Rocky Mountain route) and in our iconic railway hotels are similarly motivated. In these and other creative places, managers are hiring Chinese-speaking staff from local colleges and universities. Menus are changing to reflect Chinese tastes. Signs, flags and Chinese-language information material welcome visitors on arrival. And gift shops are being stocked with high-quality (and high-priced) products to satisfy Chinese shoppers.

HIGH-END SHOPPING is a big part of the Chinese tourism experience. Chinese tourists topped a recent survey of tax-free spending by luxury travellers in Europe, spending an average of 875 euros per trip, compared to a global average of 525 euros.[8] In 2012, a Chinese tourist set the single-day record for purchases from the duty-free stores at Vancouver International Airport by racking up a total of $70,000.[9] In an article in *The Sydney Morning Herald,* a researcher from the Chinese Academy of Social Sciences noted that some foreigners have taken to calling free-spending Chinese tourists "walking wallets." The same article noted that Harrods in London has seventy Chinese-speaking staff and one hundred ATMs that provide access to China's UnionPay system.[10] The idea is to make Harrods, in the words of a press release, "the most accessible store in Europe for Chinese shoppers."[11]

After replacing Janet's wallet at the Montblanc outlet on Bloor Street, I made it a habit to ask sales staff in other high-end stores about the importance of Chinese-speaking shoppers. At Prada, I learned that over the last two years, 60 to 70 percent of luxury goods were sold to Chinese-speaking shoppers. That's in line with experience elsewhere. According to the Beverly Hills Conference & Visitors Bureau, 60 percent of business in some local high-end stores now comes from Chinese shoppers.[12]

This keen interest in high-end shopping by Chinese tour groups was also highlighted by the people I talked to in Victoria and Niagara Falls. In both destinations, eating and shopping rank ahead of sleeping for Chinese travellers. Admittedly, that's beginning to change in other places. Tourism officials in Toronto are now seeing the arrival of wealthier, solo travellers, who, not content with the airport hotels that cater to tour groups, are opting for five-star accommodation downtown. Similarly, the Chinese shoppers in Beverly Hills are now younger, wealthier and not travelling in tour groups.[13]

China is moving along the tourism curve—from a discount market with a preference for package tours to an emerging adventurous, high-end market—much faster than most countries. One industry expert likened Chinese tourism to a species that defies scientists' expectations by evolving in a fraction of the time expected. This has some important implications for Canada. What we thought was our bad luck in not securing ADS until ten years after Australia and New Zealand may turn out to have been good luck after all. As one expert observed,

"We were late to the party, but the first half of the party wasn't very good." In other words, we missed a decade in which Chinese tour operators struggled to fit Australia and New Zealand into their low-cost, no-frills model. Early tour groups to both places shaved costs to the bone, which is a recipe for unhappiness in places that are not primarily low-cost destinations. By the time we joined the ADS mainstream, China's demand was evolving. We were able to benefit almost immediately from the emergence of travellers willing to pay for a higher-end experience, which is where Canada fits in.

WHILE I WAS IN BEIJING, I used to hear regular complaints from the Chinese National Tourism Administration (CNTA). This body, true to China's nanny-state inclinations, advocates for Chinese travellers abroad in addition to promoting tourism at home. Its complaints, which were echoed by China's ambassador in Ottawa, focused on our general failure to provide Chinese-language guest services—from the welcome at the front desk to menus, directories and newspapers—at hotels across the country. Happily, as I saw in my recent travels, this situation is steadily improving, a shift reflected in changing commentary from Chinese officials. Criticism is being replaced by suggestions, such as the idea of investing in high-end malls designed specifically for Chinese travellers, something that the Australians have done.

Getting the menu right is job one. I firmly believe that breakfast represents the uncrossable cultural divide. People who happily experiment with exotic food at lunch and dinner retreat to the comforts of the familiar at breakfast, when they are still feeling sleepy and vulnerable. Chinese people are no different. I once had a high-level Chinese delegation go AWOL on me in Vancouver because they had found a hole-in-the-wall café that offered a morning menu of fried "oil sticks," sour vegetables and watery rice porridge. None of this was available at the fancy hotel where they were staying.

New Zealand's prime minister recently returned from a trip to China to tell his fellow citizens that, if handled with a degree of Kiwi ingenuity and hospitality, tourism from China could provide an economic boost to communities throughout the country. I was struck by the response from the Accor Hotel Group, a major global chain. They announced the launch of Chinese Optimum Service Standards for their properties in New Zealand and Australia. This includes having a Chinese breakfast buffet, Chinese TV and newspapers, and a Chinese-speaking concierge service. They also commenced training for front-line staff to better understand Chinese customer expectations. Interestingly, while Chinese tourist arrivals to New Zealand were up 24.7 percent in 2012 from a year earlier, business from China at Accor Hotels in New Zealand was up 59 percent.[14]

Growth in tourism to Canada from China was up more than 22 percent in 2013. That sounds impressive, but it's only slightly higher than the overall growth in outbound tourism from China, a rising tide that's lifting all boats. Worse, our 2013 number was slightly behind growth in U.S.-bound China travel. In other words, we have to try even harder if we're to crack the top ten list of destinations for Chinese travellers (we're currently holding down the eleventh spot). This is a reasonable and eminently achievable goal for a destination as attractive as is Canada.[15]

SO, WHAT DO WE NEED to do to attract a larger share of the Chinese travelling public? For one thing, we can continue to improve when it comes to offering the services that make Chinese travellers feel at home. Doing even better when it comes to having Chinese media available in our hotel rooms would be a start. But we also need to expand the geographic reach of these efforts. Chinese tourism drops off dramatically east of Montreal, and Atlantic Canada is mainly missing in action. I talked about this on a recent trip to Nova Scotia.

I heard a number of comments about how remote the region is from where Chinese tourists normally travel. And I also heard comments about how far behind the region is when it comes to preparing for Chinese business.

Chinese travellers are currently discovering every corner of the world. Atlantic Canada is hardly out of reach. Nor is this a challenge beyond their abilities. Japanese travellers have been making the pilgrimage to Anne of Green Gables sites in Prince Edward Island for decades. People in P.E.I. have responded creatively and hospitably to this interest. Chinese tourists would enjoy Atlantic Canada's golf, seafood and fishing, its history and culture, and its shopping. There is no reason why travellers from Shanghai and Beijing shouldn't be claiming bragging rights back home with their photos of whales, icebergs and puffins. Growth in this business might also generate welcome interest in new investment, Canadian or Chinese, in hotels, restaurants and retail outlets.

That's not to say that simply polishing up on Mandarin and on Chinese cuisine is enough to expand the business indefinitely. There are structural impediments to growth. Airline connections are to the travel business what pipelines are to the energy business. If you don't have capacity, you can't do the business. As mentioned, we have seen a steady rise in trans-Pacific capacity as new Chinese carriers have added Canadian cities to their schedules. We need to continue to grow this trend. One industry specialist told me that although Japan had been seen as a somewhat mature market, the Canadian tourism industry has been able to coax new growth out of it through recent expansions in air links. There is room for a lot more seat capacity between China and Canada.

One of the reasons for focusing so intently on direct air connections is that we don't benefit as much as we should from new links added between China and the United States. Our separate visa regime means that the "two-nation vacation" is still a hassle for Chinese tourists to organize. That's a big problem. A senior person in the industry in Niagara Falls told me that our statistics wildly undercount the true number of Chinese tourists visiting Canada. This is because so many enter at Niagara Falls, New York, and are classified as arrivals via the U.S. That said, the majority of Chinese travellers on the U.S. side of the Falls are unable to cross because they don't have a Canadian visa. We need to think about the cost of requiring a separate and highly duplicative visa process for someone who has already qualified for entry to the U.S. I am not convinced that we can't find a creative way to make this easier for at least some segments of the travelling public without sacrificing the integrity of our own borders.

We have done a fairly good job of responding to the current wave of Chinese mass tourism. This has taken us some distance and can probably carry us even further. But we need to think carefully about the next wave, something that is already taking shape. This is the wave of solo travel by well-to-do, experienced and well-informed individuals from China. These travellers expect the very best in terms of food, transportation and accommodation. And they want to experience destinations, food and shopping opportunities that are out of the ordinary. Canada is a spectacular travel destination. It offers Chinese visitors much that is new and exciting, and much that is warm, welcoming and familiar. That's an attractive combination. But timing is everything. The next wave is forming now.

FIVE

The University of Beautiful Cars

The China Education Expo in Beijing is a vast and crowded bazaar in which foreign schools set up booths and promote their attractions to Chinese students. While I was in Beijing, Canada usually had the largest national stand, with fifty or sixty booths representing schools and school districts from across the country. I would spend a busy Saturday morning visiting the exhibitors, learning about their institutions and hearing about their experiences recruiting Chinese students. It was a useful opportunity to get a feel for how we at the embassy were doing in promoting Canadian education, and to get unvarnished feedback on our performance with issuing student visas.

Although I was careful not to interrupt conversations between recruiters from Canadian schools and prospective students, I did allow myself the privilege of eavesdropping. When I first worked in China in the 1980s, the government determined which lucky young people got to study abroad. Later, as people in China became more prosperous, parents became the deciders. Now it is the students themselves who weigh the relative merits of schools in Canada, the U.K., the U.S., Australia and elsewhere.

International study is still encouraged by the government of China. This comes from the laudable conviction that China needs to expose its young people to the best schools in the world. It is also born of the understanding that China still lacks the capacity to offer a high-quality education to all of its deserving students. Allowing students to study abroad is a calculated risk, but one that has been paying off. Although a portion of outbound students choose to remain overseas, enough come back to make it worth the effort. And with the economic crisis, and increasingly sophisticated recruitment by Chinese firms, the flow back to China is increasing.

Canada is a very popular destination for Chinese students. It is estimated that more than eighty thousand Chinese students are studying full-time at educational institutions in Canada, which represents just under a third of our foreign-student population. Many more take short-term summer courses that mix language training with the opportunity for tourism.[1] In the past, Chinese students were mainly interested in the undergraduate and graduate levels in Canada. But we are now seeing flows of much younger students bound for Canadian secondary schools and even primary schools. While this has a lot to do with how positively Canada's education system is viewed, it has even more to do with rising frustrations fuelled by deficiencies in the Chinese system. Education in China is brutally competitive, with students streamed out of contention for places in the handful of elite universities before they have had much chance to grow and develop. And for children in remote rural areas, the chances of successfully competing with privileged counterparts from elite schools in Beijing and Shanghai are very, very slim.

Parents in China are increasingly concerned that the country's inflexible system of rote learning poorly prepares students for a world in which creativity matters more than the ability to memorize facts. Chinese parents are also critical of what they see as a joyless, unimaginative and backward educational system. So instead of waiting until their child is of university age, many Chinese parents now try to get their offspring into the Canadian educational system much earlier. Enrolling a son or daughter in a Canadian school at a more junior level allows them time to master English and grow accustomed to Canadian ways. Canadian school districts charge significant fees for these young arrivals. The Coquitlam School District, in British Columbia, offers international students a full-year program at a tuition cost of $13,000. The international student fee for the Toronto District School Board (TDSB) is $12,500 for a full year of kindergarten or primary school, and $14,000 at the high school level.[2] Almost 1000 of the TDSB's 1400 international students are from China, a fact that prompted the board to open a marketing office in Beijing in 2013.[3]

The economic impact is, of course, much broader. Representatives of the Coquitlam School Board told me that within a week of arriving to enrol their children in school, Chinese parents are out shopping for a house and a car, usually an expensive car. "University of Beautiful Cars," a popular blog on the social media platform Tumblr, is devoted to the Maseratis and Lamborghinis spotted in the vicinity of the University of British Columbia. An explanatory note on the site attributes this phenomenon to the fact that there are many wealthy people in Vancouver, among them the parents of international students from China who are eager to snap up luxury cars in Canada for much less than they sell for back home.[4]

Recent years have seen the emergence of Canadian curriculum schools in China itself. These are run in cooperation with education officials from one of Canada's provinces, with B.C., Ontario, Nova Scotia and New Brunswick particularly well represented. The advantage of such schools is that the children remain in China while earning a North American diploma. The principal, senior administration and teachers typically come from schools in the Canadian province. Students are taught according to the provincial curriculum, and schools are inspected by visiting provincial inspectors. I visited Maple Leaf International High School in Dalian, one of a number of Maple Leaf schools in China run according to the B.C. curriculum. The school's Canadian principal was proud to tell me that, when her students get to UBC or Simon Fraser, they outperform students who were educated in the province itself.

Back in Canada, provincial education officials watch the growth of international education with a mixture of hope and anxiety. Funds generated by foreign student recruitment ease relentless pressure on budgets. In some areas, such as parts of Vancouver Island where declines in traditional industries like fishing and logging threaten to close schools, the influx of students offers communities a second chance. In the U.S., for-profit organizations are recruiting students for public as well as private schools. While some see this as a lifeline, others see it as a dangerous precedent that lets local governments evade their funding responsibilities. A recent article in *The New Yorker* posed the question, "Should a school's revenue depend on a superintendent's skill as a dealmaker, or on a principal's ability to market to well-heeled students from overseas?"[5]

In this country, wise administrators know that the success of the Canadian education model is due to the quality and integrity of the system. Their ultimate responsibility is not to raise funds but to manage and, ideally, enhance the province's education system. Bringing in bright, creative and ambitious foreign students is in itself educational, creating diversity, introducing new ideas and broadening horizons for everybody in the classroom. The perpetual renewal that comes from welcoming talented newcomers is at the heart of the Canadian advantage.

But it is naive to assume that entrepreneurial enthusiasm is always in the service of educational excellence. In Australia, rapid expansion has undermined quality, which has in turn damaged Australia's reputation as an education destination. The combination of highly entrepreneurial schools and profit-maximizing agents in target countries led to shortcuts on many admissions. The lure of access to Australia itself drove many under-qualified students to apply. They found a system that was willing to be creative, too creative, in accommodating this growing demand. The results were disappointing outcomes for students and families and a discredited system.[6] Recently, a group of academics in Australia complained that universities across the country were becoming over-dependent on foreign students. Said one: "Just as governments have become addicted to gambling revenues from poker machines, universities have become addicted to revenue streams from international students." This is in turn causing schools to relax standards and welcome candidates who are clearly unqualified, with some students described as being "functionally illiterate" due to their lack of proficiency in English. One professor complained that some of his students actually needed to bring interpreters to meetings with him.[7]

We need to be very careful about the signals we send to foreign students and their parents. If our main message is that we want smart, creative and engaging students, students who want to contribute to their academic environment and to reach out and fully experience Canadian life, that's what we'll get. But if the message begins and ends with the fee schedule, or if enrolment is really just a means for securing access to Canada itself, people will approach education in Canada as a business proposition, one that is susceptible to bargaining and negotiation. This fails the students, foreign and domestic, and the education system.

Bigger is not always better. Although growth in student numbers is gratifying, we need to spend more time thinking about the student experience in Canada. When I was ambassador, I typically visited at least one Canadian university on each of my trips back to Canada, using the time to meet with Chinese students to hear about their experience of Canada. This was almost always positive, although many students admitted to struggling with English. Others talked about the difficulties of getting to know Canadians and fully experiencing Canadian life, particularly that portion of it that happens between November and March. I recall meeting a young woman back in China who had been so intimidated by the prospect of winter in Canada that she opted to be educated in the U.S.—in snowy Buffalo, New York, just a few miles from the border.

How Chinese students deal with the Canadian winter is a good indicator of their more general ability to succeed here. Students who invest in a warm coat, get out into the weather and take up an activity such as skating or cross-country skiing are in their own way punching through the culture barrier and getting to know Canada itself. But many don't do this, or never feel confident enough to try. It is easier to stay within a comfortable cohort of other Chinese students than to take part in the wider life of the campus and the community. And that's entirely understandable. Imagine what young Canadians would do if they found themselves on a campus in Beijing or Shanghai, or a far less international city such as Shenyang or Lanzhou, only to discover that hundreds of other young Canadians lived with them in residence. While a few brave souls would forsake the comforts of the familiar and immerse themselves in Chinese culture, it's safe to assume that the majority would stay closely connected to the familiar ways of their friends on campus.

The very size of the Chinese student population on many campuses makes it easy for students to stay in a Chinese cocoon, something that can also engender unwelcome commentary. In November 2010, *Maclean's* magazine generated a huge controversy with an article that asked if some Canadian universities were "too Asian." The article was derided for trading in stereotypes about high-achieving Asian nerds and slacker, ski-bum Caucasians. And to many readers, the article and some of the commentary it inspired seemed to assign all students of Chinese (or other Asian) origin, including the many Canadians in that number, to the "foreign" student community.[8]

We need to avoid becoming so driven by the numbers that we are more focused on recruitment than on follow-through, on what happens *after* students arrive in Canada. While at least some of the energy needed for crossing the cultural divide should come from students themselves, let's not forget that we're dealing with very young people, many of whom have never been so far away from home before. Here in Canada, schools and their local communities can and should play a major role in helping to make the adjustment easier.

Some schools are trying to address this issue. The University of Toronto's Scarborough campus, for example, boasts the successful Green Path program, which welcomes incoming international students in the summer months and gives them a head start adjusting to life in Canada before school begins. The idea, as they spell it out, is to turn Chinese high school students into successful Canadian undergraduates. While the main focus is on English skills, the students learn about everything from the Toronto transit system to Canadian cuisine. I spent some time with U of T Scarborough's Green Path students and was impressed by what I saw. Students were grateful that Canadians had actually taken the trouble to think about what things look like from their perspective as young foreign visitors.

I was also impressed by what I saw at Thompson Rivers University (TRU) in Kamloops, British Columbia. The university has embraced the international agenda, actively recruiting foreign students and offering some TRU courses to Chinese and Canadian students at a partner institution in China. When I visited the campus, I met with Chinese students, many of whom were staying with local families, and all of whom seemed very connected to their community. I spent a lot of time with Roger Barnsley, the university's then president, a dynamic and inspirational leader with a strong commitment to international education. He showed me impressive new facilities built from revenues generated by international students. He also introduced me to members of the city council. They told me about how income from international students was helping to stabilize what had previously been a boom-and-bust resource-based economy. Apart from what the students themselves spent, their visiting parents were bringing in welcome revenue to local hotels, restaurants and tour operators. People in Kamloops saw this, appreciated the contribution and embraced these newly arrived members of their community.

These examples get to the heart of the Canadian advantage and the continuing Canadian challenge when it comes to international education. We are most successful in recruiting international students when we stay focused on delivering excellence in education for all students, foreign and domestic, and when we see recruitment as the first step in a long-term relationship with Canada and Canadians.

WE ARE PROBABLY nearing the end of a golden age in which China is, in effect, an exporter of students to places like Canada. China is already building its own capability when it comes to international education, something that will require us to adapt, and sooner than we think. According to its own education plan, China wants to become a major destination for foreign students by 2020. This is already beginning to happen. China is, for example, already catching up to the U.S. as a magnet for South Korean students. This tracks the steady growth in Korean business links with China, a phenomenon that has already brought a wave of Korean investors to the PRC. In addition, so many Korean students have now studied English that it is no longer seen as an edge in getting a job. Increasingly, learning Mandarin is the thing to do.[9] And some Chinese students are themselves beginning to question whether the rewards of an international education are commensurate with the investment required. As more students return from abroad, employers are less easily impressed by a foreign diploma. In some cases, students who have studied abroad are faulted for failing to acquire the Chinese cultural smarts required to succeed locally.[10]

Universities are themselves feeling the gravitational pull. Because of continuing pressures on public funding for education, many Western universities are looking to partnerships in China as a means of staying competitive. I heard a university president from Australia state that the era of the "national university" is over. He predicted that universities will have to become part of global networks, much as airlines already are. And China is emerging as a key component of any such network. The president described his university's recruitment of Chinese students in Australia and on partner campuses in China as both a cultural bridge and a $50-million business.

It is not hard to believe that, for many schools, long-term survival will be linked to some form of presence in China. Western schools have already tried a variety of approaches, everything from ambitious projects to create a campus in China, which a number of schools from the U.S., the U.K. and Australia are pursuing, to less ambitious arrangements involving joint course offerings in which students study for a couple of years in China followed by a couple at the foreign school.

Canadian schools that are interested in exploring some form of presence in China face a number of challenges. The first is that such experiments can be expensive and unpredictable. Partnering in China involves a leap of faith. Its education bureaucracy is complex, quirky and risk averse. Conditions and partners change, costs rise unaccountably, and the policy environment is opaque. The most ambitious schools are betting that this will improve over time, and that they will benefit from being early movers.

It is also often the case that the deeper and more profound the partnership with China, the higher the risk of a clash on some issue related to academic freedom. Indeed, the pressure can be applied even without a formal partnership. The University of Calgary found itself delisted from an inventory of foreign schools whose degrees are recognized in China after the university warmly welcomed the Dalai Lama on campus. It took many months to get the Chinese to relent. At the time, I pointed out to the Chinese ambassador that such unfriendly steps would cause other universities in Canada and elsewhere to reconsider possible partnerships in China. But the Chinese, confident (and correctly so) that this wouldn't happen, took their time in reinstating the university. This was a skirmish in a larger, global campaign to intimidate governments and universities and thereby diminish the international space available to the Dalai Lama.

Foreign universities, including Canadian schools, operate under the watchful eye of the local Chinese consul general, whose own career prospects ride on being able to keep unwelcome personalities, such as the Dalai Lama or champions for the Uighur community, off local campuses. Chinese diplomats trade access to China—they are the custodians of the visa process—against compliance. Their disapproval comes at a real cost. Academics who specialize in China know that if they are too outspoken, they risk being barred from visiting China, which is a costly, career-limiting development.[11]

China's skill at bullying others allows it to parlay a very weak hand—after all, China still needs access to advanced institutions in the West if it is to meet its own ambitious development goals—into a strong one. China has long intimidated its own teachers and students, ensuring that people who should normally consider themselves part of a free-thinking and borderless republic of letters have little or no voice on issues that the Chinese state deems to be contentious. An increasing number of Western institutions are debating the benefits of presence in China versus the risks of finding themselves susceptible to pressure.[12] China tends to treat the weakest and smallest players most harshly, minimizing the cost to itself while sending an intimidating message to everybody else. That said, there are ways of maintaining academic freedom without having to sacrifice relationships with China. One of the best is to be clear from the start about values and expectations, and about what is non-negotiable. It is important to be very clear about red lines at the outset in order to determine whether there are any potential conflicts ahead.

When something is going to happen that will ruffle feathers in Beijing, the most successful practitioners brief their principal Chinese contacts, firmly and calmly, about what's going to happen. This is generally timed so that it is just enough in advance to be courteous, without giving the Chinese time to crank up a painful lobbying campaign. The idea is to do as much as possible to soften the blow for your closest Chinese contacts, such as academic partners at Chinese universities or the worldly and generally tolerant education officials attached to China's offices abroad. They may actually understand what you are doing and why, but they will also pay the steepest price for failing to prevent an embarrassing incident.

Although China is today more open to dissenting views than it was even ten years ago, it is very often the case that tolerance depends on the personal protection of indulgent local hosts or partners. Because such things aren't enshrined in laws that apply to everybody, this acceptance is always conditional and subject to change. But academic freedom isn't something that is somehow negotiable or scalable. I find it painful when university administrators from the West justify concessions made to China on the basis of the greater good in the longer term. We respect our universities because they are, at their best, feisty defenders of the right to entertain ideas that challenge the status quo, ideas that make people uncomfortable and that provoke difficult debates.

China's own intellectuals are struggling with restrictions on their freedoms imposed by the new leadership in Beijing, who have already attempted to stifle discussion of things such as "Western constitutional democracy" and "universal values of human rights."[13] While courageous academics in China do occasionally rock the boat, there is still little tolerance for anything more than tiptoeing around so-called core interests, such as Tibet and the unrest in Xinjiang, and little scope for frankly addressing China's recent history, including the Communist Party's own blood-stained past.

I got to experience first-hand something of the uneasy ambiguity that prevails at even the best universities in China. Along with a few other ambassadors, I was offered the chance to speak each year to China's top law students as they gathered for the Jessup Moot Court Competition, an event that allows them to argue cases in international law in front of judges and lawyers from around the world. I always spoke about the importance of respecting the rule of law.

In 2011, the event was held at Shandong University in Jinan, a couple of hours by train from Beijing. At the time of my visit, Chen Guangcheng, a blind human rights lawyer, was still living under house arrest at a village in Shandong province. (He would later stage a spectacular escape to the U.S. embassy and ultimately be allowed to leave China.) I was torn about what to say. My mentioning the case might cause trouble, bringing down official wrath on an institution that is in many ways an incubator of reform. Nor did I want to harm relations with an important academic partner for Canadian schools. At the same time, I didn't feel that I could address China's future top lawyers without mentioning a colleague who was suffering injustice just down the road.

So I did mention the case. I started by acknowledging the respect and friendliness due from me as a foreigner and a guest, and I asked people to forgive my frankness. But I also told the law students that I respected them too much not to mention the Chen case. I reminded them that Chen had come to prominence for arguing against tyrannical family planning officials who forced abortions on poor local women, that he had already served prison time (on dubious charges), and that he been released and was technically now free. But in reality, he was under a form of house arrest enforced by local thugs. I asked the students to think about this as a signal failure to fully apply the rule of law. These bright young lawyers were off to brilliant careers in the corporate world. I wished them luck but asked them to resist the notion that the law can be neatly circumscribed, applying to contracts and companies but not to people.

The president of the university was himself a rising star and a noted progressive. And he was furious with me. The lunch he hosted after that morning session featured some tense and uncomfortable interludes. Although the president chatted happily with my German colleague, who had stuck to non-controversial themes, he was curt and defensive in his exchanges with me. What was most painful was watching this brilliant academic tying himself into rhetorical knots trying to explain away the Chen situation as an unimportant sideshow in the larger process of reform. His heart wasn't really in it, but he had to give me a dressing-down in front of his senior staff, who sat in glum silence as their boss presented his arguments. I had made my point, and accepted the stern lecture as the price to be paid.

Canadian universities have long-established partnerships with counterpart institutions in China. They need to build on this. The only thing more risky than engaging Chinese partners is *not* engaging them, leaving them to feel scorned, disrespected and cut off. Academic ties *do* represent cultural bridges, and they benefit those parts of Chinese society most likely to promote change. But bridges need to be built on secure foundations. We need to consider academic freedom, something that is central to our definition of the university, as foundational and non-negotiable.

PRESIDENT OBAMA VISITED CHINA late in 2009. The Chinese, then feeling smug and superior, were uncharacteristically churlish in their welcome. The only high point in an otherwise disappointing round of meetings came from Obama himself. Before he left China, he offered a challenge to America's young people, calling for as many as one hundred thousand of them to travel to China for studies over the next four years. This was a highly ambitious target. In 2009, it was estimated that fewer than fourteen thousand Americans were studying in China. The president's compelling challenge led to the establishment of a foundation that has worked in communities across the U.S. to encourage a much greater China-bound flow of American students. Thanks to that effort, the foundation's president was able to announce in July 2014 that the one-hundred-thousand-student milestone had been reached and, importantly, that the foundation's work will continue.[14]

I recently served as the co-chair of a national study[15] that examined how Canada is doing when it comes to educating young people about

Asia. We looked at language training programs across the country, but we also tried to get an appreciation of the extent to which Asia is part of the more general curriculum, and whether there are enough opportunities for young people to work or study in Asia. The first thing we discovered is that it is very hard to get a handle on this subject, short of surveying major school districts and universities across the country, which is what we ended up doing. Because education is a provincial responsibility, there is nothing like a national perspective. We found individual islands of progress in Vancouver, Edmonton and Toronto. Not surprisingly, much of the energy in these cities is directed at China and at training in Mandarin. It is generated by committed parents, the majority of whom are of Chinese heritage. Places where diaspora communities are relatively small, such as Atlantic Canada, are much less active. And many schools that do offer Mandarin training rely on support from China's government, which provides textbooks and teachers, and helps to set up twinning programs with schools in China.

We found little in the way of coordination between universities and the high schools in their regions, meaning that students have a hard time navigating an educational path that seems choppy and disconnected. Also largely absent in Canada are the kind of pull factors that get students interested in pursuing new and challenging courses of study in the first place. Although chambers of commerce routinely predict looming requirements for engineers and skilled tradespeople, Canadians never hear projections about the coming demand for Mandarin speakers or for people who know how to negotiate in Korea, Japan or Indonesia. Students who return from work terms and language training programs in Asia all too often report that there are no jobs waiting for them.

I thought a lot about President Obama's inspiring challenge while I was in China. Just before I left, we succeeded in having education enshrined as a bilateral priority between Canada and China. That means that cooperation in education is one of a limited number of topics to be discussed in future, high-level conversations between our leaders. The Chinese were happy to have this added. When I raised it with my own headquarters in Ottawa, there was some concern due to the fact that education is the domain of the provinces. I argued that the federal government should act as an enthusiastic partner in this respect, providing a single, high-level voice for broad Canadian object-ives set in coordination with provincial partners.

But we have yet to hear a compelling, Obama-like challenge from a Canadian leader. I suspect that this is linked to a more general silence out of Ottawa about China. Because almost any reference to China now invites controversy, it is judged better to remain silent on any related subject. This reflects the naive notion that we only seek to engage China because we support its policies or, at best, are blind to the risks associated with a closer partnership. It is hard to get across the idea that we need to study China more carefully precisely *because* it is such a difficult mix of challenges and opportunities.

I was struck by four particularly troubling aspects of our scattered and highly localized approach to encouraging young people to learn about Asia in general and China in particular. The first is that we are opting to leave large parts of the country behind when it comes to participating in the next phase of our economic development. Those regions that have large and dynamic diaspora communities are mov-ing forward, while those that aren't home to such communities, such as Atlantic Canada, have less going on. This represents a failure of governments, at all levels, to help Canadians prepare for their future.

The second problem is that, even in places where language training programs are relatively well supported, many employers seem far more focused on talent and resources flowing from China via immigration. One banker told me happily that the flow of new immigrants into Toronto made it easy for his bank to meet the demands of its growing business in China. This is indeed a huge advantage, but one that we may not always be able to count on. Immigration flows change over time. We need to take the initiative, seeing the expansion of education in Asian languages and culture, starting with China's, as an investment in our future. The Canadian business community needs to step up to this challenge since they have a huge stake in our being able to meet it successfully.

My third concern is that where we are actually providing instruction, we tend to depend on largesse from China to do so. Schools and school boards are setting up what are called Confucius Institutes administered by something called the Hanban, the part of China's government that promotes Chinese-language training internationally. Admittedly, every institution we contacted that has a Confucius Institute was happy with the relationship. But problems have been reported in Canada and elsewhere. McMaster University closed its Confucius Institute, citing concerns over hiring practices. This was triggered by the revelation that a staff member from China had been required to stay away from "illegal organizations such as Falun Gong," which is how China characterizes a practice followed freely and legally by many Canadians.[16]

Even more recently, the Toronto District School Board decided to delay the launch of its own Confucius Institute, a controversial project board members felt had been sprung on them by the board's then chair. It didn't help that he resigned suddenly, just as the board was set to review the agreement. The board's reluctance to go ahead with the deal has in turn led to concerns that its rebuff will hurt efforts to recruit in China, the source of 75 percent of the TDSB's foreign students.[17] The Chinese government has since moved to terminate the agreement with Toronto.[18]

I have visited Hanban's headquarters in Beijing and was impressed by the people I met. I felt I was meeting educators with a compelling passion for helping foreigners learn Chinese. But these dedicated officials don't operate in isolation. It would not surprise me if they were under regular pressure from the Chinese government to uphold such obnoxious policies as the cruel and relentless effort to crush Falun Gong globally. This suggests that public institutions in Canada and elsewhere need to think very carefully about the limits of any partnership with Hanban.

Toronto isn't the first place in which a globe-trotting school administrator cut a deal in China that surprised and unsettled colleagues back home. But it may be among the last, at least in this part of the world. I think that we're reaching a turning point in Canada and the United States, by which I mean that while Confucius Institutes will likely continue to proliferate in the developing world, they will no longer simply be given the benefit of the doubt by overly eager North American partners. That's not a bad outcome, especially if schools and school boards make it clear that they are not about to trade away academic freedom in exchange for a container of books from China. It also suggests that we are beginning to see Hanban as only one possible component in a much larger national effort to embrace Chinese-language training. We need to build our own indigenous capacity in Canada to teach Chinese.

My fourth and final concern relates to Canadian students themselves. Many of the students I encountered were quick to point out that the lack of job prospects after graduation is a real disincentive for taking the time to study a difficult language such as Chinese. I heard this perspective enough to accept that the lack of jobs is a significant impediment. But I was also left with the sense that some students view the opportunity to learn Chinese or to work and study in Asia somewhat passively. It is as if these things have no value until they are activated by an employer. What was missing in many cases was a sense of passion for acquiring the key to an immense and vibrant culture, or the necessary confidence (and, yes, at times overconfidence) in the notion that effort, enthusiasm and energy are always rewarded, although not necessarily in the most expected way.

We need to see our educational links as a two-way street, and we need to accept that having at least some exposure to China, to its history and culture, to its role in the world, is part of being an educated Canadian. But we need to invest the time, effort and money to make this happen.

SIX

Buying a Piece of Canada

hinese people are making a big impact at street level in Canada through investment in real estate. The notion that foreign buyers are snapping up local real estate has a long if not entirely honourable tradition in our country. Germans once loomed large in Canadian anxieties, given their proclivity for buying property in places such as Muskoka and coastal British Columbia. The Japanese have figured in this debate, too, particularly in the 1980s, when the soaring Japanese economy and a rising yen fuelled concerns about investors from Tokyo buying city blocks in Vancouver for a price that in Tokyo would purchase the land occupied by a bar stool in the Ginza. Vancouver-based urban planner Andy Yan, who has devoted a lot of time and careful analysis to the topic of foreign investment in the real estate market, points out that Vancouver's Lions Gate Bridge was made financially viable following an investment in the early 1930s by the Guinness family (yes, *that* Guinness) in the West Vancouver development known as the British Properties. And despite the fact that Canadians are among the dreaded foreigners buying up property in Florida, Arizona and Hawaii, we still manage to get worked up when Americans display similar acquisitiveness on our side of the border.

Lately, the conversation has turned to what Chinese investors are up to in Vancouver, Toronto and other Canadian cities. This has emerged as a topic for discussion in the absence of reliable data. According to Canada Mortgage and Housing Corporation (CMHC), which is just beginning to study foreign investment, investors of all origins—meaning people who bought property without intending to live in it—accounted for about 17 percent of the condo market in Toronto and Vancouver in 2013, something that runs counter to the prevailing wisdom. As one economist observed: "When you talk to developers in the [Greater Toronto Area] and even in many pockets in Vancouver, they tell you that 70% of presales and close to 50% to 60% of final sales are by investors—this is the flow—not the stock as reported by CMHC."[1]

Additional ambiguity exists around just who these investors are and where they come from. People who talk about "Chinese" investment, for example, often miss the point that much activity is almost certainly driven by people of Chinese origin who have become permanent residents of Canada and are in the process of becoming Canadian citizens. So the word *foreign* doesn't completely apply to their purchases. Whether the word *investor* applies is harder to determine. Unlike previous generations of immigrants, many Chinese applicants have decidedly international lifestyles and careers, meaning that many official permanent residents are in no big hurry to permanently reside in Canada. This has in turn prompted recent changes to the Citizenship Act, lengthening the residence requirement and making it much more specific in an effort to reinforce "attachment and connection" to Canada.[2]

Recent changes to our immigration system also included the termination of the Immigrant Investor Program (IIP), a decision that affected more than sixty thousand waiting applicants, the majority of them from China. Under the program, applicants with a net worth of $1.6 million and over would put up $800,000 in a five-year interest-free loan to the Government of Canada. Over time, the federal government expressed concern about what was described as "fraud" in the program. This mainly referred to the widespread practice of immigrant investors applying under the parallel and larger program operated by the province of Quebec, only to settle elsewhere in Canada, with Vancouver being the most popular destination. While Quebec would still benefit from the investment part of the transaction, the place where the immigrant actually settled would be left to cover costs for health care and education.[3] Although the Quebec program continues, the federal government has vowed to crack down on applicants who are attempting to game the system by applying to Quebec but settling elsewhere.[4] The government was also disappointed by what it saw as the modest amount of economic impact the program generated. The meagre results were attributed to the fact that many applicants showed little interest in living in Canada full-time. In the wake of the cancellation, disappointed investors threatened to sue the government, but the reaction on Chinese social media was largely positive. That's because many netizens in China assumed that the beneficiaries of the program were corrupt officials looking to stash ill-gotten cash in a complicit Canada.[5] It is estimated that between 16,000 and 18,000 corrupt officials have fled China since the 1990s, taking with them 800 billion Yuan (roughly $150 billion) in ill-gotten funds.[6]

Given the absence of hard data, people are quick to see what's happening through the prism of their own often biased or self-interested perceptions. Ian Young, the Vancouver-based correspondent of Hong Kong's *South China Morning Post*, regularly writes about this tendency. He offers compelling arguments for seeing the phenomenon for what it is, distinguishing "between the mythical proposition of non-resident Chinese 'investors' celebrating Lunar New Year by buying apartments or swooping down in helicopters, and the rather simpler, statistically sound, reality: That tens of thousands of rich immigrants, mostly Chinese, have recently moved to Vancouver and are using their foreign-acquired funds to buy homes, thus fuelling the city's chronic unaffordability."[7] According to Young, "of the 36,973 rich migrants known to have moved to British Columbia under the now-defunct immigrant investor scheme from 2005 to 2012, 30,013 were Chinese."[8] I agree with Young, and particularly with his point about the need to banish conspiracy theories and exotic stereotypes. This is, in its nature and scope, an entirely new phenomenon. We're being exposed to a piece of the Chinese dream, a process whose reverberations are having a significant impact at neighbourhood level in some Canadian cities. It's worth more careful thought and analysis than we are currently devoting to it.

Two things are particularly worthy of closer study. The first is the potential impact of such a vast amount of pent-up Chinese demand on housing markets that are relatively small by global standards. A lot of money is flowing into the Vancouver and Toronto markets. That's good news for those who have homes to sell, for real estate agents and for those who provide the goods and services that go with a high-end lifestyle. But it's not good news for young people who are looking to buy in those same neighbourhoods. And, as the local economy heats up, it makes it much harder for people on fixed or otherwise limited incomes to remain in the now-fashionable downtown core. That's a tragedy on the personal, individual level, and one that creates larger social problems as these same people struggle to live in far-flung suburbs where necessary services such as shops, hospitals, parks and libraries are farther away.

The second issue we need to think about is the connection between this process of acquiring a new address in Canada and the acquisition of Canadian citizenship. In his book *Millionaire Migrants*, UBC academic David Ley writes eloquently about the downside of treating a Canadian passport as a commodity on offer to so-called immigrant investors. The program works on the assumption that an entrepreneur who succeeds in one business environment, such as the fast-paced, lightly taxed and highly competitive one in China, can readily succeed in a very different Canadian context. This creates expectations on the part of new arrivals that are rarely realized given the very different tax and business conditions prevailing here. Such newcomers are often criticized for treating citizenship as a business proposition—after it has been presented to them as such. When their Canadian business plans fail—and, according to Ley, many do—at least one member of the family finds it necessary to return to Asia to generate some income, only to be penalized for not showing sufficient commitment to a new life in Canada.

Other immigrant-receiving countries struggle with the same challenge. It's hard to balance openness and generosity to newcomers with hard-nosed practicality about what it takes to succeed here, and what skills and experience we most need. But just because it's difficult to get this right doesn't mean we shouldn't try. We've been relying on the dubious notion that an applicant's net worth is one of the most reliable indicators when it comes to predicting the likelihood of a happy and successful transition to Canadian life. What does this say about us to people who are considering moving here? It certainly fails to give pride of place to the qualities and values that have always attracted people to Canada. Having cancelled the IIP, we have another chance to get things right. The federal government has introduced a new program and hopes that it will do a better job of generating economic benefits. This should have encouraged some hard thinking by those of us who are already citizens about the obligations as well as the privileges of being Canadian. This is a sensitive topic. About the only time we approach it, and gingerly at that, is via a conversation about rising house prices. But that discussion inevitably peters out in the absence of reliable statistics. As one academic observer puts it, "we're trying to solve a major social policy issue on the back of the housing market."

Even in the absence of actual data, it is safe to assume that buyers from China are important players in Canada, if only because they are

so active elsewhere. Chinese real estate investment in London has registered a dramatic 1500 percent increase since 2010, totalling more than
one billion pounds by late 2013.[9] Chinese investment in Australian
real estate topped AU$4 billion during the 2011–2012 financial year.[10]
One consultancy estimated that Chinese buyers currently account
for 18 percent of new home purchases in Sydney and 14 percent in
Melbourne, a number that should rise by 30 percent by 2020, or an
additional AU$44 billion in property purchases.[11] The U.S. National
Association of Realtors estimates that Chinese buyers accounted for
18 percent of the US$68 billion foreigners invested in U.S. real estate
for the year ending March 31, 2013.[12] Canada also shows up in polling
as a highly popular destination. According to the *Hurun Report Chinese
Luxury Consumer Survey 2014*, Canada represents the third-most-desired
emigration destination for wealthy Chinese, after the United States
and Europe.

The notion that Chinese buyers are active in Canadian real estate
is also reinforced by evidence from realtors themselves.[13] I met with
a Toronto realtor who specializes in serving the Chinese market. She
has been in the business long enough to have seen a steady evolution
in demand. In the 1990s, the action was from Hong Kong (due to anxieties about the coming return to Chinese rule). This dwindled over
the next decade, and has since been replaced by demand from the
much larger mainland market. In pointing to factors that drive this
demand, she listed predictable things such as Toronto's diversity and
quality of life, but she also stressed the importance of education as an
impetus. Many Chinese parents buy a condo to house their child while
he or she is studying in Canada. While at it, a significant number of
her clients purchase additional units, buying something for themselves
or for their own parents. These come in handy when visiting the kids,
but they also provide the opportunity to safely park some money in a
secure second address, a place to go if China becomes too polluted,
crowded, corrupt or unstable.

As the agent walked me through one model unit, she pointed out the kind of issues she needs to consider on behalf of her Chinese clients, such as whether a stylish ceramic cooktop and discreet overhead fan can handle the heat and sizzle that are part of wok cookery. But her responsibilities transcend kitchen design. It is her job to advise Chinese clients, who are buying virtually sight unseen, about which neighbourhoods are safe, convenient and likely to hold their value. She helps them make the trade-off between buying in suburban Markham, which is very popular with Chinese immigrants, or selecting something closer to downtown. Another agent told me that including the phrase "near the University of Toronto" in a listing is as important as being sure to add the word *new*.

A Vancouver realtor who specializes in high-end listings estimated that, over the last five years, roughly 45 percent of his clients have been Chinese people who are looking to "park" cash and family members in Canada. Typically, the main wage earner stays on in China to make the most of more lucrative opportunities. At some high-end showings, as many as 80 percent of his clients have been Chinese. Educational opportunities and the West Coast lifestyle are the main draws. *The Economist* recently took a look at this phenomenon in an article that highlighted research by economist Robin Wiebe of the Conference Board of Canada. Wiebe's work points to compelling correlations between growth in China's gross domestic product and Vancouver real estate prices. The article includes a telling quote from Andy Yan about the challenge of determining the impact that foreign investment has on the Vancouver housing market: "Everyone knows it's there, but it's proving it that's the problem. We know it's not wage growth; and it isn't the economy here. All we know is that in Vancouver, real estate has been de-coupled from the local economy."[14]

At the end of the day, it's this decoupling of the real estate market from the local economy that feeds the social policy problem mentioned above. When the housing market is priced far above what local people can ever hope to afford, they must either forego the dream of owning their own home or move elsewhere. It is true that this problem can't be solved "on the back of the housing market." Policies designed to boost broader economic growth, education levels and social mobility are all part of the solution. But that doesn't mean ignoring smart policies that directly address the short-term and very human cost of a runaway housing market.

So let's assume that at least a portion of the money flowing out of China into international real estate is ending up in Canadian cities. Is this something that should worry people, or is this yet another in a series of waves of investment that have carried new energy and prosperity into our society? A healthy investment market is key to generating new housing stock. It's what makes renting possible as an affordable option. But it's worth thinking carefully about the extent to which investment, wherever it is from, can skew or influence the market in ways that make the larger community less diverse and affordable. Popular real estate investment destinations such as New York and London are now looking at the phenomenon of absenteeism and its effect on neighbourhood life. Vancouver is beginning to look at this, too.

Undeterred by the lack of available hard data, Andy Yan measured absenteeism among condo owners by looking at power usage among condos in a variety of Vancouver neighbourhoods. Yan assumed that units drawing minimal amounts of power were likely unoccupied. He found that absentee rates as calculated by this measure vary across Vancouver, rising to higher levels in desirable waterfront neighbourhoods such as Coal Harbour. But he also makes it clear that it matters little whether the absentee owners are "from Calgary or Shanghai." The important thing is that someone, somewhere consider the negative impact of absenteeism on the vibrancy of a neighbourhood, avoiding the emergence of what Yan calls a "zombie city."[15]

Investment also leads, understandably enough, to strategies to maximize profit. The problem is that too much emphasis on profit

alone can have a negative impact on the diversity and perceived quality of life in the neighbourhood. In residential real estate investment,
smaller is often better, a perception that leads to a proliferation of tiny
units called micro suites, which are attractive to investors but not of
much use to families. Investors buy into these projects years before
construction with a small down payment and flip them when, several
years later, the unit (or units) are ready for the market. In a 2013 panel
discussion of foreign investment in real estate in Vancouver, writer
and activist Sandy Garossino suggested that many of the city's condos
aren't purchased to house people, but amount instead to "really expensive safety deposit boxes."[16] At the same forum, Andy Yan made the
important point that, to the extent that real estate investment is part
of a trend by wealthy people around the world to park money, we may
need to "re-think parking rules."

The very absence of data means that many theories about the
impact of investment on Canadian real estate tend to be expressed in
emotional and dogmatic terms. Some, mainly in the real estate industry, are quick to claim that fears about foreign investment inflating
local prices are wildly exaggerated. Many on the other side of the
argument are so preoccupied with the problems attributed to foreign
investment that they fail to see the human dimension of the issue.
By this, I mean a flow of people that has enriched and diversified
Canadian life. Regardless of what side people are on, the discussion is
all too often driven by anecdote. A few years ago, Toronto was buzzing
with the story of a Chinese student who nonchalantly bid $400,000
more than the asking price to secure a bungalow in Toronto.[17] Ian
Young says that the B.C. variant of this anecdote is about wealthy
Chinese buyers scouting properties by helicopter. In both cases, such
accounts have taken on larger, symbolic status, fuelling urban anxiety
and mythmaking.

Some analysts point out that inflexible regulations and local red
tape contribute far more to rising prices than does demand from foreign

buyers. In an efficient market, they argue, rising demand should simply trigger an increase in the supply of houses. Others argue that it's more complicated. Inefficiencies in the market do play a role, but this is greatly exacerbated by huge, pent-up demand from China, helping to drive prices to record levels. I asked a Vancouver realtor about the possibility that demand from foreign buyers is pricing some long-term residents, many seniors among them, out of the market. "That," he said, "is the sad reality. But we can't stop the train."

When investment originates in places, such as China, where it is hard to get large amounts of money out legally, and where corruption is a problem, it is safe to assume that some of the money flowing into Canada is, if not hot, at least lukewarm. Simply bringing the money to the table often involves bending rules on both the Chinese and Canadian sides. Between April 2011 and June 2012, agents from the Canada Border Services Agency seized close to $13 million from Chinese nationals at the Vancouver and Toronto airports, an amount that represents 59 percent of the illegal cash seized at both sites. In these instances, people had failed to declare that they were bringing into Canada currency in excess of $10,000. In most cases, the cash was returned after a fine was paid. The average amount smuggled was $16,000, although one man had $177,500 stowed away in various places.[18] It is assumed that a significant amount of this was destined for the real estate market. One popular method is to have multiple friends and relatives bring in or transfer enough cash for the purchase.[19]

China may be taking steps to regularize the money-transfer process. In 2014, state-owned China Central Television (CCTV) caused a splash when it alleged that the Bank of China was facilitating money laundering by wealthy clients seeking to move cash abroad. The Bank of China, rattled by this rare attack from another SOE, explained that it was operating a pilot program out of several branches in southern Guangdong province designed to help clients cover the cost of emigration, including buying a new house. Strange as the episode was, it is not at all uncommon for the Chinese government to test potentially risky programs at a local level. For its part, CCTV was anticipating, correctly, that the majority of its viewers would be most concerned not by the transfer mechanism but by where the wealth came from in the first place.[20]

That's a concern for the government of China, too. When Australia expanded its own immigrant investor program recently, China issued a public request that Australia not allow the program to be used by Chinese fraudsters.[21] As part of an ambitious anti-corruption campaign, China has dispatched teams to a wide range of countries to pursue corrupt officials who have absconded with funds. This international part of the anti-corruption campaign is called Operation Fox Hunt 2014, and the U.S. and Canada are key targets for its investigators. Both places are popular with corrupt officials because both are highly desirable locations in which to house family members and educate children, and neither has an extradition treaty with China.[22]

We are at a moment when wealthy people all over the world are, in the words of Andy Yan, "parking" some of their wealth in real estate in locations that are both desirable and likely to hold their value. Given the fact that potential demand in China is huge and that it has been pent up for decades, Chinese investors are bound to come in for most of the attention. As Yan argues, we need to focus more carefully on the parking rules themselves, and worry less about where the money comes from. Addressing this fully in cities such as Vancouver and Toronto requires much more civic (and civil) debate than we have seen to date. Ideally, it should be based on fact rather than anecdote— something that argues for collecting data that can help us better understand what's really happening in the market.

Any such discussion would certainly benefit from a review of recent experience in jurisdictions that do place some limitations on foreign investors. In Australia, for example, foreign investors are barred from buying existing housing, the idea being that foreign investment should

contribute to the growth of the country's housing supply. Other jurisdictions have imposed or are exploring taxes on non-resident owners.[23]
While the real estate industry hates this idea, it opens up some interesting policy options. If we levied such a tax in Vancouver and Toronto,
for example, its proceeds could be used to support the construction of
affordable housing in the downtown sections of both cities.

We should also carefully review existing safeguards against corrupt
practices, including whether or not enhanced supervision and enforcement measures are required when it comes to discouraging flows of
hot money and the unwelcome arrival of corrupt officials.

Our thinking also needs to be more creative and connected when
it comes to assessing the economic impact of immigration. The notion
that the IIP had a negligible impact on the economy will be challenged
by businesses selling into the high end of consumer markets in cities such as Vancouver, Calgary and Toronto. To the extent that these
high-net-worth individuals were buying homes, they were in the high-
price end of these and other Canadian markets. I spoke with a realtor who estimated the impact of the program at about six hundred
purchases each year in Toronto, where she works. That doesn't seem
like a big number until you consider that, in 2013, just under two thousand homes sold for more than $1.5 million in Toronto, up 18 percent
from 2012.[24] So, it's likely that the program drove a significant percent-
age of high-end sales there and in other cities, along with markets for
expensive cars, furniture and private school fees. That may or may not
be a desirable outcome, but we should at least think it through, and
include local jurisdictions in the discussion.

I asked a Vancouver agent about high-end demand generated by
investor immigrants in his city. "If we didn't have them," he said, "we'd
have no business." He also told me that Chinese clients were quick to
use the demise of the program as a bargaining chip, telling realtors
that since demand is almost certainly going to diminish, they're going
to have to sharpen their pencils and offer better deals. The impact of

cancelling the Canadian IIP is beginning to be felt more widely. By late August 2014, there were reports that a similar U.S. program was reaching capacity due to a sudden "surge" in applications.[25]

In December 2014, the federal government ended months of speculation by unveiling a significantly different version of the IIP. Much, much smaller, it will offer permanent residency to some fifty investors who have a net worth of $10 million and are willing to invest $2 million in a venture capital fund.[26] It will take some time for the impact of the program to be felt, and while there are other opportunities for wealthy people from China and elsewhere to invest in Canada, it is hard to believe that reducing the IPP to a trickle won't be felt at street level in Vancouver and Toronto.[27]

I am more than confident that the IIP *did* need an overhaul. But it would have been useful to set it in the context of a more fundamental and more inclusive discussion about what it is to be a resident, a neighbour and a citizen. That kind of honesty is a prerequisite for developing policies designed to ensure that our cities remain welcoming, affordable, prosperous and livable. Being open to discussing this doesn't in any way imperil our commitment to building a diverse and tolerant society. But it depends on having more facts than we do now.

After years of being poor and unable to travel freely, China's citizens are discovering the world. A tidal wave of demand has been unleashed. This is helping to drive global trends in tourism, education and real estate, which are having a significant impact on the world's most livable cities, Vancouver and Toronto among them. China's people will almost certainly continue to feel the magnetic attraction of Canadian life. This is a welcome if at times almost overwhelming phenomenon, but it doesn't have to remain an essentially mysterious one. This is yet another way of saying that knowing more than we do now about China and its people, where they're going and why, is essential if we are to steer our own course successfully.

CHINA AND
CANADIAN SECURITY

SEVEN

The Unfinished Empire

The sun was beginning to burn through light cloud cover, banishing
the early morning chill as Janet and I made our way around the
eastern flank of the Gate of Heavenly Peace. We emerged into
Tiananmen Square and took our places in a huge grandstand that
was filling with ambassadors, guests from overseas and other people
lucky enough to have a ringside seat for the spectacle that would
follow. It was the early morning of October 1, China's National Day.
This being 2009, we were about to witness the special celebrations
marking the sixtieth anniversary of the founding of the People's
Republic of China.

From time to time, I gazed up at the top of the gate, to the place
where, exactly sixty years ago, Chairman Mao had stood to address his
victorious followers at the end of the civil war against the Nationalists.
Mao is reported to have said, "The Chinese people have stood up," a
ringing phrase that has captured imaginations and motivated patriotic
Chinese for decades. That some people who were in the square at the
time recall Mao as having said something a bit more bureaucratic in
his heavy Hunan accent, simply announcing the establishment of a
new government, hasn't diminished the legend.

As the minutes wore on, I could see former premiers Zhu Rongji and Li Peng, and former president Jiang Zemin taking their places atop the gate. I had first seen Jiang in the mid-1980s, when he was the mayor of Shanghai and I was working at our then new consulate general in the city. His enormous black-framed glasses (which, along with old-man pants hitched up to near shoulder height, figured in parodies of the former leader) marked him out clearly, despite the distance between my place, near street level, and his position high above.

By mid-morning, the sun was blazing in a blue sky. Its appearance right at show time had conspiracy theorists in the foreign crowd muttering about Chinese efforts to manipulate the weather, a conversation that could be expected every time it snowed unexpectedly, or when the Beijing weather was unseasonably hot, cold or wet. Janet and I were mainly concerned about making it through the next four hours with nothing to shade us but our programs.

In the late 1990s, when I ran Canada's unofficial outpost in Taiwan, we would attend another national day parade each October. In Taipei, the anniversary marked is that of the revolution, launched on October 10, 1911, that brought an end to the Qing dynasty and ultimately created China's first experience with republican government. Conceived by Sun Yat-sen, the first Chinese republic was an experiment in idealism that descended, sadly and steadily, into corrupt and heavy-handed single-party rule. The republic would struggle through tumultuous decades, with Sun and his successor, Chiang Kai-shek, attempting to preside over a China torn apart by warlords and contemptuously occupied by the Japanese. Chiang's Nationalist Party (the Kuomintang or KMT) clung to power at the end of World War II, only to be defeated by Mao in the ensuing civil war and banished to the island of Taiwan in 1949.

The October parades that I watched in Beijing and Taiwan could not have been more different. By the time I was living in Taiwan, it had given up its Cold War bellicosity. The island was now a democracy, with a free press and a very lively civil society. Taiwan's parade was folksy and low key. Instead of showcasing tanks and planes, it was a chance for bands and dance troupes from all over the island to show their stuff. Another difference, springing from that same folksiness, was that all the guests were provided with baseball caps to protect them from the even hotter sunshine of subtropical Taiwan. At the parade in 2009, however, I was without such valuable headgear. Since my cap was emblazoned with the flag of the Republic of China, anathema to true believers in Beijing, it had been consigned to storage in Canada. I missed it that sunny morning by the Gate of Heavenly Peace.

As we squinted into Tiananmen Square, we could see a procession approaching from the west. China's president and Party chairman, Hu Jintao, was standing in a gleaming Red Flag limousine, staring straight ahead as he sped in the direction of the People's Liberation Army (PLA) troops massed just east of us on the Avenue of Eternal Peace. Hu wasn't dressed in his normal dark business suit, wearing instead a Mao jacket buttoned high on his neck. As he approached each section of troops, he would call out, *"Tongzhimen, xinkule!"* ("Comrades, you are working hard!"). And each unit would in turn shout back, *"Wei remin fuwu!"* ("Serve the people!"). This was an important bit of theatre. The head of China's Communist Party was inspecting the men and women responsible for maintaining the Party's unquestioned rule. The Party's chairman was greeting the Party's army.

The PLA parade was the first of a two-part production. It would be followed by its political equivalent, a chance for the Party to make its case to the people of China. In the second part, floats recalled the eras of former leaders Mao, Deng and Jiang, and culminated in a paean to current president Hu Jintao. The message, somewhat awkwardly stitched together, was that the heroic party of the revolution had become the party of prosperity and stability. Doing this under the watchful gaze of Mao, whose portrait still peers out over Tiananmen, requires a continuing suspension of disbelief by China's citizens.

Earlier, as the military parade began, as troops and tanks rumbled into the square, the weight of recent history was oppressive, reminding many of the events of June 4, 1989. That was when the PLA rolled into Tiananmen and obediently turned their weapons on idealistic young people who were judged a threat to the Party's hold on power. On this October morning, it was as if the leadership hoped to bury those memories in an avalanche of patriotic fervour. This would be a military parade like no other in the nation's history. In the past, the marchers might have been Chinese, but the most potent weapons had been Russian. But on this day, China was showcasing its technological prowess. Many of the aircraft filling the skies (I had never seen so many planes in the air at one time), as well as many of the tanks, personnel carriers and missiles rumbling and clanking along in front of the grandstand, had been designed and made locally. I quickly learned that I didn't need to ask which ones were appearing for the first time. I simply listened for the whir and click of the cameras wielded by the foreign military attachés in the audience, all of them as intent and excited as birdwatchers at spring migration.

And among all the equipment were soldiers, sailors and air force personnel high-stepping in formations that were surreal for their machine-like uniformity. Also interspersed were large numbers of what are called People's Armed Police (PAP), heavily armed paramilitary units that crush civil disturbances within China, leaving the PLA largely free to deal with external threats. As a civilian observer, I often find it hard to distinguish between the PAP and the PLA. This is not entirely surprising. China's leaders fear the threat from within as much as the threats from outside. Today, both forces were equally imposing.

One attaché explained, somewhat defensively, that the Chinese were going beyond the requirements of military discipline, reaching a fussy showiness that was more appropriate for Radio City Music Hall than the parade square. The marchers certainly appeared to have been selected by central casting. Each was of an identical and impressive stature. Every cap was level with the one beside it, and polished boots swung up and snapped back down in unison. Other sour observers muttered about unsportsmanlike tricks, like sticking pins in the collars of uniforms to keep necks and heads rigid. The tension broke when a formation of women high-stepped into sight. They had guns cradled in their arms, and were shouting slogans with martial fervour. But the effect was bizarrely softened by their short, cherry-red skirts and their white boots. This strange tableau brought a smile to the normally sour visage of President Hu Jintao, a scene that was replayed endlessly on TV.

I would see the Chinese security forces deployed in significant numbers many more times during my travels in China, and I would learn that there was more to their job description than state ceremonial duties. I next saw them on a visit to Kashgar in China's distant west. Kashgar is farther from Beijing than Vancouver is from Toronto, and is worlds apart in terms of culture and identity. Kashgar sits at the western edge of China's vast Xinjiang (literally, "the new frontier") region, a vast, resource-rich territory that is home to the Muslim Uighur people.

Visiting the region, you are reminded that, in addition to being a dynamic, emerging and urgently modernizing country, China is also a surprising throwback, a lone survivor of the ancient era of empires. Xinjiang was added to the Chinese empire at a time when Rome was flourishing. It has been lost and regained several times since, and is currently the scene of a tense standoff between Chinese security forces and Uighurs who see their religion, language and culture as under threat from a westward migration of Han Chinese. The new Han migrants are eager to benefit from the booming economy of a region that is important for its energy and mineral resources and, increasingly, as a road, rail and pipeline corridor linking China to Central Asia, the Middle East and, ultimately, Europe.

Xinjiang is a region in transition. Urumqi, the capital, is now increasingly full of the garish office towers that are part of all the other "second tier" cities in China. But as you travel even further west, it is hard not to think that you have left the modern nation-state and are reconnecting with the China of dynasties and empires. I fell in love with Kashgar because it is one of the few cities in China that looks and feels different. It is in fact so different that parts of the city and surrounding countryside were chosen to represent Kabul in the film version of *The Kite Runner.* But change is coming. I was disheartened to learn of typically ambitious (and jarring) Chinese plans to make Kashgar "the next Shenzhen," meaning another sprawling and soulless Chinese metropolis. Already, cheap modern structures are nibbling at the edges of the old city, a highly visible example of the cultural dislocation that is at the heart of Uighur anxieties. The government professes to being committed to preservation. But what I saw was more like a sad and shabby theme park, accurately described by a UNESCO representative in China as "one of the black spots of heritage conservation."[1]

This tension broke into violence just months before I arrived to take up my posting. In July 2009, gangs of Uighur toughs rampaged through Urumqi brandishing knives and, in many shocking cases, pulling Han Chinese people from cars and hacking them to death. Later, Han Chinese gangs returned the violence, attacking Uighurs. When I visited in October 2009, the region was under heavy security. The army and police were everywhere. Security officials went as far as cutting off all internet service and international telephone links across the entire region. I had timed my visit to the region to end on a Friday. I wanted to observe prayers at the mosque on the Muslim day of worship. During many visits to Afghanistan, I had seen the Canadian Forces on operations in and around Kandahar, and was impressed by how carefully they balanced their security precautions with the sensitivities of local communities. Canadian soldiers went to great lengths to keep "long guns" (meaning rifles) out of sight when visiting schools or when calling on tribal elders.

No such sensitivity was on display in Kashgar. As I sat on the sunny steps of the mosque, I watched worshippers filing in through the imposing cordon that the security forces had put in place. Armoured personnel carriers ringed the plaza in front of the mosque, and heavily armed troops filled the spaces between. Worshippers filed in through a narrow passage between the vehicles. The effect was imposing and humiliating, and spoke volumes about the continuing tragedy of Chinese misrule in Xinjiang. The Chinese defensively point to very real links between Uighur extremism and global terror networks. In a shocking recent incident, knife-wielding assailants, believed to be Uighurs, slaughtered twenty-nine travellers inside the train station in Kunming in China's southwest. Chinese netizens were furious when, in their view, Western media focused not on the victims but on the alleged roots of the problem back in Xinjiang. This has been followed by even more acts of terror in Xinjiang and beyond.

But even while condemning terrorism, it is hard not to see a connection to China's absolute tone-deafness when it comes to local sensitivities. Writing about conditions in Xinjiang, Pakistani journalist Ahmed Rashid makes the point that "Islam only becomes a threat when Muslims are repressed and treated as third class citizens."[2] On a visit to a satellite tracking station during my visit, I noticed that all the screens were being monitored by Han Chinese. I asked whether any Uighurs were employed. "Oh, yes," was the enthusiastic reply from the Han manager. "They make great cleaners."

I would see more evidence of this misguided approach to the governance of what China calls minority peoples when I later secured permission to visit Tibet. This is difficult for ambassadors to do, with permission only grudgingly granted long after the application is made. Normally, the Chinese insist on packing ambassadors into regional groups and shuttling them around on tightly organized official programs. Happily, the Americans are considered to be such a handful that I was left on my own. The first time I applied, I was only given approval to travel months later, at the end of May, which coincides with one of the busiest seasons for incoming Canadian VIPs. I had a stream of high-level visitors arriving in Beijing and couldn't possibly be away. I asked if I could shift my visit by a couple of weeks, but was turned down. It would be more than a year before I got another chance.

Like Xinjiang, Tibet has also been the scene of ethnic violence. Frustrated monks rioted in the Tibetan capital of Lhasa in early 2008, an uprising that was swiftly and brutally put down. Here, too, simmering resentment is fed by the steady flow of Han Chinese migrants, something that is changing the nature of the place. This is but the latest chapter in a sad history. Tibetan writer Dawa Norbu described the first stages of this dismantling of the old Tibetan world with the arrival, in the 1960s, of China's Cultural Revolution: "Prayer-flags were pulled down. The whole point of the exercise was to completely humiliate the believers and drive them into submission to the new doctrine. What was sacred yesterday was made into an object of utter ridicule today. What were the veritable sources of pride and confidence yesterday were rendered into humiliation and shame today. The whole orderly cosmology was reversed. The earth replaced the sky, and the sky the earth."[3]

The visitor is constantly reminded by Chinese officials that Chinese investment is bringing in modern infrastructure and new conveniences. But this torrent of Chinese money is also threatening to turn Tibet, starting with much of Lhasa, into an indistinguishable component of the new China. I found it interesting that among elites in Beijing and Shanghai there is a growing interest in Tibetan Buddhism. But at the same time, China's leadership is busily blocking the well-springs of that faith. The Dalai Lama, the person most clearly associated with Tibet's spirituality, is anathematized, routinely vilified in Chinese talking points and transformed by a vengeful Beijing into a bone of contention with any country that dares to offer him a welcome.

Organizing my visit involved waging a lengthy struggle with my controllers in the foreign affairs section of Tibet's regional government.

Their objective was to completely fill my schedule with official briefings, lunches and dinners. My plan was to do only the meetings that were absolutely required, and to carve out enough time to see what was happening with my own eyes. This included visiting Norbulingka, the unassuming and relatively modern building that had been, until the late 1950s, the summer residence of the Dalai Lama. It was from this residence that the current Dalai Lama slipped out of Tibet, and out of the reach of the Chinese. Visiting the palace, which is furnished as it was when the Dalai Lama lived there, was a bit like stepping back into my grandparents' apartment circa 1959. It is full of heavy furniture, musty rugs, antique appliances and kitschy pictures. But it has a comfortable, lived-in look, as if the occupant has just stepped out on an errand. This feeling of continuing connectedness was reinforced as I watched Tibetan pilgrims file through the rooms. Chanting softly, they paused before objects, a radio here or a picture there, bending to come in close to nuzzle and caress. It was as if something of the previous occupant could be experienced through contact with the things that had once been part of his daily life. It was touching to watch, and easy to feel that it might be true.

My other must-see destination was the Jokhang temple, the heart of Lhasa and the holiest shrine in Tibetan Buddhism. Small shops and eateries line three sides of a plaza in front of the temple. This is all relatively unobtrusive, except for the neon lights of a Chinese fast-food place. If you raise your eyes above the shops, you will see that the rooftops are busy with security people gazing down into the square, watching for any signs of disturbance. I crossed the square and joined the ceaseless circle of pilgrims walking clockwise around the temple. A friendly Tibetan helped me to understand which parts of Tibet various groups of pilgrims were from, pointing out distinctive robes, cloaks, headgear and hairstyles.

As we walked, we watched for Chinese security patrols pushing through the crowd at regular intervals. The patrols move counter-clockwise, searching the onrush of pilgrims for any sign of trouble. Their against-the-grain approach is an apt symbol of China's anything but subtle approach. What was most jarring for me wasn't the presence of the troops, but that each unit was trailed by a soldier carrying a fire extinguisher. This isn't because the temple, slick with yak butter and full of the open flames of countless lamps, is a fire hazard, but because the latest desperate and heart-breaking manifestation of resistance is self-immolation. The job of the last man in the squad is to prevent the appearance of any new martyrs.

IT DOESN'T TAKE LONG to figure out that much of China's security consciousness is focused inward, and particularly on the two huge regions that it has long struggled to incorporate into its empire. But that is not to say that the view out beyond the empire is any more reassuring. In fact, China has very good reason to worry about its neighbours. It has fought with most of the bigger ones over the course of the last century, and, with the possible exception of Pakistan, has no country nearby that it can entirely trust or consider like-minded.

Sino-Japanese relations are at their lowest point in recent memory. The navies and air forces of both East Asian powers are operating dangerously close to one another as they argue over a cluster of rocks that is, depending on your view, part of China or the very tail end of the Japanese archipelago. The conflict became more serious with China's sudden imposition of an Air Defense Identification Zone (ADIZ) over the region, a move that had airlines scrambling to comply with new rules requiring the filing of flight plans with Chinese agencies. It also prompted both Japan and the United States to challenge China's move by flying their own military aircraft through the region without seeking such permission. The sudden move has generated worries among some that it is another example of Beijing's selective, cafeteria-style approach to the rules, as one writer put it: "part of a larger pattern of Beijing's refusing to adhere fully to existing international norms and standards, even as it pursues the benefits of a system whose functioning they underwrite."[4]

The dispute runs much deeper than recent territorial manoeuvring. It has much to do with Tokyo's inability, and possibly its unwillingness, to convincingly express contrition for the brutality inflicted by Japan's imperial army before and during World War II. This has prevented Japan and China from building the trust necessary to accommodate China's rise (and Japan's slow decline) without increasingly worrisome confrontation. That said, China contributes to the tension by constantly invoking anti-Japanese feelings to stoke nationalism.

The situation is less confrontational but equally unpredictable on the Korean peninsula. When I served as a trade commissioner in Seoul more than thirty years ago, small discrepancies in my carefully compiled import statistics could be attributed to infrequent and highly secret shipments from China, which was otherwise viewed with hostility and fear. Today, South Korea eagerly embraces China as a trade and investment partner.

Meanwhile, North Korea, China's long-time ally, is increasingly viewed by the Chinese as a dangerously unstable liability, but one that it cannot disown or abandon. Chinese leaders cringe when foreigners compliment them for their unique influence over North Korea, knowing in their hearts that their leverage is limited. China's main concern is that the collapse of North Korea would bring an avalanche of economic migrants into China and, far worse from a Chinese point of view, bring an American-influenced and democratic Korea right up to its very borders. China feels an abiding loyalty to one of its few remaining fellow communist states, but keeps a watchful eye on its worrying and unpredictable belligerence.

Meanwhile, China's relations with Russia are nominally better. China and Russia are currently partners in the Shanghai Cooperation Organisation, a forum which they and a number of neighbouring authoritarian states such as Kazakhstan and Kyrgyzstan use as a Central Asian counterbalance to NATO. But although China and Russia find common cause in opposing developments such as Western intervention in Syria, theirs is a marriage of convenience. China is probably torn by Russia's meddling in Ukraine. On the one hand, they would quietly approve of anything that distracts and demoralizes the United States and its allies. On the other, cross-border interventions run counter to China's zeal for the doctrine of non-interference. Working out a major natural gas deal during Vladimir Putin's 2014 visit to Shanghai was an opportunity to discomfit the U.S. and its European allies. But this doesn't signal lasting Sino-Russian friendship.

China split with the then Soviet Union in the late 1950s, leading to a period of tension that culminated in major border clashes a decade later and ominous preparations on both sides for a possible nuclear war. Although those days are long past, Russia looks uneasily at its sparsely populated Far East, which is bordered by large and dynamic Chinese provinces hungry for the region's abundant resources. And Chinese investment in what were the Central Asian republics of the former Soviet Union means that China, rather than Russia, is becoming the dominant power in Central Asia.

China is working hard to establish its relations with the neighbouring countries of Central Asia because it sees this as a matter of necessity. China's reach west is partly motivated by the need to secure resources, but it also reflects China's desire to stabilize the region so that it doesn't undermine the security of China's own west. It hopes that forging ties with these less-than-democratic states will facilitate what China terms anti-terror cooperation, but what often amounts to joint efforts to crush groups sympathetic to Uighur nationalism.

China's leaders are well aware that instability beyond their western borders is increasingly felt in China itself. I recall meeting a woman in Urumqi who ran an NGO helping people afflicted with HIV/AIDS. Rates were spiking in some parts of the territory. When I asked why, she explained that it was due to intravenous drug use fuelled by the increasing availability of Afghan heroin, a tragic by-product of the chaos in a country with which China shares a tiny and remote border connection.

China and India emerged as modern nations at roughly the same time: 1947 for India and 1949 for China. These neighbours were early allies and leaders in the non-aligned movement. But managing their mountainous border became increasingly difficult in the wake of India's decision to grant asylum to the Dalai Lama when he fled Tibet in 1959. The situation deteriorated to the point that China launched a decisive cross-border military strike in 1962 that caught India by surprise, and led to a humiliating rout of the Indian army.

The uneasy relationship between the two giants continues, with China deploying troops along the high-altitude frontier and the Indian media crowing about the development of new missiles capable of hitting Chinese cities. On my visit to eastern Tibet, I received a typically detailed briefing about the region from the Chinese officials in charge. Certain counties in the district were described as "remote and rarely visited." On cross-checking against my own map, I discovered that their supposed isolation is largely due to the fact that they are actually part of the northern Indian state of Arunachal Pradesh.

A by-product of tension with India is China's close and enduring relationship with Pakistan, a bond enabled by China's seeming indifference to Pakistan's troubling connections to global terrorism and nuclear proliferation. Indeed, late in 2013, China extended loans to Pakistan for the construction of new nuclear facilities. But it can't be reassuring to China's leaders to know that their best and just about only friend is Pakistan.

As China's economic power has grown, so too has its influence over neighbouring Southeast Asian countries. This authority was greatly facilitated in the first decade of the present century by America's near total distraction with wars in Iraq and Afghanistan. But the situation is changing here, too, as China is increasingly faced with regional

challenges, many of its own making. China publicly stresses its benevolent intentions, and works hard to convince people that it is unique
among world powers in not having a history of territorial expansion.
But it has steadily undermined its own argument by pushing aggressively for recognition of what it calls the "nine dotted line," a Chinese
amendment to maps of the region laying claim to a vast area of the
South China Sea, swallowing up territory that is also claimed by
Vietnam, Brunei, Malaysia and the Philippines.

China backs up this claim through the aggressive presence of armed
vessels operated by its increasingly far-reaching navy and by a number
of other maritime agencies. This has provoked a feisty response from
Vietnam, which has a long history of fending off Chinese advances.
The most recent chapter was a bloody border war in 1979 that gave
the Chinese much more than they had bargained for.

The Philippines has also abandoned a policy of friendship at all
costs with Beijing. But bereft of anything like a modern navy, it is finding itself overmatched. Predictably, China has reserved some of its
most aggressive behaviour for what it perceives as its weakest adver-
sary. China's ships mount what is termed a "cabbage strategy," succes-
sively surrounding distant, disputed islands, and establishing what it
hopes is a precedent-setting presence.

The vast circle that we have drawn around China closes with
Taiwan, the island that lies between the Philippines and Japan. Taiwan
is home to that remnant of China's republican government that fled
the mainland after its defeat by the Communists in 1949. The defeated
regime brought with it leading figures from across Chinese society, not
just in government and the military, but in business, the arts, education and even China's top chefs. This elite community superimposed
itself on a distant and somewhat forgotten portion of China, one that
had in fact been ruled by the Japanese from 1895 to 1945. The result
was a very uneasy marriage between a Mandarin-speaking ruling class
and a Taiwanese-speaking local population that had been heavily

influenced by Japan (and who, indeed, are among the few formerly colonized peoples to look back on the Japanese era with something approaching nostalgia).

As uneasy as the situation was (the island was the scene of a brutal crackdown on the local inhabitants by the newly arrived Nationalists), the main focus in the 1950s was fending off threats from now-Communist mainland China, which had made reunification[5] a core national objective. Over time, Taiwan changed. It stopped thinking of itself as a temporary outpost of a government that claimed to rule all of China. Its leaders gradually set aside dreams of returning to recapture the mainland. Slowly, governance was localized, and more clearly focused on improving conditions on the island itself. And even more slowly, it was democratized: restrictions were relaxed on opposition parties, the media and dissent in general. There was now room for serious discussion about whether the island and its people were a once and future part of China, or whether Taiwan had become something different and was deserving of some form of separate, autonomous status. By the time I arrived to run Canada's unofficial office in Taiwan in 1998, this debate defined the main divide in Taiwanese politics. I was on the scene in Taiwan in March 2000, when the Nationalist Party (the KMT), which had run Taiwan since 1949, was defeated in an election by the Democratic Progressive Party (DPP), which is more focused on the Taiwanese identity of the island and its people.

China's approach to Taiwan has evolved, too. It has many missiles pointed at the island, and its military still trains to retake it. But China is also relying on its immense economic leverage, a factor that has grown as Taiwan has evolved from a rising economy that makes goods to a wealthier economy that invests in making goods elsewhere, for the most part in mainland China. The relationship is warmest when the KMT is in power (and they have since staged a comeback), because they are the party most invested in the Chinese-ness of Taiwan. But, regardless of which party is in power in Taipei, China still works hard

to limit and roll back Taiwan's efforts to have anything like an autonomous presence on the world stage. And Taiwan remains a "core interest" for China, meaning that, regardless of the cost in terms of its
international standing, China would unhesitatingly use force to prevent the island from seeking full independence.

THIS CIRCLE TOUR ILLUSTRATES how full of challenges the
immediate neighbourhood appears to China's leaders. They feel beset
by domestic threats in Tibet and Xinjiang, and hemmed in by their
mainly unfriendly neighbours. But the greatest threat, at least in the
minds of China's political and military leaders, lies far on the horizon.

China's Communist leadership has tended to view the United States
with a mixture of awe and profound suspicion. Deeply impressed by
America's economic and military might, China's leaders have also
long been convinced, and not entirely without reason, that the United
States seeks to destabilize their regime. They see the threat as being
both direct—evidenced by U.S. actions such as selling arms to Taiwan
or flying surveillance aircraft along China's coast—and indirect. Some
people in China see U.S. efforts to support human rights, for example,
as a Trojan horse carrying with it the people and ideas that will topple
the Communist regime.

Recently, however, although suspicions still remain, much of the
awe has been lost. The America that seemed omnipotent in the wake
of the First Gulf War is, in the view of China's leadership, no more.
America's long, hard slog in Iraq and Afghanistan has contributed significantly to this reappraisal. Added to this is the fact that the reputation of the U.S. in China has been greatly diminished by the global
financial crisis. Sitting in on meetings with very senior leaders, I was
more than once struck by the degree to which personal satisfaction, a
sort of Chinese *schadenfreude*, colours their perceptions. Some of the
most senior members of the leadership were at pains to express their

very real satisfaction at seeing the United States, long used to lecturing the Chinese on how to manage their economy, humbled. What I also detected in this commentary was a degree of naïveté about "American" views and intentions—a broad category that runs from uncritical praise of China to unrelenting criticism, with much carefully nuanced thinking in between—and a profound underestimation of American resilience.

Of course, it was not as if China had to come to this almost intoxicating sense of self-confidence entirely on its own. The hugely successful Beijing 2008 Olympics, coupled with China's dynamism in the face of the economic crisis, helped to shape a new narrative about China internationally, which in turn influenced China's perception of itself. By the middle of 2009, the prevailing global storyline was that China could do no wrong. According to such reports, it had found the means to escape economic gravity, essentially spending its way to ever-increasing prosperity. This admiration was only heightened when, in 2010, China passed Japan to become the world's second-largest economy. Included in breathless assessments of China's seemingly inevitable rise were observations that part of China's success was due to its efficient governance. Its leaders, capable technocrats, were held up for admiration as U.S. lawmakers squabbled on the edge of the fiscal cliff.

Deng Xiaoping had famously instructed his colleagues to "keep a low profile, and bide our time." He felt that there was no need to attract attention and create anxieties internationally while engaged in the business of rebuilding the country. His successors also considered it wise to emphasize the country's developing status. This enabled them to fend off requests for China to bear a greater burden in the international community. But by 2009, that narrative was harder to sell. Nor was there much inclination even to try to sell it. The foreign policy agenda was being shaped by new actors, including the top brass of the PLA, nationalistic journalists and academics, and hyper-patriotic young netizens who were coming of age at what seemed to be China's moment.

The result was an astounding display of Chinese chutzpah, a process marked by uncoordinated assertiveness with Japan and the countries of Southeast Asia, and an unbridled churlishness with international actors ranging from the Vatican to the Nobel Committee.

China has never been unwilling to take on potential adversaries, relying on what its strategists refer to as "active defence" to surprise and overwhelm potential threats before they become actual.[6] Up until recently, China's leaders have tended to pick their fights carefully, rarely taking on more antagonists than they could manage at one time. But by 2010, it seemed that China was embroiled in disputes with most of its powerful neighbours. Some analysts have suggested that China's more assertive foreign policy from 2008 through 2011 can be divided into two separate phases. The first, which lasted until late 2009, and saw China on the offensive with its neighbours, reflected its sense that the United States was in permanent decline and was disengaging from Asia. This has been wryly described as an example of "premature triumphalism."[7] In fact, China's very assertiveness helped enable a formidable American response.

By 2010, China, taking note of America's re-engagement in East Asia, began to modify its approach. It stepped back from some of its more assertive behaviours and moved to the defensive, angrily condemning what it saw as U.S. interference in its region. China was outraged, for example, when the U.S. sent an aircraft carrier into the Yellow Sea in the wake of North Korea's shelling of South Korean civilians. They were also enraged by the decision to rotate U.S. Marines through training exercises in Australia's Northern Territory. (In the wake of this, a Chinese official told me that his government was furious with Australia. The Chinese are always keen to play one country off against another, so my interlocutor added, only partly in jest, that China's policy line would now be to "reward Canada and punish Australia," something that I imagined lasting until Canada itself managed, inevitably, to annoy an increasingly sensitive China.)

China is not without a few threats of its own. It acquired and has recently refit a Soviet-era aircraft carrier. This represents only the very first, small step in the long and arduous process of actually learning how to conduct carrier operations at sea, a discipline that the U.S. Navy largely pioneered and continues to overwhelmingly dominate. But the acquisition speaks to the expanded blue-water ambitions of China's navy, which had hitherto been seen as a coastal force.

Much more threatening to U.S. defence planners is China's apparent mastery of the technology required to launch cruise missiles capable of striking and sinking a carrier at sea. If there was any doubt about China's new confidence, even in relation to the powerful United States, it was banished in early 2011, when the PLA arranged to unveil a new stealth fighter aircraft only hours before the then U.S. defense secretary, Robert Gates, was scheduled to call on China's leaders. There was some head-scratching when it seemed that even China's leaders had been caught by surprise, but the in-your-face message from the PLA to the top man at the Pentagon could not have been clearer.

What we're seeing in East Asia is confirmation that notions such as balance of power actually do have real-world applications. America's active engagement in East Asia, reinforced through a network of bases and the presence of combat troops on the Korean peninsula, played a key role in preserving stability in the region from the end of World War II to the start of the twenty-first century. Concerns that U.S. resolve was weakening generated both opportunism and anxiety. The tension we have been seeing between China and Japan and between China and almost everybody else in the South China Sea results from the perception that the region has a security vacuum that needs to be filled. China, not surprisingly, sees itself as the best candidate for that role. This has in turn caused Japan to consider whether the constraints imposed on it after World War II, designed to limit its military ambitions, need to be reconsidered.

While most states in the region welcome a renewed U.S. commitment to East Asian security, the situation is now very different. The United States must determine how to play its traditional role without literally bumping into the ships and planes of a PLA that now believes that its mission has greatly expanded. Indeed, there was justifiable consternation in Washington in August 2014 when a PLA plane conducted an aggressive barrel roll perilously close to a U.S. plane that was conducting a surveillance flight well outside China's territorial waters.[8] China argues, with some justification, that it has sea lanes to protect, territorial disputes to resolve and growing interests in exploiting the economic potential of the seabed in the vast territories it claims. It has been working hard to repackage that challenge as an opportunity.

At his June 2013 summit with President Obama, China's president, Xi Jinping, suggested that the U.S. and China develop "a new type of great power relationship." Optimistic observers see in this an earnest desire to break from the template of the past. Conventional wisdom holds that a rising power (think of pre–World War I Germany) and a declining power (think of same-era Britain) can only achieve rebalancing through conflict. But China's vision of a different way of managing great-power relations comes with a catch. In outlining his proposals, Xi seemed to be arguing for what amounts to a division of spheres of interests, with the U.S. being left untroubled in the eastern Pacific and China free to pursue its destiny in the waters that begin somewhere west of Hawaii. Xi has since taken to speaking about the need for a new Asian security structure that pointedly excludes the United States. That's cold comfort to the other countries of East Asia, where many see active U.S. engagement as a necessary counterbalance to China. It is also not good news for the United States, since such exclusion would effectively decouple the U.S. from the world's fastest-growing economies. What's needed instead is an entirely new perspective in which the U.S. and others accommodate all the reasonable and legitimate expectations that come with China's rise, including the fact that China will inevitably be more militarily present in the region, while China responds by embracing more of the rules and responsibilities that come with enhanced status.

If this sounds easier said than done, it is. But that doesn't mean that it's impossible or unattainable. And it is hugely important. Let me use Taiwan as an example of why it is essential that the United States retain its influence in the region. Chinese rhetoric about confronting Taiwan has cooled since the return of the KMT to power on the island in 2008. Despite the fact that the Communists and KMT are old civil war foes, they largely agree on the Chinese-ness of Taiwan, an understanding not shared by Taiwan's other major party, the DPP, which focuses much more on the local, Taiwanese language and culture of the island.

That said, both Taiwanese parties seek to retain as much autonomy for the island as they can without directly confronting China, and both welcome the close engagement of the United States, including its regular sales of military equipment to the island's armed forces. China, whose military modernization has now given it the edge over Taiwan's military, has never renounced the use of force, and could be expected to steadily raise the pressure on Taiwan should it perceive that the U.S. is reconsidering its security commitment.

As I saw first-hand during my time in Taiwan, this careful balance of power has created a safe environment for the emergence of democracy. The political process is not always pretty, but it gives a voice to all of the island's communities and ensures that they are consulted on issues that shape their future. This has put the lie to those who have in the past speculated as to whether democracy (often caricatured as "Western-style" democracy) is compatible with Chinese culture. What the U.S. owes China in this process is the assurance that it will not renege on its promises to abide by a One China policy that is widely understood to preclude support for Taiwanese independence. The United States has played an important role in restraining Taiwanese impulses to do things that would cross red lines and provoke China.

The antidote for the Taiwan problem is time. Time is certainly required for the people of Taiwan to work out the nature of their future relationship with China. But time is an even more important commodity on the other side of the Taiwan Strait. China needs time to develop a higher degree of national self-confidence and political maturity. The more patient and respectful China is, the greater the possibility of a future relationship with Taiwan that is close and positive. By this I mean a relationship that celebrates a common sense of Chinese-ness, where it exists, and that allows both places to share in the economic dynamism of the region. But such an understanding would also need to be sufficiently generous to respect Taiwan's unique history, culture, language and democratic political system, and to acknowledge the dissenting views of the many people in Taiwan who don't self-identify as Chinese. Getting both sides to that state of readiness is going to take patience and goodwill. Taiwanese confidence in China's goodwill and respect for democratic principles, never particularly strong, has been weakened further by Beijing's reluctance to allow truly free elections in Hong Kong. The United States remains the single most important source of assurance that Taiwan, and China, will be allowed the years, and possibly decades, needed to work out a new and mutually beneficial relationship.

In the meantime, accommodating the military dimension of China's rise will require that the U.S. and its allies develop better lines of communication with the PLA. This has not been easy in the past, partly because of the PLA's penchant for secrecy and opaque dealings, but also because of a natural disinclination to reach out to potential adversaries. In 2013, the U.S. Navy's top officer, Chief of Naval Operations Jonathan Greenert, made a compelling pitch for closer cooperation with the Chinese. He hosted his Chinese counterpart for a visit that included a tour of one of the U.S. Navy's fast-attack submarines. Later, during a town hall meeting with U.S. sailors, Greenert was asked about the risks of being so transparent with potential Chinese adversaries. He replied, "You can't just look at each other and say, 'You're here, I'm here, and leave me alone.' We must have a dialogue.... 'How will we talk to each other when we come across each other?'"⁹ This wasn't a one-off gesture. The U.S. also invited China to participate in an annual naval exercise off Hawaii in 2014. The Chinese came with an official contingent that took part in the exercises and, not far away, a surveillance ship that spied on them.¹⁰

In late August 2013, the Canadian destroyer HMCS *Algonquin* collided with the supply ship HMCS *Protecteur* while both ships were en route to Hawaii. As a result, Canada's single largest warship on the North American west coast and the only ship capable of sustaining lengthy operations in the Pacific were both temporarily out of commission. But it got worse: an engine room fire in early 2014 left *Protecteur* dead in the water, and with it, our hopes of playing a constructive role in an increasingly tense region.

This was happening as the crisis in Ukraine erupted. The Canadian Cabinet met in a rare weekend session to discuss the problem in Europe. We would end up deploying six F18 fighters, other aircraft and a frigate on NATO missions related to Ukraine. Our interest and activism is to our credit. But what are we to make of the corresponding silence from the government about what might be considered a crisis in our Asia policy, such as it is, or that our embarrassing travails in the Pacific barely even made the news in Canada?

Canada needs to face up to the fact that the most dangerous security challenge of the coming decade is taking shape not in Eastern Europe, despite the antics of an insecure and economically vulnerable Russia, but in East Asia. That's not a particularly welcome message. We have spent the last decade buying the equipment we needed to fight in the deserts of Afghanistan, and we also have to deal with the demands of patrolling our own Arctic waters, so the Pacific challenge comes at the most inconvenient time imaginable.

We could, of course, sit things out. But no decisions are cost-free. The government has lately been signalling Canada's interest in making a mini-pivot of our own back into Asia. For the last few years, Canadian ministers have been attending various regional meetings to proclaim that Canada is back. This is delivered to East Asian counterparts who remember earlier bouts of Canadian activism. And while they are scornful of our lack of staying power, they do welcome a more engaged Canada, if only because Canadians—at least, the Canadians of their fondest memories—represent a contrast to brasher Americans and Australians.

The reason for our new-found activism, or perhaps, more correctly, vocalism, is that we are beginning to worry about being excluded from new institutions designed to encourage greater cooperation on trade and security in the Asia Pacific region. Canada lobbied for and ultimately secured agreement to join the Trans-Pacific Partnership (TPP), a trade agreement under negotiation with countries including the United States, Japan, Australia, Vietnam, Singapore, Chile and Mexico. Obtaining access to the TPP was not automatic or easy for Canada. While our protected dairy sector is often held up as the main impediment, the real problem is that we're simply not considered to be a player anymore. Months before we secured agreement to join the TPP, I bumped into an old friend from the U.S. negotiating team who was characteristically blunt, explaining to me that we simply don't show up enough to be taken seriously.

We have had less success securing access to the East Asia Summit, which brings together the leaders of East Asia with counterparts from countries such as the United States, Australia, New Zealand, Russia and India. Nor have we been invited to join an organization called the ASEAN Defence Ministers Meeting-Plus (ADMM-Plus), which brings the senior defence officials of Southeast Asia together with partners from China, Japan, India, Russia, the United States, Australia and New Zealand. We're outside because we have largely been absent from the region for the last twenty years, other than occasionally showing up at key conferences and, rarer still, sending one of our few available frigates on an area visit.

But we should not underestimate the impact of even a modest commitment. In 1995, I helped to organize the visit to Malaysia of the then new Canadian patrol frigate HMCS *Regina*. At the time, *Regina* and her sister ships were widely admired for being technologically advanced and highly functional—ideal attributes for countries that are well short of super-power status but have serious maritime interests and responsibilities. The Canadian navy did a remarkable job conducting briefings for their counterparts in the Royal Malaysian Navy. Although they were obviously proud of their advanced technology, the Canadian sailors brought a disarming modesty to the proceedings that won them many friends.

Deploying naval ships on international duty serves a variety of purposes. Navies conduct training missions, join in counter-terrorism and anti-piracy work and help deliver humanitarian assistance. Indeed, the good work of the U.S. Navy in the wake of the 2004 Indian Ocean tsunami, and the goodwill this generated, is credited with helping the United States to make its eventual pivot back to the region. It is also true that a smart and effective forward defence against illegal migration begins on the far side of the Pacific. And as my experience in Malaysia illustrates, having a navy capable of operating with partners in Asia provides a compelling testimonial about Canada's interest, engagement and quiet competence as a regional player.

It is in our interest to take a leaf from Admiral Greenert's book and start our own conversation with China's navy. A more regular Asia Pacific presence by Canada's navy would send the message that it isn't just the Americans who value stability and balance in the region, and it isn't just the Americans who want to ensure that East Asia remains open and connected to the wider world. This helps to defuse the tendency to think of the future as a tense Sino-American showdown.

Many countries have a stake in accommodating China's peaceful rise, and many share the expectation that China will manage this responsibly. In other words, we should join the Americans, Australians, New Zealanders, Singaporeans and others in welcoming China's growing capacity to help fight crime and piracy, to deliver humanitarian aid when it is needed and to pursue cooperation rather than confrontation.

This won't be cheap. We are already struggling to do even the basics in securing our Arctic waters. Some would argue that being more present in the Pacific can only come at the cost of being less present in the Atlantic. We need to accept the fact that we have by far the world's longest coastline to patrol, *and* that there is a growing need for us to meet new responsibilities in the Asia Pacific region. There are no shortcuts here. We require a navy capable of doing both jobs.

But this doesn't have to begin with a massive ship-building program. Deploying even a modest naval presence to Asia would be a welcome first step in our own oft-promised re-engagement with the region. We should also make it clear that participation in exchange programs in Asia, including programs with China, are *de rigueur* for Canadian Forces personnel destined for high-level commands. Above all, we need to better understand the extent to which engaging China's military, confidently and intelligently, contributes to global, regional and Canadian security.

EIGHT

China's Long Reach

We have looked at security issues within China, along China's frontiers and, given China's growing assertiveness, out in the blue waters of the Pacific. But there is yet another dimension to the changing security environment that comes with China's rise, one that is increasingly apparent to Canadians. China aggressively engages any perceived challenges to its interests, no matter how far or foreign. And it is not shy about pursuing opportunities to advance national power and competitiveness through clandestine activities in other countries, Canada included.

The last year has brought several incidents in which individuals of Chinese origin now living in Canada have been accused of spying for the PRC. And in a dramatic and unprecedented announcement in late July 2014, the Canadian government revealed that computers at National Research Council Canada had been hacked "by a highly sophisticated Chinese state-sponsored actor."[1] China reacted predictably, issuing its usual blanket denials. But in a worrying development, Canada's cyber-spying allegation was followed ominously closely by the detention in China of a Canadian couple who ran a café near the border with North Korea. China announced that the Canadians

Kevin and Julie Garratt were under investigation for the "suspected theft of state secrets about China's military and national defense research."[2] The café was popular with Christians, suggesting another possible motive for the detentions, which came at a time when China was engaged in one of its all-too-frequent crackdowns on so-called foreign religions. But it was hard not to believe that China, tired of being the target of international criticism for its espionage, was making an example of Canada, a high-profile but non-threatening target. That this could destroy the lives of a well-meaning Canadian couple who had been of help to many in China was of little or no consequence. China was playing hardball with us.

How did we get here? Nobody should be surprised that Canada is among the targets of a vast, well-funded and highly effective Chinese espionage effort. China is a skilled and active practitioner of traditional spying techniques. According to many analysts, what characterizes Chinese tactics is a patient approach in which a range of agents, many of whom are informal recruits, are tasked with gathering small amounts of information or equipment. This intelligence gets pieced together into larger and more useful patterns as information is accumulated. In distinguishing between the Russian approach to espionage and Chinese practice, analysts sometimes invoke a hypothetical mission to secure a large sample of sand from a beach. The Russians, according to the experts, would send in a submarine, which would in turn land a well-equipped team to excavate a portion of the beach overnight. The Chinese, on the other hand, would have five hundred people stroll around unobtrusively. But each would quietly collect a pocketful of sand.[3]

In a recent investigation by Reuters of Chinese efforts to obtain U.S. defence technology, one analyst talked of Chinese efforts to "flood the zone with buyers," recruiting hundreds of people to make small purchases of high-tech items that cannot legally be sold to China.[4] There is little reason to believe that such efforts are mounted only south of the border. In the wake of the 2004 report to Parliament by the Canadian Security Intelligence Service (CSIS), an unnamed Canadian intelligence source described China as the country most aggressive in seeking to illegally acquire Canadian technology. The source attributed much of this effort to the work of visiting students, scientists and business people recruited by China's intelligence agencies.[5] In their 2009 book about espionage in Canada, Fabrice de Pierrebourg and Michel Juneau-Katsuya write, "Of all the countries that happily dance across the Canadian border to shoplift our technology, China is far and away the busiest and the most aggressive."[6]

Often the appeal is to patriotism, asking someone of Chinese origin to do something for the motherland. In late 2013, police charged a Canadian man of Chinese origin for allegedly attempting to transfer plans for new Canadian navy ships to Chinese sources.[7] In the spring of 2014, a Montreal man of Chinese origin was indicted by the FBI for his alleged involvement in a plot to steal U.S. agricultural technology secrets.[8] And in July 2014, a Chinese man with a home in Vancouver was arrested in Canada based on FBI allegations that he had been hacking into the computers of aircraft giant Boeing.[9]

But, as Canada is discovering, when it comes to Chinese espionage, the biggest problem isn't human intervention, but cyber. And the target isn't necessarily state secrets in the traditional sense, but technology. The U.S. estimates that Chinese hackers have stolen tens of billions of dollars in American technology.[10] There is certainly no reason to believe that Canada is not also a target. Indeed, a former security advisor to Nortel Networks has alleged that the company that was once the pride of Canada's high technology sector was fatally undermined by extensive penetration and technology theft from hackers inside China.[11] Awareness of the scope and success of Chinese cyber espionage has been building in the U.S., spreading from the intelligence community to Congress, the military, business and the media. Indeed, the China bureaus of a number of major U.S. media outlets such as *The New York Times* and *The Wall Street Journal* have themselves been hacked. Investigations into persistent cyber attacks ultimately led to the U.S. indicting five Chinese nationals, accusing them of hacking into U.S. company databases to steal commercial information.

But the impact of revelations about China's cyber-espionage has to an extent been blunted by the tit-for-tat effect of American Edward Snowden's damning allegations about the extensive eavesdropping conducted by the U.S. National Security Agency in China and elsewhere. The Snowden allegations have provided China with a welcome distraction from accusations about its own cyber-espionage. However, my sense is that, whatever the United States and its allies have been up to, the Chinese mount the more insidious and aggressive program.

In a groundbreaking 2013 report, the computer security firm Mandiant included details of attacks by Chinese hackers against the Canadian subsidiary of a firm then called Telvent. The company designed software enabling pipeline operators to remotely access valves and security systems across vast networks. Telvent's database included "detailed blueprints on more than half the oil and gas pipelines in North and South America."[12] As one industry analyst, reacting to the attacks, put it, "This is terrifying because—forget about the country—if someone hired me and told me they wanted to have the offensive capability to take out as many critical systems as possible, I would be going after the vendors and do things like what happened to Telvent."[13] Assigning blame in this murky business is something of a mug's game. What's far more evident is that there is a much livelier debate in the West about the trade-off between personal privacy and national security. As a result, whatever the U.S. and its allies do to rein in their own cyber programs, they will continue to face a vast, ambitious and highly effective threat from China.

Snowden's allegations will also have a chilling effect on trade in technology and other sectors. That's because he suggested that the U.S. and its allies have asked technology companies to engineer back doors into their products that would make it easier for home-team intelligence agencies to penetrate them. This will provide additional justification for protectionist measures that, under the guise of security concerns, restrict market access to favoured local firms. China has already announced that state-owned firms will be barred from working with U.S.-based consulting groups, warning that the U.S. uses its consulting companies to find out everything it wants to know about China's state companies.[14] We have also seen attacks in China's state media against U.S. technology firms such as Apple, Google and Facebook. And the China offices of Microsoft and chipmaker Qualcomm have endured aggressive anti-monopoly investigations.[15] In August 2014, Chinese media reported that the PRC would develop a homegrown computer operating system to lessen the country's dependence on U.S.-based suppliers such as Microsoft, Google and Apple.[16]

This line of nationalistic attack is not unknown in the West, having been applied to Chinese firms in general and to telecoms giant Huawei in particular. That's because Huawei has grown rapidly from being a small, provincial-level firm in China to becoming the world's largest provider of telecoms equipment. I was amazed on my first visit to the company's elegant campus in China's southern city of Shenzhen. It brought me back to my early days as a trade commissioner in China in the mid-1980s, when a big part of the job involved helping Canada's Nortel. Years later, as I toured Huawei's product display centre, I felt that I was looking at the company that Nortel might have become had it survived. There is an irony in this because some of the allegations about Chinese hacking of Nortel link the activity to efforts to enhance Huawei's competitive position.[17] That said, while I don't discount the possibility of damaging attacks by Chinese hackers, I was one of many who witnessed the growth of a profound and ultimately tragic degree of corporate arrogance at Nortel in the last years of its operations. So we should not underestimate the extent to which the company's final crisis was self-inflicted.[18]

Intelligence agencies in the U.S., Australia, Canada and elsewhere have sounded warnings about Huawei's global growth and ambitions. A U.S. congressional committee recommended that the Chinese company be blocked from participating in the construction of national infrastructure or other sensitive projects, and that it not be allowed to merge with U.S. companies. In 2012, Australia blocked Huawei from tendering on a national broadband network. And although Canada has been more welcoming, we have made it clear that national security provisions would be invoked to restrict access to bid on the government's own communication system. A terse response from the prime minister's spokesperson during a 2012 media scrum spoke volumes: "I'll leave it to you if you think that Huawei should be a part of [the] Canadian government security system."[19]

We owe it to ourselves to think about Huawei more carefully. It is entirely sensible to be very wary of risks associated with working with a Chinese telecommunications company, but we also need to be clear that there are costs involved in shutting the door. Huawei has won market share because of its ability to cut costs. That is sometimes described as an unfair advantage or a predatory tool, but we should be slightly suspicious when those criticisms are voiced by Huawei's less successful competitors. Huawei has won contracts in Canada with operators such as Bell, Telus and Wind because of a cost advantage that ultimately benefits Canadian consumers.

And waving the security flag can distract us from some hard thinking about some shortcomings of our own. I recall a conversation with a Canadian who had worked for major Western telecoms manufacturers in China. I asked him about Huawei and its tactics. His response was blunt: "When Huawei beat us, it was normally because they were cheaper and better." But there is even more to it than that. We are still home to the surviving bits and pieces of technological expertise that made Nortel great. Huawei has, to its credit, begun to invest in research and development in Canada, providing jobs to some of the people left unemployed by Nortel's collapse. This effectively connects Canadian talent to broader market opportunities internationally, China included.

The U.K. has sought to work with Huawei by requiring the company to fund a centre in Britain in which its products are inspected to ensure that they don't contain back doors for Chinese intelligence. It is an innovative approach, but not without its critics. Some have complained that the British effort amounts to little more than an arrangement for Huawei to police itself.[20] That said, the U.K. approach attempts to do something more than shut the door on a big, highly competitive player in the global telecoms market. In many ways, it is a paradigm for the challenge of engaging a rising China. The trade-off is between risk avoidance—which is becoming increasingly costly as China becomes bigger and more important—and the less travelled path of risk mitigation. This isn't an area where our intelligence agencies seem able to help us much. While they are effective, and even eager, in pointing to the risks, they are much less helpful at telling us how to manage them. That's no longer enough.

This isn't a challenge that we can or should leave entirely to the government to manage. Common sense will carry security-conscious Canadians a long way. Security experts de Pierrebourg and Juneau-Katsuya are compelling advocates for some practical, no-brainer actions that Canadian companies should (but don't always) take, such as screening new staff more carefully or restricting access to sensitive technology and trade secrets. They also make the point that senior executives often overrule corporate security people out of a misguided desire not to appear rude in front of overly inquisitive Chinese guests. Nor are government employees always good role models. In a 2013 security exercise, close to two thousand employees of Justice Canada gullibly clicked on a fake link embedded in an email, the kind that is typically used by hackers to gain access to a target's confidential information in what are called "phishing" expeditions.[21]

CHINA IS ALSO ACTIVELY ENGAGED in trying to reach out and influence people in Canada to support ideas and causes it considers important. This is not in itself sinister. In fact, it's not unlike what I used to do as a diplomat in Seoul, Shanghai, Kuala Lumpur, Taipei and Beijing. But I did my job in the open, and the currency I used to win access to people was nothing more than lunches and dinners at my home, a bottle of Icewine as a Chinese New Year's gift or the occasional invitation to see a visiting Canadian performer or film.

In 2010, Dick Fadden, the then head of CSIS, stated that there is strong evidence that some countries operate a very different advocacy program in Canada, one in which municipal officials and even provincial ministers are covertly cultivated over time.[22] He hinted broadly that China was one of the countries doing this. Perks such as international travel are used to build up a relationship. Over time, the targeted officials are expected to take decisions that advance specific Chinese objectives, meaning that, as Fadden stated, "decisions aren't taken on the basis of the public good." The remarks caused a sensation, but mainly because the interview was aired on the CBC just a few days before the Chinese president arrived in Canada for a state visit. The allegations were angrily dismissed by the Chinese.

China is not squeamish about wading into Canadian life to challenge anything that runs counter to its own hardline views. Chinese embassies and consulates don't hesitate to confront local politicians, cultural organizations or school officials in cases where they have expressed support for causes that China considers taboo. There have also been persistent allegations that Chinese diplomats organize Chinese students in the U.S., Australia and Canada to mount pro-China demonstrations designed to drown out opposition voices. John Fitzgerald, a respected colleague from my Beijing days, returned to his native Australia to make the claim that "Chinese Australians are being lectured, monitored, organized, and policed in Australia on instruction from Beijing as never before."[23] Asked about Chinese informant networks at Australian universities, an Australian intelligence official said, "They have more resources in Sydney University than we do."[24]

We should not assume that China is more scrupulous when it comes to the diaspora in Canada. I recall a late-night argument with Chinese officials who were pushing us to stifle protests outside the Ottawa hotel where their president was staying. This ended abruptly when it was pointed out that most of the noise was coming from the well-organized contingent of pro-China activists. A common problem arises when a Canadian municipality, school or cultural institution aligns itself with something that directly or even indirectly supports the Falun Gong. Sometimes the Canadian organization is even unaware that the organization it is supporting is actually linked to the Falun Gong. But this will be quickly and forcefully pointed out to them by the local Chinese consulate. The message will carry a blunt reminder about the benefits of seeing things China's way, with not-so-subtle references to an upcoming visit, a cultural exchange under negotiation or a research partnership. This is odd coming from a country that regularly and sanctimoniously invokes non-interference in the affairs of other nations as a fundamental principle of international relations. And Chinese officials blithely ignore the fact that Falun Gong's peaceful protests are the organization's only means of responding to decades of brutal repression by China.

Sometimes the conflict is even more public. When I was running the Asia Pacific branch of Foreign Affairs back in 2003, China's deputy consul general in Toronto wrote a letter to the *Toronto Star* in which he defended China against allegations that it had not done enough to prevent the spread of the SARS virus beyond its borders. In the course of the letter, he accused the Canadian citizen who had made the allegations of being a member of a "sinister cult" because of his connections to Falun Gong. When the Canadian duly sued the Chinese official, the Chinese ambassador in Ottawa asked Foreign Affairs to ride to the rescue, citing diplomatic immunity. But diplomatic immunity applies only to people working at embassies. Consular officials, like the author of the letter, are covered by much narrower protections, clearly limited to the natural, day-to-day performance of their duties. And it is up to a judge to determine whether a specific activity qualifies for this carefully limited protection from prosecution. In this case, the judge determined that making an intemperate attack on a Canadian citizen in the pages of a major newspaper isn't something that qualifies for immunity. The ambassador in Ottawa was furious with me. Our exchanges were some of the most heated that I've ever had. But in the end, China withdrew the official rather than face a trial.

CHINA'S IMPACT on global security is partly a product of its insecurity at home and within its East Asian neighbourhood. Emboldened by what it perceives as American decline, it risks following the tragic path of other overly assertive rising powers, a path that almost always leads to confrontation. This is of more than academic interest to Canadians. As tensions rise in the western Pacific, we need to think about our long-term economic interests there, about the security of allies such as the U.S., Australia and Japan, and about our own long-term security. We can play a role in helping to accommodate China's peaceful rise, but if we are to do so, we will have to invest in a navy that can carry out missions in the Pacific.

We also need to accept that a prickly and insecure China will, for the foreseeable future, feel free to interfere in Canadian society in an effort to blunt actions and messages that it sees as unhelpful. It is also likely that China's economic development strategy will continue to include a clandestine element that involves stealing foreign technologies. This raises the question as to whether it is ever appropriate to speak out in the face of Chinese espionage or other illegal activities. If the attack is sufficiently serious to cause a major problem in our national infrastructure, the answer is a resounding yes. This is the kind of serious information that democracies share with their citizens. The Chinese would prefer that incidents like this remain secret and that we remain uninformed, which would be enormously convenient for them. But this is just one of the many areas where our systems differ. And, remember, simply stating the facts (as we did in calling attention to recent cyber attacks against the Canadian government) is not the same as gratuitously insulting the Chinese government or, worse, the Chinese people.

What about the argument that such frank speech threatens the safety of innocent Canadians living in China? Were we to accept this, it would amount to a level of blackmail that would fatally undermine China's relationship not just with Canada, but with just about every nation that cares about its citizens. And China would be hugely disadvantaged if it were to allow itself to be so cut off from the wider world. All that being said, Canadians living in China need to understand that they do not enjoy the protections they take for granted at home, and that the Canadian government is limited in terms of what it can do in the face of capricious actions by the Chinese state.

We need to be frank in acknowledging espionage and interference by China as serious and continuing threats. But we no longer live in a world in which simply closing the door on China is an option. Nor should we be intimidated. I try to keep in mind one of the key takeaways from the recent writings of China-watcher James Fallows, namely to "take China seriously as it goes through remarkable change and development, but without being afraid of it."[25] We can't simply opt out of the messier and more problematic aspects of China's rise. Our world is changing, regardless of how we feel about it. Shutting our door to China is not in our own self-interest. Instead, we need to be vigilant in monitoring Chinese behaviour, frank in speaking out when misbehaviour is detected and innovative in designing measures for our own protection.

CHINA AND CANADIAN WELL-BEING

NINE

Saving Little Fatty

On September 30, 2009, the eve of that auspicious National Day that I described earlier, Janet and I were invited to a reception in the cavernous Great Hall of the People in Tiananmen Square. Each year on that day, China's premier delivers a short state-of-the-nation address to the great and good of Chinese society, and to foreign guests, including the diplomatic corps. Ambassadors in their first year have the added privilege of attending a brief meet-and-greet with the premier before the speech. Then, during the speech, they are seated in the front rows among the Chinese celebrities. Like other new ambassadors, I had by this time already called on the Chinese president to present my credentials (a short letter to the president from the then governor general, Michaëlle Jean, introducing me as Canada's ambassador).

My session with the premier was not a one-on-one meeting. The newly arrived ambassadors lined up in alphabetical order before each of us was summoned for a brief conversation with the evening's host, something that provided just enough time to extend greetings, make a pleasant comment and move on. Chinese protocol typically leaves nothing to chance. We had been instructed to say no more than two

sentences, something I planned to do in Chinese to spare the interpretation time. As I walked up, the chief of protocol turned to the
premier and said, "This is the new Canadian ambassador. He speaks
very good Chinese." That's an overly generous accolade in my case,
and one that you will hear from the ever-courteous Chinese even if
you've struggled to string the words for "thank you" together correctly.
The premier's weary face tightened at this prospect, but I kept it short,
taking less than a minute to give him greetings from the prime minister and the people of Canada, remind him that we were marking the
seventieth anniversary of the death of Norman Bethune, and express
the hope that he might visit Canada soon. His face brightened, and I
was moved on.

I rejoined Janet as guests surged into the main hall. Giant Chinese
basketball players chatted with tiny gymnasts. Grizzled veterans of the
civil war shuffled past tycoons in expensive suits. The silver and gold
of elaborate headdresses, flashing here and there, testified to the presence of people from China's ethnic minority regions. A large crowd
buzzed around a table full of fit and confident young men and women:
China's astronauts!

Our table was much more sedate, featuring an older and quieter
collection of scholarly looking men and women. They were, we
quickly learned, China's most distinguished doctors. As we made our
introductions, it was easy to see why we had been seated at this particular table. Most of the doctors had done some training in Canada,
and all of them had at least some current connection with a Canadian
university or research institute. Their presence reminded me of continuing connections in a sector that has always been central to our relationship with China. Canadian doctor and activist Norman Bethune
is undoubtedly our most high-profile medical ambassador. Although
he was made famous in China through Mao's essay presenting him
as a symbol of selfless internationalism, Bethune's real contribution
to China and to the medical world of his day was as an innovator of

systems and equipment. He constantly tinkered with new tools and procedures, sometimes using himself as a guinea pig.

As I had mentioned to the premier, in 2009 we were marking the seventieth anniversary of Bethune's heroic death (he contracted blood poisoning after cutting his finger while operating on a Chinese soldier as the invading Japanese advanced). To honour the anniversary, embassy colleague Patrice Cousineau had arranged a wonderful exhibit of rare photos of Bethune, showing him at work on the front lines and in all-too-brief moments of relaxation. I remember being struck by the obvious physical toll apparent in his face and frame as the weeks of privation and danger mounted.

I was so impressed by the photos that I suggested that we use them as the inspiration for a larger travelling exhibit that would tour China in 2010, the fortieth anniversary of our diplomatic relationship. The objective was to allow Bethune the man, the Canadian and the medical innovator to emerge from behind the slogans and trappings of revolutionary heroism. Collaborating with partners in Canada and China, we came up with an exhibition that followed Bethune's life from his boyhood and education in Canada, through years of medical apprenticeship and political radicalization, to pioneering surgical work on the battlefields of Spain and China. It was a major draw in cities throughout China.

After the exhibit finished touring, I arranged to display a reproduction of one of the posters from the show in Canada's official residence in Beijing, where Janet and I lived. It was a famous two-panel piece that illustrates Bethune's creativity. The first panel shows Bethune carefully inspecting a humble wicker pannier that Chinese peasants hung over the backs of their donkeys for the important purpose of carrying manure to their fields. The second panel shows Bethune unveiling what he called the "Marco Polo Bridge," an arched wooden case modelled on the pannier design, housing a mobile surgery kit. Fitted on the back of a donkey, the case enabled Bethune to transport his operating theatre to the most remote battlefields. I used to bring Chinese guests to have a look at the poster before inviting them in to dinner. It always touched them. But I would go beyond the traditional Bethune story to observe that Canadians come to China to listen as well as to learn, and that many of the most successful chapters in our history together are based on respectful collaboration.

I had cause to remember the Canada–China medical connection again at an event in the autumn of 2010. I had been invited to speak at a ceremony marking the hundredth anniversary of the founding of the West China School of Medicine in Chengdu, in the southwestern province of Sichuan. As I sat in the grandstand waiting for my turn to climb up to the podium, I attempted to count the audience. It was arrayed like an invading army, drawn up in blocks of one hundred on the field in front of me. By the time my name was called, I was at seven thousand attendees and counting.

I was there because back in 1910, the school's founders had included a Canadian couple, missionary doctors named Omar and Retta Kilborn. The Kilborns had arrived in China in the 1890s. They met on the steamboat that navigated the dangerous shoals and currents of the Yangtze, and married when they reached Chengdu. It was a dangerous time. The Qing dynasty was entering its terminal phase and anti-foreign riots were common. Both Kilborns worked tirelessly to introduce Western medicine in that then-remote part of China. Omar took a lead role in establishing the Chinese Red Cross Society and showed great personal courage working to alleviate the suffering of wounded soldiers during the 1911 revolution. Retta introduced women's medicine in the region, and led local efforts to eliminate the cruel practice of binding girls' feet. They joined with other missionary doctors to establish what would become a large and thriving hospital and medical school.[1]

I was reminded of Canada's medical connection to China yet again on a visit to the city of Dali in Yunnan province, which is even

deeper in China's southwest. I had been seeking out, quietly and carefully, members of some of the Protestant house churches that thrive in
the area. I am keenly interested in the subject of religious freedom in
China, and wanted to be sure that the embassy had first-hand knowledge of what was happening to these sometimes embattled believers.

During my visit I was introduced to a very welcoming old couple,
she in her eighties and he in his nineties. They had met while working
in the hospital in Dali in the years after World War II, when it was run
by Protestant missionaries. The mission had been evacuated in 1952,
as the Communists tightened their control over civil society in China.
Later, during the Cultural Revolution, both the husband and the wife
had been harshly punished for their past association with foreigners.

Both spoke lovingly of one foreigner in particular: Dr. Jessie
McDonald, a Canadian woman who had spent decades in China.
"Dr. Mac" was, like Retta Kilborn, a medical pioneer, one of five
women in a cohort of 350 medical students at the University of Toronto
in 1905. She travelled to China in 1913, and experienced first-hand
the tumult and chaos of the early republic. She stayed on to see the
misery brought by the Japanese invasion. As the Japanese pushed into
central China, she was forced to leave the country via Shanghai, only
to circle around China by ship and re-enter it via the remote southwest. She travelled the mountainous Burma Road, ultimately reaching
Dali, where she spent a decade providing much-needed medical support to the local Chinese and to the non-Han minority peoples who
lived in the neighbouring hills. She built a hospital and also trekked
out to remote clinics, at sixty doing work that would have exhausted
a much younger person. She was among the last of her missionary
community to leave Dali after the Communist victory (the red cross
on the wall of the hospital had been painted over with a slogan urging
that the imperialists be kicked out). She paused, the story goes, to ring
the church bell one last time on her way out of town.[2] McDonald died
in 1980, but was recalled by my two hosts with a touching spontaneity.

WE SHOULDN'T THINK of our collaboration with China in health and medicine as limited to our shared past. Globalization has made it urgently important that we pay attention to public health trends in China. In this case, altruism is joined with self-interest, because what happens in China doesn't necessarily stay in China.

I saw this first-hand as I worked with colleagues in Foreign Affairs in 2003 to deal with the rapidly growing impact of the SARS epidemic. SARS, a deadly and highly contagious respiratory disease, appeared in south China in late 2002. Chinese officials, anxious to avoid blame for the outbreak, dragged their feet, failing to advise the World Health Organization (WHO) about the outbreak until months later. Because I was running the Asia Pacific branch of Foreign Affairs, I was involved in our early efforts to respond to the developing crisis. In the first weeks, this mainly meant providing advice to Canadians who happened to be in the most affected areas—China, Hong Kong, Taiwan and Singapore—and ensuring that our own offices remained open and able to help those same Canadians.

But everything changed when the outbreak reached Canada. A woman who had contracted the virus in Hong Kong travelled back to Toronto, infecting others in an outbreak that ultimately claimed forty-four lives in Canada, all in and around Toronto. The city became the subject of a WHO travel advisory, something that triggered widespread anxiety about visiting Toronto. As a result, in addition to its appalling human toll, the epidemic ultimately cost the city more than $700 million in lost tourism and retail sales.[3] But the impact was felt far beyond Toronto. My team at Foreign Affairs could barely keep up with the cases of Canadian travellers being quarantined, denied entry or otherwise stranded all around the world. The entire country was treated as an affected zone.

We learned from this. Later, when I was ambassador in China, one of my most valuable colleagues was Dr. Felix Li, who represented the Public Health Agency of Canada (PHAC) at the embassy. He was our front line in China when it came to health, building links with Chinese officials and improving our awareness of emerging health threats. PHAC's monitoring of local media reports throughout China was recognized by the Chinese themselves as an important part of their early-warning system. China has clearly learned from the SARS crisis. The country's recent response to outbreaks of bird flu have been, by most accounts, efficient, transparent and largely effective in preventing the spread of the disease.

When Prime Minister Harper visited China in 2009, health was identified, appropriately enough, as one of a limited number of priorities for cooperation. That's in tune with a Canadian tradition that runs back to the Kilborns, and recognizes the impact that a vast, under-regulated but globally connected China has on world health. Less obvious, but of growing importance, is China's own role as a medical innovator. Part of the difficulty in coming to terms with modern China is trying to grasp that it can be both painfully backward and at the same time impressively innovative. Its medical schools are increasingly linked to global networks, and its huge population means that China is a formidable source of data for medical research. Sheer numbers also mean that the state of China's health has a significant impact on global outcomes. Commenting on recent Chinese success in combatting tuberculosis—prevalence dropped by 57 percent from 2000 to 2010—two Italian experts wrote that "any major Chinese advance in controlling Tuberculosis will inevitably move all global indicators in a positive direction."[4] China's experience in dealing with the disease on a large scale—even as the prevalence of TB declined, one million new cases were recorded in 2010—provides encouragement and positive examples for other big, developing countries.[5] But despite progress in treating a wide range of diseases, huge obstacles remain to be overcome. A recent study showed that less than one third of cancer patients in China survive for five years after diagnosis compared to 70 percent in the United States.[6]

China can and does make a positive contribution to global health in other ways. Late in 2013, a Chinese company was pre-qualified by the World Health Organization for global sales of its vaccine to combat Japanese encephalitis. The company can produce large volumes at relatively low cost, which is wonderful news for countries in the developing world. What makes this even more noteworthy is that the manufacturer was aided by technical support from a U.S. NGO, thanks to a grant from the Bill and Melinda Gates Foundation.[7] This is a good example of how we can leverage a smart partnership with China into broader, regional influence. As China's capability grows, it becomes an important source of high-quality, low-cost health care solutions for itself and others, and an increasingly interesting partner for medical research or more narrowly commercial collaboration.

WITH GROWING PROSPERITY in China, personal habits are changing, as are patterns of disease. Problems we have long struggled with, such as diabetes, heart disease and stroke, are becoming more prevalent in China as lifestyles become more sedentary, and as fast food becomes more popular. The one-child policy hasn't helped. Single offspring (mainly boys because of sex-selective abortion) are spoiled outrageously, and spend far too much time playing video games and eating junk food. And since plumpness has long been associated in China with prosperity, we have seen the emergence of a generation fondly referred to as *xiao pangzi*, or "little fatties." What's even stranger is that the older generation in China has largely kept to the healthy and abstemious ways of their own early days, when a lean lifestyle wasn't a choice but an inevitability. Parks are full of seniors doing every exercise imaginable: walking backwards; slapping trees; wielding swords; writing watery characters with giant, broom-sized calligraphy brushes; kicking feathered shuttlecocks; or tangoing, waltzing and foxtrotting into a healthy old age. When I was young, the government humiliated us into fitness through a commercial that saw Canadians huffing and puffing behind a "sixty-year-old Swede." In China, it would be your eighty-year-old grandmother.

Because health is recognized as a shared priority, Canada and China have regular meetings chaired by their respective ministers of health. China's health officials are keenly interested in Canada's experience in combatting the problems that come with a modern, Western-style diet, such as heart disease and diabetes. China is also eager to learn more about how we deliver—and pay for—our health care. I recall sitting in on one meeting of health ministers in Shanghai where the main topic was how to preserve universal public access to health care in the face of growing demand for private care. The Chinese were keenly interested in Canada's experience, knowing the extent to which our debate is shaped by proximity to for-profit clinics in the U.S. The Canadian side was even questioned about revenue streams generated by hospital parking lots and cafeterias. China is moving quickly to find new sources of revenue to finance health care. The government has announced plans to have private institutions provide 20 percent of hospital care by 2015, leading the *Financial Times* to talk about a "pyramid of hundreds of potential private hospital deals, as investors target the new Chinese gold rush."[8]

Meanwhile, Chinese people are hugely dissatisfied with a health care system that is unable to cope with demands for advanced treatments and better services. And few Chinese patients wax eloquent about the bedside manner of their doctors. Resentment is building to the extent that brutal assaults against doctors have been recorded in a number of cities. Part of the resentment has its origins in flawed policy. Because China has tried to keep medical costs down by capping doctors' salaries, many doctors in China have become glorified pill pushers, supplementing their meagre incomes by accepting payments from pharmaceutical companies to prescribe their medications. Recently, large multinational firms have been caught up in this scandal, allegedly offering Chinese doctors benefits including foreign travel in return for promoting specific medications.

As the Chinese system has become more specialized, segmented and profit oriented, the patient is frequently lost in the system. That reality has inspired an innovative partnership between the University of Ottawa's faculty of medicine and Shanghai's elite Jiao Tong University. The focus will be on patient-oriented primary care, something that is seen by the Chinese as a Canadian strength. At the same time, the Canadians will have access to research data generated in a medical system vastly larger than our own.[9]

Another emerging area of concern is eldercare. The simple fact is that China is getting older. In September 2013, China's *Caixin* magazine reported, "About 14.3% of the population, or some 193 million people, were aged 60 or over at the end of last year, according to census figures. That demographic group is expected to expand to 34% by 2050. The Ministry of Civil Affairs estimates 36 million seniors nationwide are disabled or partly disabled, which means their health care needs require special attention."[10] In other words, the population of disabled or partly disabled seniors in China is greater than the population of Canada. Other research looking out over the same time period paints an even grimmer picture, suggesting that "China is on track to have almost half a billion elderly people by 2050 and most of them will have chronic diseases but no treatment."[11]

Changing patterns of life in China mean that grown children are so busy working, and often so far away from their original family homes, that they are unable to care for their elderly parents. And the one-child policy, combined with improved life expectancies, means that four grandparents and two parents are looking to a single child to support them through long years of retirement. Add to that the fact that issues such as disability and dementia have been stigmatized in China, with victims hidden away, or that many Chinese seniors rely almost totally on traditional Chinese medicines of limited efficacy, and you can begin to see the work that needs to be done to better support the elderly in China.

Toronto's Baycrest hospital, which is affiliated with the University of Toronto, is among the leading Western institutions helping China to respond to this growing demand. Baycrest and others are counselling patience and careful analysis, despite the severity and urgency of the problem. The worry is that China, with its preference for hardware-over-software-based solutions, will see the issue as a real estate problem—and opportunity, triggering a boom in the construction of eldercare facilities. While providing affordable accommodation for seniors is important, effective eldercare needs to be understood as part of a larger, whole-of-life health care strategy.

The very idea of sending elderly family members off to live somewhere else bumps up against a number of cultural barriers in China. It isn't just discomfort associated with sending respected family members away; there is also a touching sense of frugality and self-sacrifice on the part of the older generation. In the words of one retirement home operator, "Some families insist we don't tell the parents how much it costs ... or they won't stay."[12]

China is also looking to Canada for broader advice on other operational issues, such as how to get more bang for its health care buck. It has not escaped the Chinese that Canada is able to deliver quality health care to communities scattered across a huge territory. The first lesson for China's doctor-centred system is that you need to empower a range of other health care professionals, starting with nurses. The second lesson involves the smart use of technology. One of the happiest memories from my time in China was of working with Dave Turpin, the then president of the University of Victoria. He had come to Beijing with a group of colleagues to introduce CanAssist, an innovative program in which researchers from across the UVic community come together to develop solutions to make life easier for disabled people. We gathered a group of Chinese doctors—including one of the highly respected specialists I had met at that National Day dinner—to watch as the team demonstrated their work. My favourite example was a user-friendly joystick that enabled a music-loving girl to access the songs on her iPod, despite the limitations imposed by cerebral palsy.

And on my 2010 visit to the West China School of Medicine, after paying tribute to the Kilborns, I attended an event to mark the collaboration between the university's hospital and a group called Canadian Surgical Technologies and Advanced Robotics, which is part of the London (Ontario) Health Sciences Centre. The Canadians were helping the Chinese hospital raise its standards in a few key areas so that it could be accredited internationally.

AS THE ENCEPHALITIS vaccine story illustrates, for all its problems, China is also home to some important solutions. Although China does struggle, not surprisingly, to provide quality care for 1.3 billion people in a territory almost as large as Europe, it is home to many impressive universities and medical research centres. And, as the University of Ottawa is discovering, China's vast population enables the collection of huge amounts of data to study trends, making the achievement of breakthroughs much faster than might otherwise be possible.

I had the great privilege of meeting the inspiring Canadian athlete and activist Rick Hansen when he came to Beijing in 2011 to mark the twenty-fifth anniversary of his first visit to China, an important component of his original Man in Motion world tour in 1986. Rick was paralyzed in a traffic accident as a teenager, but overcame this trauma to become a celebrated Paralympian and, over time, a compelling public advocate for the disabled. His foundation has raised significant funds and promoted important research into the treatment of spinal cord injuries. I first arrived in Shanghai only weeks after Rick's original 1986 visit to China. A key supporter during that first visit was Deng Pufang, the son of Deng Xiaoping. The younger Deng had been paralyzed following a brutal assault by Red Guards during the Cultural Revolution. The fact that he had received his life-saving medical treatment in Canada helped cement their friendship.

Twenty-five years later, I watched as Rick again took on the Great Wall, using the visit to inspire a new generation of Chinese citizens. He made it clear that the flow of ideas and inspiration is now two-way. The foundation wanted to cooperate with counterpart organizations in China to benefit from the deep pools of research data available in a country that, because of its size and uneven level of development, sees far too many disabling accidents. And while the sheer volume of data is important, so too are the talents, energy and experience of Chinese doctors and medical researchers who are, according to Rick, "world leaders" in the treatment of spinal cord injuries.[13] Rick's visit caused me to reflect on the evolution in our long partnership with China in health and medicine. A story that began with the Kilborns and their intrepid colleagues in nineteenth-century Sichuan still has new chapters to be written.

TEN

Air, Water and Animals

By now we have seen so many stories about pollution in China that new batches of bad news almost fail to register. Almost, but not quite. *The New York Times* reported in April 2013 that outdoor "air pollution contributed to 1.2 million premature deaths in China in 2010, nearly 40% of the global total."[1] The Chinese publication *Caijing* reported that China's environment ministry has for the first time acknowledged the presence of "cancer villages," marked by abnormally high rates of the disease, presumably due to environmental problems.[2] According to one report, 20 percent of rivers are simply too polluted for any form of contact.[3] Beijing's consumption of water so exceeds local supplies that the city is worse off than many countries in the Middle East.[4] Rapid population growth in and around Beijing, and elsewhere in dry northern China, has so strained water resources that officials have been forced to build a hugely expensive and highly controversial project to divert water up from central China.[5] And for months in 2013, Chinese netizens were grimly addicted to stories about the alarming discovery of thousands of dead pigs in the Huangpu River, which flows through downtown Shanghai.

THE EARLY PART OF MY POSTING as ambassador coincided with the last months of a relative improvement in air quality in Beijing, the legacy of $10 billion in work undertaken before the 2008 Olympics. Factories were moved out into the hinterland, new subway lines replaced bus routes, and bare hillsides were reforested with trees.

Chinese officials happily reported an increase in "blue sky days." But that blueness masked more sinister problems. Although authorities released official air quality statistics, the U.S. embassy conducted its own monitoring and posted the results on social media. Wide discrepancies were evident between the numbers Chinese officials posted and the readings from the embassy. That's largely because the U.S. embassy's data tracked the presence in the atmosphere of much smaller particles than were covered in the more positive official reports. These smaller particles, generated by car exhaust, factory smokestacks and coal fires, are insidious because of their ability to work their way into the bloodstream. Ontario's Ministry of the Environment singles out fine particulate matter as having "the greatest impact on health."[6] China objected to this rival and embarrassing monitoring, describing it as a form of interference. Officials at the foreign ministry in Beijing were particularly incensed when the U.S. embassy began describing the worst days as "Crazy Bad,"[7] a controversial but apt description that was later modified to "beyond index," something that has been described as akin to being "downwind from a forest fire."[8]

That counts of these smaller particles would be rising is not surprising. Despite the vanished factories and resurgent tree cover, Beijing, Shanghai and other major cities are choking in automobile exhaust fumes. In July 2013, the *China Daily* reported that twenty thousand cars were being added to Beijing's streets each month.[9] The winter months are typically the most polluted in Beijing. Far more coal is burned and car exhaust hangs in the still air trapped by the hills that surround the city. For Janet and me, each winter of our stay in Beijing was worse than the one before.

By January 2012, Beijing was beginning to descend into what would later be termed an "airpocalypse"—weeks of "crazy bad" air quality. I remember bringing the advance team from the Prime Minister's Office to the Temple of Heaven, a site the PM would himself visit weeks later. It is one of my favourite places in Beijing. The vast park around the temple is filled with elderly Chinese performing traditional Tai Chi, playing chess and singing patriotic songs. In my memories from the 1980s, the conical tower of the temple seems always to be set against the bluest of skies. But on this January day, the tower was indistinct, wrapped in a brown haze. My throat began to feel raspy as I walked with the team along the ceremonial path that leads to the temple. Before long my throat was on fire and I could barely speak.

By the next January, fine particulate matter in Beijing's air was forty times higher than the exposure limit recommended by the World Health Organization.[10] Writing in *The New Yorker*, columnist Evan Osnos described how pollution was changing "the rules for Beijing living." As he put it, "In Beijing we talk about air purifiers the way that teen-age boys talk about cars. More than once, I've gone into a friend's apartment and put an admiring hand on a top-of-the-line IQAir HealthPro, and said, 'Niiiice.'"[11] In a piece in *The Atlantic*, Emily Brill wondered whether air quality in Beijing was worse than the clouds of dust that hung suspended around Ground Zero after 9/11. Although some scientists were reluctant to comment on what they saw as an apples-and-oranges comparison, Thomas A. Cahill, professor emeritus of physics and atmospheric science at the University of California, Davis, and someone who has measured air quality at Ground Zero and in Beijing, was unambiguous, stating, "I would personally rather breathe the air at the World Trade Center."[12]

The situation descended into farce when, after Shanghai was hit by its own airpocalypse in late 2013, one patriotic journalist tried to argue that dealing with air pollution builds citizenship and promotes a sense of humour. Another argued that it could enhance air defence efforts, since the smog would baffle optically guided weapons. They were laughed into silence by the reaction on Chinese social media.[13]

None of this escapes the attention of China's leadership, which sees concern about pollution as one of a small number of potentially explosive issues—like inflation, unemployment, corruption and income inequality—that could trigger social unrest. They are wise to be so concerned. A recent Pew Research Center survey found that the problem is already acute. In 2013, 47 percent of Chinese respondents listed air pollution as "a very big problem," up 11 percent from 2012. Forty percent had similar concerns about water pollution, up from 33 percent a year earlier.[14] Chen Jiping, a member of the Chinese People's Political Consultative Conference, a high-level advisory body, pointed to anxiety about the environment as the leading cause of civil disturbances, or "mass incidents," in China: "The major reason for mass incidents is the environment, and everyone cares about it now.... If you want to build a plant, and if the plant may cause cancer, how can people remain calm?"[15] There is a very significant disagreement between those senior policy-makers in China who are driven to maintain economic growth—seeing it as key to ensuring social stability—and those who see the environmental cost of such growth as unsustainable.

This is one of the most challenging debates shaping China's future. Think of the argument around automobile policy alone. Not only is the growth of the auto industry in China, now the world's largest manufacturer, seen as an important driver of the economy but car ownership, once an unimaginable luxury, is now an exciting possibility within the reach of a growing middle class. When I served in Shanghai in the 1980s, I could drive from my home, which was in a new housing development near the airport, to the office that we ultimately opened in the heart of downtown in about twenty minutes. The only cars on the road were taxis and official vehicles. Now that journey is often an hour-long bumper-to-bumper crawl on a tangle of expressways. The day of the owner-operator vehicle has more than arrived. So while it is easy for critics in the West to suggest that China needs to do something about automobile emissions, it's considerably less easy for China's leaders to figure out just what that is.

But they are not sitting on their hands. A plan unveiled in 2013 called for cuts to coal utilization by industry and for the removal of the most heavily polluting vehicles from the roads. Strict limits on licence issuance in China's big cities will also have an impact, although by now the new growth markets are China's booming second-tier cities inland.[16] While some environmentalists complained that the curbs did not go far enough, others were impressed by China's willingness to act.[17]

In 2007, China surpassed the United States to become the world's largest emitter of CO_2, which is a principal greenhouse gas and a leading contributor to global warming.[18] Thanks to China's continuing rapid growth, which is still largely fuelled by coal, and the increasing use of natural gas in the United States, this gap is increasing.[19] By September 2014, China's total emissions were greater than those of the U.S. and the E.U. *combined*.[20] Among other things, this means that growing emissions from China cancel out the beneficial impacts of progress elsewhere. A recent Dutch survey said that the single most cost-effective way of halting the dangerous rise in global temperatures is for China's emissions to peak just after 2020, something that is highly unlikely unless Beijing adopts even more radical policy changes.[21]

This has two significant implications for China internationally. The first is that it exposes China to criticism from many countries, previously seen as allies, that are concerned about global warming. This is particularly acute for the Pacific Island states most affected by rising water levels. The second implication is that China's dismal performance on emissions undercuts its position that, when it comes to fighting climate change, the biggest sacrifices should be made by the major powers of the developed world. China's lack of commitments under the Kyoto Protocol was one of the reasons the U.S. did not sign on, and was used by Canada as a reason for abandoning our own commitments.

Our timing on leaving the protocol wasn't great. We announced our withdrawal from Kyoto as Canada's environment minister returned from a major conference in Durban, South Africa, at which China had for the first time signalled an openness to capping emissions (albeit to be worked out at a future date) and a willingness to discuss an instrument that would be legally binding for participating countries. China brought a new sophistication to its participation at the meeting. It was clear that Chinese negotiators had learned a great deal since the last major climate summit in Copenhagen, when their intransigence generated widespread criticism. This new poise at the negotiation table was almost certainly linked to their growing experience in setting environmental policy at home.[22]

Canada's environment minister, Peter Kent, either failed to notice this evolution in Chinese thinking or decided that it was insufficient. He was in the minority in this view, given that many international observers were favourably impressed by China's new flexibility.[23] Kent irked the Chinese by publicly blaming them for obstructing progress, by which he meant blocking language that would have been even more binding on countries. To follow this up by coming home and withdrawing from the Kyoto accord was doubly unhelpful to China, undercutting their argument, designed for people back home, that any Chinese commitments would be balanced by continuing actions by rich countries. This earned Canada stinging rebukes from both India and China, with the Xinhua news agency describing our decision as "preposterous" and "irresponsible."[24]

Engaging China on environmental policy is a priority for the E.U. in general and informs the diplomacy of important member states such as the U.K. in particular. Britain sees such activism as being in its own long-term interest. There was a time when we thought the same way. Canada made a significant contribution to helping China build its own cadre of environmental policy-makers through assistance from the Canadian International Development Agency (CIDA). Strangely enough, CIDA had a fixation with keeping Canada's contribution under wraps. This was partly due to a well-intentioned but ultimately excessive fidelity to the international nature of the work. CIDA officials thought that it would be unseemly for Canada to take too much credit for a project in which a handful of other countries were active. We were ultimately so successful that even the Chinese were, for the most part, unaware of our contribution. Nor were many Canadians aware of it. I remember having to brief our own visiting ambassador for the environment about CIDA's environmental work in China. This is another example of Ottawa's failure to connect. We should have used the experience gained in China to inform and enhance our broader international work on an important global issue.

Canada does collaborate with China on a smattering of projects funded by Environment Canada and other agencies. But our ambivalence about our own environmental policy leaves our efforts tentative and somewhat incoherent. Worse, our clumsy squabbling with China at Durban damaged our credibility, just as possibilities for exciting collaboration with China were improving.

As is true with global health, when it comes to the environment, China is part of the problem and part of the solution. Working with China in the international system to reduce global emissions is clearly in our interest. That doesn't mean we should give China a free ride, but it does mean we should act in ways that are smarter and more likely to nudge China in the direction most associated with its self-interest and our own. It would help, of course, if our own credibility on climate change were stronger, but that's not a reason for hanging back and staying out of a global discussion in which China is an increasingly important player.

Engaging China on the environment became even more important following the Asia-Pacific Economic Cooperation (APEC) meeting in Beijing in November 2014, when China and the United States
announced a major agreement on combatting climate change. Under
it, China agreed to cap CO_2 emissions "around" 2030. This would
be achieved through efforts including an ambitious pledge to have
"around" 20 percent of China's energy come from renewable sources
by that time.[25] For its part, the U.S. undertook to double the pace of
its emissions reduction efforts, so that total emissions would be 26 to
28 percent lower than 2005 levels by 2025.[26] Skeptics immediately
suggested that there was less to the deal than met the eye, particularly since China's proposal appeared to be in line with at least some
pre-existing growth projections, and since the country's emissions will
continue to rise for the next fifteen or more years.[27] It's also clear that
President Obama will have his hands full making progress while fending off a Congress that is over-supplied with climate change deniers
and coal promoters.

But it is important to put the announcement in perspective, seeing
it as the latest step in a steady evolution in thinking evident in both
Washington and Beijing. It is also likely that continuing pressure from
a Chinese public that is increasingly worried about air quality will continue to motivate leaders in Beijing. Finally, the announcement will
almost certainly inject new optimism and momentum into broader,
global climate change negotiations. The announcement creates a challenge for the current government in Canada, which has consistently
claimed that its own climate change ambitions need to be calibrated
with those of the United States, and which has also pointed to Chinese
inaction as an excuse for our own lack of progress. And it leaves us on
the sidelines of a hugely important global discussion.

While the ultimate objective of international activism on climate
change and other environmental issues is to reverse a steady deteri-
oration in the very air we breathe, closer collaboration with China

on the environment would also open attractive new opportunities for Canadian firms in the sector. We already have a number of companies making a difference in areas such as water purification, energy-efficient vehicles, and environmentally friendly building systems and materials.

Typically, Canadian environmental firms face two challenges in China. The first is one of scale. China's problems are often so vast as to swamp the capabilities of small, cutting-edge Canadian firms. The solution here is to begin slowly, starting carefully with trial projects that are small enough to manage but big enough to build mutual confidence. As they gain experience, some firms seek partners in China capable of helping extend their reach and capabilities. A key consideration here for any firm is to ensure that all intellectual property is sufficiently protected, including from the firm's Chinese partner.

The other challenge is that most environmental projects in China are accessed through some level of government. That underlines the need for an introduction from some level of government in Canada. As mentioned previously, we have an uneven track record here. Some cities—such as Vancouver, Calgary and Waterloo in Ontario—are more active and more effective than others. This isn't good enough. We can't afford to be partially engaged if we want to play a bigger role in a sector of such huge potential.

CHINA'S RAPID DEVELOPMENT comes at a vast cost to its citizens, who have little say as rampant industrialization and urban sprawl lay waste to air, water and land. But that cost is also being borne in other countries. This has long been acknowledged by China's near neighbours, and more recently, rising emissions from China have pushed the impact out across the Pacific and into the North America.[28] But the cost also includes plants and animals from every corner of the world, now under pressure as unscrupulous suppliers compete to indulge the exotic tastes of China's prosperous consumers.

A bizarre incident in April 2013 provided a tragic illustration of what's at stake. A Chinese ship ran aground in the Philippines, damaging a coral reef, a living organism so special and so sensitive that it had been given World Heritage status by UNESCO. Worse, the hold of the ship was full of pangolins, or scaly anteaters, an animal whose numbers are under intense pressure despite being protected by a ban on international trade. Chinese consumers believe that the ground-up scales of pangolins have medicinal benefits. When I first lived in China in the 1980s, it was not uncommon to see live pangolins caged in front of restaurants. Picky consumers wanted to be sure that they were getting fresh product. Restaurant owners are more circumspect now, but the trade is still huge. In the words of Jonathan Baillie, conservation programmes director at the Zoological Society of London, "All eight pangolin species are now listed as threatened with extinction, largely because they are being illegally traded to China and Vietnam. In the twenty-first century we really should not be eating species to extinction—there is simply no excuse for allowing this illegal trade to continue."[29]

Pangolins are by no means the only animals under threat. In August 2013, Janet and I paid a return visit to the natural history museum in Dublin. We enjoy its fascinating and disarmingly old-fashioned collection of stuffed animals, birds and fish from Ireland and abroad. Huge glass-panelled cases display the bones of the giant Irish elk, a stuffed Irish wolfhound, clusters of hares, weasels and foxes, and various mounted fish taken from the sloughs, rivers and coastal waters of the Republic. In the international section, I was brought to a halt by the strangely altered appearance of a stuffed rhino. A gaping white patch marked the place where its horn had been. A sign explained that the horn had been removed as a precaution against theft, something that had already happened at a number of European museums. I would later learn that this precaution had been futile. Thieves, undeterred, broke into the museum's storage area, overpowered the guards, and made off with this and other horns in the collection.[30] What drives demand is a lingering and unshakable belief, particularly in China, in the medicinal qualities of powdered horn.

Far, far worse of course is the relentless poaching of live rhinos in Africa, where they are being brought close to extinction. Elephants face a similar fate. Pilfered tusks are supplying the growing demand for ivory among the wealthy classes in China and Vietnam. Fortunately, the Chinese government is taking at least some steps in response. China and Hong Kong have recently destroyed tons of ivory confiscated from smugglers. That's a welcome gesture, although some point out that China has yet to move decisively to shut down ivory trading in its domestic market.[31] There is also reason to doubt whether senior officials in China are uniformly committed to shutting down the illegal trade in ivory. According to the Environmental Investigation Agency (EIA), Chinese officials used visits to Tanzania by China's former president Hu Jintao and by current president Xi Jinping as opportunities to smuggle large amounts of ivory out of the country courtesy of the presidential aircraft. Indeed, so much ivory was purchased in advance of the Xi visit that, according to EIA, prices on the black market doubled.[32]

Added to this is the relentless pressure from Chinese consumers on any animal unfortunate enough to be equipped with a penis or other body part reputed to have aphrodisiacal qualities, a demand that is fuelling the poaching of tigers, bears and other species.

China's growing appetite for other natural products can have unintended negative consequences on wildlife. In their book *China's Silent Army*, Spanish journalists Juan Pablo Cardenal and Heriberto Araújo travel the world to see first-hand the impacts of China's growing reach. Although they display a deep respect for the determination and sacrifice of the hard-working Chinese labourers and small-time entrepreneurs who are on the front lines of this phenomenon, the overall picture is grim. One of the book's saddest chapters reports on the steady destruction of the great forests of Siberia, a rampage made possible by Chinese demand for wood products of all qualities and by the lawless, mafia-style business environment of modern Russia. As forests are felled and shipped to Chinese border mills, the fodder for animals such as wild boars also disappears. This in turn eliminates a food source essential for the survival of tigers. So, the magnificent Siberian tiger is doubly threatened: directly by poachers and indirectly by loggers.[33]

Before waxing too judgmentally about the devastation being wrought by a rising China, it is worth recalling that China is hardly the first country to be guilty of such rapaciousness. The Dublin museum and others like it in Canada and elsewhere in the West remind us of our own propensity to hunt, collect and consume our way through the natural world. And this isn't just a part of the historical record. Although China is the world's largest importer of illegally traded species, number two is the United States, where the business is fuelled by demand for exotic pets.[34] And before snickering at China's fixation with wild animal aphrodisiacs, we might want to consider the proportion of time, money and energy Western pharmaceutical companies devote to curing erectile dysfunction (versus, say, producing lower-cost remedies for encephalitis).

That said, China poses a particular problem because rising prosperity is generating surging demand for endangered species, a problem that is exacerbated by widespread corruption in China and in many of the developing countries where China is now active and influential. Chinese firms strike secret deals with impoverished regimes, allowing them to operate outside the surveillance mechanisms set up to prevent trade in endangered plants and animals. China's international fishing fleet is a cause of particular concern since in many of its preferred destinations, particularly off Africa, fishing is essentially unregulated. That means that the extent of the catch taken by the Chinese fleet, which is the world's largest, is currently a mystery.[35]

Some of the most worrying recent trends are taking shape in China itself. China is, for example, experiencing a boom in animal theme parks, in many of which the animals are expected to perform for the delighted guests. Just as North Americans are turning against the idea of confining killer whales in tiny habitats so that they can amuse us with their rare intelligence, China is getting interested in the idea. The world's largest aquarium has opened in China, and reports indicate that it has acquired a pair of wild-caught killer whales from Russia. In the words of David Neale, animal welfare director at Animals Asia, "The real worry is ... precedent. I've been in and out of China for the past 12 years ... and the development in the marine parks is aston-ishing. The numbers of wild-caught dolphins and wild-caught beluga whales that are in the country now is into the hundreds. The worry that I have is that other parks will want to bring killer whales into their marine parks as well."[36]

Demand from Chinese zoos and wildlife parks is also driving the trade in chimpanzees illegally shipped out of Guinea and other African countries. Chinese investors are surging into Guinea in search of min-ing projects, but they are leaving with more than minerals. According to Doug Cress of the Great Apes Survival Partnership, "Chimpanzees are being caught, stuffed into crates and packed onto a flight with no questions asked. Each one costs around US$25,000 [in China], with gorillas brought into Guinea and shipped off selling for around US$40,000 each. Current export controls at the airport are unsatisfac-tory and we believe corruption and gross incompetence by officials are allowing this trade to thrive."[37]

In 2012, Interpol estimated that, in the previous three years, 130 chimps were shipped out of Guinea illegally (it is possible to legally trade apes bred in captivity). That may seem like a modest number until you consider that poachers typically kill ten family members for every ape they capture.[38] Guinea was ultimately penalized for this traffic by the responsible regulatory agency, the Convention on International Trade in Endangered Species of Wild Fauna and Flora (CITES), which barred the country from all trading, even under otherwise legal permit, in the species it oversees. But China, which is typically treated with deference by international organizations, escaped sanction. It has even been commended by CITES for its domestic policies.[39]

China is also home to a vast number of farms on which wild animals are harvested. By some estimates, up to twenty thousand bears are being kept in tiny cages in farms across China. Farmers slice into the bodies of captive bears to siphon off bile, which goes into making shampoo and toothpaste.[40] Needless to say, those animals that survive the crude surgery waste away through the course of a long, cruel ordeal in captivity during which they are regularly milked for bile.

Tigers are also farmed in China. While farm operators argue that this is a conservation effort, the trend is widely condemned. Apart from representing an indignity to a wild species, the practice makes it easier to kill and consume tigers, thus feeding demand and keeping the illegal trade alive. *The New York Times* points out that some five thousand tigers are kept on farms in China, a development that is fuelling ugly new trends in an ongoing assault on this magnificent animal. In one disturbing instance, police raided a house party in which guests were busy "watching a tiger being slaughtered and butchered, then gorging on meat that's considered an exotic delicacy."[41]

But there are gleams of hope on the horizon. We are seeing a growing willingness in China and Hong Kong to eliminate shark fin soup from restaurant menus. Close to one hundred million sharks are killed annually, with much of the demand generated by the popularity of shark fin soup.[42] The emerging reprieve is partly due to efforts in China to curb expensive and ostentatious consumption by public officials.[43] Perhaps as important is the activism of Chinese basketball star Yao Ming, who has spoken out against consuming shark fin soup, and in support of efforts to protect elephants. He is part of a growing trend in urban China to do more to protect the environment at home and abroad.

I encountered this new consciousness when Canada's effort to open China's market to seal meat was brought to a halt by local activists

in Beijing, no doubt supported by the international campaign against
the seal hunt. Diplomatic work occasionally introduces issues that,
while not so stark and unambiguous as to require resignation, leave
you feeling torn and uneasy. I'm not a big fan of the seal hunt, but I
reminded myself that I was serving as the ambassador of Canada, not
the ambassador of the Republic of David Mulroney. I did my professional best in an ultimately fruitless effort to open the market. But the
Chinese opposition caused me to think carefully about how others see
the hunt, about the futility of our cold, science-based argument when
it comes to the fate of living things, and about the price that support
for the hunt exacts in terms of our reputation and ability to influence
others. It made little sense that more of our agenda with China was
being allocated to preserving the seal hunt than to figuring out how
we, as important maritime nations, might work together to protect the
world's oceans.

Anti–seal hunt activism in China might seem surprising. We are far
more used to hearing about what appears to be a widespread disregard
in China for the protection of wildlife. But I didn't for a moment doubt
that the views I was hearing about the seal hunt were genuine and
heartfelt. The reaction from our critics was evidence of the emergence
in China of a new sensibility in relation to the natural world.

When I first lived in China in the mid-1980s, pet ownership
was largely restricted to birds and fish. We lived in one of the first
Western-style subdivisions in Shanghai, launched in the mid-1980s
as the city was reclaiming its status as an international centre. In the
early mornings I would see the manager of the then-new Volkswagen
plant exercising his German shepherd inside the chain-link fence of
the communal tennis court. The local staff of the subdivision, mainly
farmers who had worked land now occupied by Japanese-built bunga-
lows, watched in horrified fascination as the big dog let off steam in
that small enclosure.

Twenty-five years later, my Beijing mornings would begin at 6 A.M. as I walked Sherpa, a Chinese-born English bull terrier, along the canal behind the embassy. He would stop frequently, all too frequently, to sniff and greet a procession of golden retrievers, Labradors, boxers, poodles of all sizes, chihuahuas and, of course, Pekingese. Urban China was falling for dogs and everything that goes with owning one, including high-end pet food and doggy supply stores, vets, spas and boarding kennels.[44] The authorities made half-hearted attempts to enforce a rule that said only small dogs would be tolerated inside the heart of the city. But this was widely interpreted by pragmatic locals as merely a suggestion that you walk your big dog at sunrise and well after sunset, when things weren't too busy. Since Sherpa was on the borderline in terms of shoulder height, I hurried him toward the diplomatic sanctuary of the embassy when the police, like almost everyone else we passed, took too much of an interest in his large, egg-shaped head and strange, rolling gait.

This surge in dog ownership is happening at a time when dog meat is still seen as a nourishing dish in parts of rural China, an embarrassing fact for city dwellers, and a subject not normally discussed in polite company. But the two cultures do clash. While I lived in Beijing, dog-loving activists converged on a truck carrying hundreds of dogs for slaughter. They blocked its forward progress and ultimately paid close to $20,000 so that the entire truckload could be freed.[45]

A major dog-meat festival at Yulin in South China has been the subject of increasing public criticism for the number of dogs killed (estimated to be as high as ten thousand per day when the event took place in 2012) and the inhumane slaughtering methods used. There is also speculation about where the dogs ultimately come from, given that dog theft is not uncommon in China.[46] In fact, in the late summer of 2014, seventeen men were prosecuted for selling dog meat that was both stolen and poisoned. They had been shooting strays and pets with dart guns laced with cyanide and other toxic chemicals.

Police estimated that some sixty tons of contaminated dog meat were ultimately sold.[47]

Despite being held early to keep a low profile, the 2014 edition of the Yulin festival was disrupted by conflicts between traditionalists, for whom a meal of dog meat and lychee is a mid-summer tradition, and animal rights activists who see the event as symptomatic of a widespread and criminal contempt for animal welfare. For its part, the embarrassed city government did its best to duck the controversy, declaring "that it did not sponsor the event and would strictly enforce food safety regulations. Civil servants, teachers and medical staff were also ordered not to eat dog meat at restaurants. And restaurants serving dog meat were ordered to cover the word 'dog' on their signs."[48]

China, like every rising economic power, is taking a heavy toll on the resources of the natural world. While there is considerable truth to the argument, often voiced in China, that we are criticizing the Chinese for things that we were doing ourselves until the recent past, the notion that we should simply look the other way is unthinkable. Change is indeed coming from within, but it isn't yet sufficient to reduce pressure on a range of species. Simply put, we don't have enough tigers or tropical timber left to wait out internal debates in China. Worse, a particularly noxious side effect of China's global reach for resources is that it often fuels corruption in states in which elites trade resources for personal gain. This is an area where China needs to accept, sooner rather than later, its full responsibilities under international agreements that it has already signed—such as CITES. For their part, officials at CITES need to stop giving China a free pass, pretending that it is behaving the way they would like it to behave.

Sometimes the best solutions are already close at hand. A recent study found that snow leopard populations on the Tibetan plateau are most effectively protected by the presence of Buddhist monasteries in the region. In Tibet, Buddhist monks enjoy a rare degree of respect and authority and have proved highly effective in curbing poaching of the big cats by local hunters and herdsmen.[49] Quoted in the press release that accompanied the study, George Schaller—a conservationist noted for his long dedication to the preservation of the snow leopard,[50] and co-author of the report—said it best: "Buddhism has as a basic tenet the love, respect, and compassion for all living beings. This report illuminates how science and the spiritual values of Tibetan Buddhism can combine their visions and wisdom to help protect China's natural heritage."[51] This has in turn encouraged animal welfare organizations to work with monasteries, helping the resident monks enhance their skills when it comes to monitoring and protecting the cats.[52]

So, in addition to doing more to hold China to account internationally, we need to think more carefully about how to encourage, empower and energize China's own diverse and often unrecognized environmental champions. It's not too much to say that this is as important as the air we breathe.

ELEVEN

The Food We Eat

B efore closing this discussion of how China is influencing our well-being, we should consider the question of food safety. The first thing to understand is that this is one of the most contentious issues in today's China. In its survey of issues concerning the Chinese public, the Pew Research Center found that the number of people who see food safety as a "very big problem" rose from 12 percent in 2008 to 38 percent in 2013.[1]

I experienced this first-hand when I posted to weibo photos of a visit I had made to a major Chinese dairy in Inner Mongolia. The objective of the visit was to promote closer links with the Canadian dairy industry. It was a surreal experience. The dairy itself is the size of several football fields and, unusual for a production facility in China, it is almost entirely automated. Raw milk is delivered to one end of a vast industrial space full of pipes, tanks and blinking consoles. The finished products at the other end are milk, cheese and some very tasty yoghurt. Some of the raw milk is trucked in from farms in the region, but much of it comes from the dairy's own herd, which is housed nearby (and which we hoped to improve with some high-quality cattle imports from Canada). Throughout the visit, my hosts nervously stressed how important food safety is. They pointed out sanitary precautions at every stop on our tour.

But the feedback from our weibo followers was overwhelmingly negative, warning me against any association with an industry that is reviled in China. In response, I explained that the purpose of my visit was to build links to Canada that would only improve safety and quality. But that did little to mollify our outraged followers. And for good reason. Shipments of tainted baby formula made from powdered milk had sickened tens of thousands of Chinese babies in the period just before the Beijing Olympics. Ultimately, six children died. It turned out that some milk suppliers had spiked milk products with the chemical melamine to make it appear to have a higher protein content. What is perhaps most shocking about the incident is that after its initial discovery, it was covered up, almost certainly to avoid negative publicity before the Games.[2]

Although this was one of the most notorious food safety crises, it was hardly unique. It wasn't even the first large-scale case in the dairy industry. Nor did it lead to a degree of national soul-searching sufficient to effect lasting change. In some cases, food safety problems are rooted in pervasive environmental degradation. Soil pollution, for example, has contributed to alarming heavy-metal contamination in rice.[3] By one estimate, the amount of poisoned soil in China is equivalent to all the farmland in Manitoba, Ontario, Quebec and the Maritimes.[4] But to a shocking extent, the problem also flows from human greed. It is almost impossible to police millions of local entrepreneurs, some of whom are all too willing to cut corners in ways that endanger public health. Authorities in Shanghai were forced to crack down after it was discovered that people were getting sick after using drinking straws that had been manufactured in basement factories where waste plastic was being recycled.[5]

When I lived in Beijing, one of the most worrying stories was of the prevalence of "gutter oil," or cooking oil retrieved at night from drains and sewers and resold to restaurants by day. The manager of a company that transforms oil recovered from sewers into biofuel estimated that his industry probably accounted for only 10 to 20 percent of demand for recycled oil, leaving the remainder to find its way into the food system.[6] This being China, the problem has trigged entrepreneurial innovation. One manufacturer is reportedly testing chopsticks that can warn diners if food has been cooked with contaminated oil.[7]

Such alarming stories point to massive regulatory failures, something that is compounded by pervasive corruption. This in turn points to a deeper problem at the heart of Chinese anxieties about this issue: a widespread failure of public morality that threatens the very ties that should bind a society. Worrying about the absence of altruism and general neighbourliness in Chinese society is a staple of social media chatter, stoked by regular reports of accident victims left to die, ignored by uncaring passersby, and by all too many accounts of people adulterating food and drug products to make a quick profit. The cumulative impact of stories like these is significant because it generates a widespread lack of trust that is hard to overcome. Better surveillance and better science can help when failings in the food system are due to rare technical malfunctions or naturally occurring pathologies. But how do you respond to a seemingly widespread criminality that leaves everyone vulnerable?

One answer is to turn away from mass-produced food. China is currently witnessing a huge hunger for locally grown organic products.[8] But supplies are limited. For many, the easiest answer is to turn to imports from countries judged to be safe and reliable. Because of the infant formula scandal, Chinese demand for foreign-produced milk powder is surging. It was "up a staggering 45 percent in some months" of 2012, according to Agriculture and Agri-Food Canada.[9] And Chinese visitors to Hong Kong are notorious for clearing store shelves of baby formula, with similar behaviour in places like the U.K. prompting retailers to limit the number of cans sold to single shoppers.[10] New Zealand is becoming known as the "Saudi Arabia of milk" thanks to its success in China. New Zealand's overall exports to China were up 45 percent in 2013, largely due to explosive growth in demand for its milk. Indeed, demand from China has enabled New Zealand to become the world's biggest milk supplier.[11]

In 2013, an enterprise known as Canadian Dairy Manufacturing Inc. (CDM) was launched in Toronto by Chinese investors with the objective of shipping powdered infant formula exclusively to China. Early reports suggested that the company had lined up close to $700 million in sales over five years through Chinese distributors.[12] That Canada could get into this business surprised many, since our supply management system means that milk exports from Canada are deemed by the WTO to be subsidized, which significantly restricts our access to global markets. Infant formula, however, is considered to be in a separate category as a further-processed product, and the dairy industry in Canada continues to be of the belief that nothing constrains us from supplying it to China on a competitive basis. One expert I spoke to suggested that simply having the made-in-Canada label on the tin means that Canadian-produced infant formula would command a premium price in China.

But at the end of 2014, almost two years after the project was high-lighted as a success story in the course of a visit to China by former Ontario premier Dalton McGuinty,[13] CDM was not yet up and running. So, if Canada is to join the ranks of countries helping to meet China's demand for infant formula, it may fall to another manufacturer to lead the way. Meanwhile, Saputo, a large Montreal-based supplier of milk and cheese, has taken another route to supplying China and other Asian markets. It recently bought a major Australian producer of cheese and butter and is looking at other international acquisitions.[14]

Some foreign suppliers of powdered milk have discovered that the higher profile that comes with growing market share can generate unfriendly attention from the Chinese government. As demand surged for foreign powdered milk, the suppliers faced allegations of excessive markups. The Chinese government ultimately levied fines totalling

US$100 million on six firms, five of them foreign.[15] Many interpreted this as a way of assisting the domestic industry, although any move that made foreign milk powder more affordable (several suppliers slashed prices even before the investigation had concluded) cannot have been entirely good news to China's own producers.[16]

In 2013, New Zealand's major dairy exporter, Fonterra, was required to react quickly to concerns about possible botulism contamination in some of its products. This later prompted President Xi Jinping to admonish New Zealand's prime minister about the importance of food safety, something that many Chinese netizens found a bit too much to take. They acknowledged that the New Zealanders had reacted quickly and transparently, something that could be a lesson for China's own firms. One person even commented online that Chinese officials should be required to have their own children consume local milk powder.[17] Although the botulism concerns ultimately proved to be unwarranted, the New Zealand supplier took a major hit in the Chinese market, with at least some of the damage due to persistent negative reporting by China's state media.[18] Fonterra has since announced plans to consolidate its position in China through the acquisition of 20 percent of a major local dairy firm.[19]

More recently, the fast-food industry in China has been shaken up by revelations that major firms such as McDonald's and KFC have been serving meat that was well past its expiry date. I was initially surprised by this, because such firms had formerly enjoyed reputations for being relentless in their insistence on using only quality ingredients. They relied on tactics such as surprise visits to local suppliers to check on conditions. But business analysts warn of what they refer to as "quality fade." In the words of *The Wall Street Journal*, "As multinationals have localized production and management, in many cases their standards have reverted to the local mean."[20]

Despite allegations of foreign firms cutting corners in an underregulated Chinese market, it is hard not to believe that many foreign brands will continue to command a premium in China because of their continuing association with higher quality and higher standards. Analysts in Australia, seeing food and drink exports to China surge, talk about the nation's China-trade focus shifting from "mining to dining."[21] The CEO of Air Canada told me that one of the advantages that attracts Chinese passengers to his airline is the opportunity to sample food that comes from Canada. That's why Clearwater puts its logo on the claws of the live lobsters it sells in China, ensuring that shoppers can feel confident they are buying high-quality *Canadian* lobsters, "considered by many," the company proudly points out, "to be the finest in the world."[22] And it's why we have seen a surge in sales of everything from Canadian Icewine to cooking oil. The "Made in Canada" logo makes a big difference.

Authors Damien Ma and William Adams point out that about 450 million people in China have yet to attain a standard of living that makes it possible to eat meat once a day. But this is changing quickly. As Chinese people become more prosperous, demand for meat and other food products previously out of their reach will increase, a process that will drive food prices up globally.[23] This will in turn put new burdens on the environment. Meeting China's demand for meat will, for example, require the intensive cultivation of vast new herds of livestock. In addition, China's demand for refrigeration will only increase as its food service industry evolves and improves. According to *The New York Times*, "An artificial winter has begun to stretch across the country, through its fields and its ports, its logistics hubs and freeways. China had 250 million cubic feet of refrigerated storage capacity in 2007; by 2017, the country is on track to have 20 times that."[24] The report goes on to note that this development won't come without a heavy cost. Refrigeration is a major generator of electricity demand, and gas leaks from refrigeration are a major contributor to global warming.

If nothing else, these trends should prompt us to rethink our own wasteful habits when it comes to food production, processing and consumption, and to step up efforts to engage China on environmental issues. We can also hope that the impact of growing demand from China, in addition to promoting broader interest in healthier and more sustainable eating habits, prompts technological changes enabling us to produce, transport and process food more efficiently.

SIMPLY MEETING THE CHALLENGE of feeding China's own population is driving major Chinese companies to go global. The need is becoming more urgent as pollution and climate change reduce the land suitable for agriculture in China. In 2013, a major Chinese meat processor bought Smithfield Foods, a U.S. company that is one of the world's largest pork producers. China's state-owned enterprises are looking to invest in large agricultural land holdings in Europe and Latin America. And the country's major state-owned trader of grains, China National Cereals, Oils and Foodstuffs Corporation (COFCO), is moving to acquire companies active in the trade of commodities including sugar, soybeans and wheat.[25] These moves reflect China's ambition to play a more important role in the global supply chains for key foodstuffs. While this is partly motivated by a desire to ensure food security at home, China also sees the trade in food and agricultural products as a two-way street. China's import bill can be at least partially offset through revenues generated by a range of new food exports.

Although Canada enjoys a huge surplus with China when it comes to food and agricultural products, we are already importing roughly $1 billion in fruits and vegetables, fish and processed food from China. In most cases, consumers are unaware of the Chinese content in the food they eat. Many of our own processed foods, such as sauces, fruit juices, and even baby food, rely on Chinese ingredients. I started thinking about this after getting to know an American rabbi in China who ministers to the foreign community. I was intrigued to discover that he also travels the country inspecting Chinese factories supplying ingredients for kosher food. In September 2013, Bloomberg reported that Chinese inspectors had cracked down on fruit juice plants that appeared to be processing apples unfit for human consumption. At least one of the plants was a major supplier of apple juice to Canada and the United States.[26]

Before getting too worked up, it's worth remembering that food quality problems originate in many places, including Canada. But China's size, production capacity and the imperfections in its under-regulated and uneven system mean that it is in a risk category of its own. The globalization of the food business already makes it difficult if not impossible to simply shut our doors to Chinese products until its entire system has been upgraded and reformed. Chinese products are already built into our food chain, just as Chinese products are built into supply chains in other sectors. That's a positive development in terms of price and variety, and an inevitable consequence of globalization.

When I served as ambassador, I was a regular caller on a Chinese agency whose long name was the General Administration of Quality Supervision, Inspection and Quarantine, known to us simply as AQSIQ. They were the gatekeepers for a range of Canadian products—meat, canola, fruits and berries—we were trying to sell in China. There were times, such as during the long effort to reopen markets for Canadian canola, when it seemed that the Administration was a front for Chinese protectionism. The problem with such suspicions, whether justified or not, is that they can interfere with your ability to actually listen to what Chinese officials are saying. There is a danger in spending so much time arguing your case that you begin to miss cues that you need to understand.

Each time a delegation from Agriculture Canada visited Beijing, we would invariably travel to the offices of AQSIQ to review our wish list of Canadian products that we were trying to get into the Chinese market, and to give the Chinese an update on the items that they were trying to sell to Canadians. In the early going, the dialogue was completely disconnected. We would vigorously make our points and then basically tune out the Chinese, figuring that they were still a long way from being able to meet our standards. We were so intent on making our points, and so fixated on the rightness of our cause, that we weren't sufficiently attuned to growing frustration on the Chinese side about access for products as diverse as cooked chicken and dog food. Getting Chinese chicken into Canada seemed a long shot to us. And, given past problems with contaminated dog food and pet treats from China in Canada and the U.S., we weren't overly concerned about appearing unresponsive on that file either.[27]

But after some unexpectedly acrimonious exchanges with the Chinese, we huddled to rethink our approach. While we were pushing for seemingly unlimited access for Canadian products in China, it appeared to the Chinese that we weren't willing to take even the first steps to help Chinese producers get their products into Canada. As we thought about this, it became clearer that what the Chinese were actually asking for wasn't immediate access to Canada, but that we send inspectors to China to examine their best factories. If we found problems, they wanted us to point them out, thus helping them to understand where they were falling down. What they wanted wasn't necessarily access, but respect. Slowly and carefully, we started a process, a dialogue. This opened doors for Canadian products that had previously seemed closed, and it started the Chinese on a long road to compliance with Canadian standards.

The way ahead with China will require us to blend respect with an equal amount of caution and vigilance. We need to be open to products from China, even food products, so long as we can be satisfied that they meet Canadian standards. Such openness is the quid pro quo for maintaining our own access to China's much larger market. Our approach needs to be based on up-to-date and fact-based assessments, not on prejudice or a misguided sense of generosity. This argues for an even larger presence in China by Canadian inspectors and industry specialists.

China's impact on global health, the environment and the safety of the food we eat is increasing with the dynamic growth of its economy. This means that we have to pay much more careful attention to what's happening on the ground in China as we draft our own policies relating to health, the environment and food safety. Working harder at understanding the nature of China's impact on global well-being means that we can better protect ourselves in those significant areas where China is still part of the problem, and better position ourselves where it is now part of the solution.

CHINA AND
CANADIAN VALUES

TWELVE

The Buddha of Compassion

henever I speak about the Canada–China relationship in Canada or in China, I mention the fact that a mature relationship should include the ability to discuss potentially difficult subjects, such as differing views about human rights. We should do this out of the respect that we have for China as a member of the global community. China is not some lawless pariah state. We expect it to obey both international laws and its own. Speaking frankly is also something that flows from the respect that we have for the people of China, including the many who have worked hard to advance human rights at home and abroad.

In 1948, a Canadian named John Humphrey helped to draft the *Universal* (italics mine) Declaration of Human Rights, a document described by Eleanor Roosevelt as "the international Magna Carta for all Mankind." The emphasis on universality begins in the preamble: "Whereas recognition of the inherent dignity and of the equal and inalienable rights of all members of the human family is the foundation of freedom, justice and peace in the world ..." This broad and generous inclusiveness makes human rights a legitimate topic of conversation among responsible nations. China's relationship with the document dates back to the days of the pre-Communist Republic of

China, which was among the signatories in 1948. Although the document predates the People's Republic of China, the PRC effectively accepted it when they replaced the Republic of China, by then exiled to Taiwan, in China's seat at the UN.[1]

China is not generally inclined to acknowledge the "universal" scope of the document, and instead prefers to advance a notion that human rights policy needs to be considered in developmental or incremental terms when it comes to developing countries like itself.[2] I generally hear some version of that argument when I discuss the subject with groups on both sides of the Pacific. Sometimes the question is put as an issue of fairness: "Why do Western countries focus on human rights while ignoring economic rights? Doesn't the fact that China's government has pulled hundreds of millions of people out of poverty count for something?" My short answer is that it certainly does, and that a respectful and successful dialogue with China needs to spend at least some time acknowledging the spectacular improvement in people's livelihood that the PRC has delivered. Acknowledging this should also engender some sympathy in the hearts of foreign critics, given the enormous difficulties that China faced in the past, and still faces. A human rights dialogue is about helping to effect positive change, not scoring points.

Sometimes the questions I get are less about fairness and more about the propriety of discussing human rights at all. Often the questioner is angry, and Canadian questioners tend to be even angrier than Chinese ones. In these cases, the questions often start with "Who do we think we are?" and almost inevitably reference disgraceful chapters in our own history. This includes the head tax we applied to Chinese immigrants until 1923, and its successor, the equally shameful Chinese Exclusion Act, which denied almost all Chinese people access to Canada and was only repealed in 1947. My response to this particular argument starts with an acknowledgment of its validity: We do indeed have our own misdeeds to acknowledge. But these are, in almost all cases, acts that we have tried to atone for through public apologies and corrective measures, including some form of compensation, albeit long overdue. Even more important, because we can talk about these things, because they are the subject of media scrutiny, scholarly research and activism by interest groups, and because victims and their families can hold current governments to account, we can feel more confident that such outrages won't happen again. Almost none of this is true in China.

Questions from Chinese interlocutors sometimes focus on concerns about human rights as a smokescreen for efforts to constrain China just as it is coming into its own. Is human rights promotion just another Western tactic for destabilizing China? That could only be true if human rights were some kind of dangerous concept unfairly applied to China. And it would only be accurate if China itself wasn't a centre of creative thinking and courageous activism in support of human rights. China's 1911 revolution owes much to the vision of Chinese reformers who were critical of the decadent and intolerant late-Qing regime. That said, much commentary about human rights in China is based on the premise that a divide exists between self-interested Western notions of human rights, which are designed to advance a political agenda wholly unsuited to China, and Chinese notions, which are more appropriately focused on harmony, stability and prosperity.

Some argue that, given China's influence, if the UN were to produce a Declaration of Human Rights today it would look very different, starting with the fact that it would be less likely to speak of universal rights. Proponents of this view also emphasize the importance of being sensitive to significant cultural and historical differences between China and the West. This is a useful reminder. But it should not become an excuse for accepting as natural and necessary China's restrictions on such basic rights as being able to speak freely or expect a fair trial. Nor should we concede that these are essentially "Western values," or that they are somehow conditional, dependent on a state of economic development that the Communist Party can forever locate in a future that never arrives.

Widespread acceptance of this argument is bad news for Tibetans and Uighurs and for almost everybody else in the PRC other than the leadership of the Communist Party. But it's also bad news for Canadians. We believe such values are universal not because the UN happens to say they are, as important as this is, but because of shared beliefs about the dignity of every human being. Devaluing people anywhere devalues them everywhere.

It's not as if senior Chinese officials are afraid to discuss human rights with foreigners. You don't make it to the top of the system in China without displaying considerable toughness, coolness and competence. When the relationship is good, they simply deflect the question with a few brief remarks about China's developing status, adding in some bland assurances that China meets all its commitments. When relations are less rosy, the response includes stern reminders about the importance of respecting China's sovereignty and the need to avoid interfering in its domestic affairs. If Tibet or Xinjiang have been mentioned, you may be in for a lecture on the evils of feudalism or religious fundamentalism. The next step is a not-so-friendly reminder of the benefits of having a good relationship with China.

China has in the past attempted to channel bilateral discussions about human rights into the confines of a dialogue between foreign diplomats and officials of China's foreign ministry. These mechanisms are by design slow moving, rigid and largely unambitious. The Chinese also typically try to prevent the kind of inclusiveness that is seen as essential when discussing human rights in the West. Interested NGOs and other human rights experts must content themselves with pre-consultations with their own diplomats. They feel frustrated, and justifiably so, when they are largely kept out of the actual discussions with the Chinese.

Canada abandoned its own such dialogue with China following a 2006 report that pointed out many of the shortcomings of the process.

While I agreed with the critique, I disagreed with the decision to end the dialogue. I have a somewhat Chinese view of diplomacy: Never discard an exchange, dialogue or annual meeting that might be useful later. You don't have to put it in the centre ring or make it your main effort, and you should certainly be honest about any limitations or problems. But you should never close off any vehicles for communication with the Chinese on a topic you consider important.

In my way of looking at it, mechanisms such as the human rights dialogue are like small, and admittedly fragile, levers used to nudge and ultimately move the imposing rock of Chinese policy and practice. Viewed from afar, the rock seems stationary despite all the effort. But if you take a closer look, studying small signs in the soil around it, the rock is slowly shifting its position. That only happens because multiple levers are deployed—remember that other countries have some version of the same dialogue—and because Canada itself deploys other levers, too, a topic I will return to below. Of course the most important and effective levers are in the hands of the Chinese themselves, wielded by visionary officials, by idealistic young people, by artists, journalists, intellectuals and other champions of human freedom.

Recently, Canada has tended to be both impatient and unimaginative in its approach to human rights engagement with China. We abandoned our only official dialogue mechanism and then failed to think creatively about the number and nature of levers still available to us, about how to deploy them in a concerted way, maximizing their effect. Some levers get more attention than others. Journalists, for example, seem fixated on the frequency of our simply mentioning human rights with senior people in China. And because journalists are fixated, so too are Canadian politicians. Don't get me wrong: having senior people raise human rights issues is extremely important, and, done properly, it is one of the most effective levers available to us. But over the last twenty years, it has taken on something of a routine, tick-the-box quality. Ministers worry that if they don't mention human rights, no matter what topic they are in China to discuss, they will appear uncaring when a reporter asks about it after the meeting.

My own view is that human rights should always be on the agenda of the prime minister and the foreign minister. I am much less convinced that human rights should inevitably be on the agenda for everyone else, such as, for example, the minister of finance in a meeting with China's Central Bank governor. I would prefer to be more strategic, deploying other high-level Canadian visitors when there is a timely, compelling reason to intervene. That's because other Canadian ministers are generally meeting Chinese counterparts who are themselves a long way from the human rights file in Beijing, and who will duck the question if we can't find a good reason for making them reflect on a specific case. If we're not careful, the frequency and predictability of our interventions cause them to lose their punch.

It's better to wait for opportunities when we can actually have an impact and expect a thoughtful response. It is very important to point to specific actions that your counterpart can take to make the situation better. In one case, during our regular dialogue between the Canadian minister of health and her Chinese counterpart, we focused on getting much-needed medical attention to a prisoner whose welfare was of concern to us. China's health minister, himself a doctor, took the question seriously. Chinese mayors and provincial governors are good people with whom to raise specific cases in their territories. It is important to do this carefully and respectfully. The idea is to get cooperation, not to embarrass or enrage. In the most sensitive cases, I normally suggested having the discussion when the two senior officials had some quiet time together. You are more likely to get a thoughtful and nuanced answer in that context than by raising the issue in a room full of note-taking officials. In those cases, senior Chinese leaders, unwilling to look weak in front of their own staff, will deliver the official line.

In addition to making your points, you have to listen very carefully to what you are hearing from your hosts. When I visited Tibet in 2011, I was welcomed by a senior official who happened to be Tibetan (although the most senior person in the region, to whom my host reported, was Han Chinese). Much of our discussion was covered by the local media. I was very careful to be sure that I delivered important messages about human rights and that I avoided giving up, even out of natural courtesy, a positive quote that could be taken out of context by the state-sponsored media. All too often, they cobble together the positive quotes into a report that seems to suggest support for the Communist Party's firm hand. It was a difficult discussion. At its end, I was presented with a reproduction of a classical *thangka*, a traditional Tibetan painting on silk. Months later, I met an American of Tibetan origin, who told me that he had followed media reports of my visit. He then asked if I understood the full significance of the *thangka*. I was embarrassed to say that I didn't. It was, he said, a likeness of the Buddha of Compassion, of whom the Dalai Lama is considered, by many devout Tibetans, to be a manifestation. Was I being sent a signal, or simply being reminded that things are more complicated than they appear in talking points? At the very least, it brought home to me how dangerous it is to be so intent on making a point that you overlook the possibility of complexity or ambiguity on an important issue.

WHEN WE RAISE HUMAN RIGHTS cases in China, it's important to have an outcome in mind that is within reach, or that at least holds out the possibility of some forward motion over time. While the ultimate goal is freedom for courageous lawyers, embattled journalists and harassed religious believers, persistence might first yield improved conditions for them or their family.

It goes without saying that if the Chinese have done something positive, we should acknowledge it. Ideally, we should be attempting to establish an actual conversation with the Chinese, engaging them in a way that will encourage something more than the angry delivery of unhelpful talking points. Delivering a stinging rebuke is immensely satisfying—for about five minutes. But if it leads to the abrupt end of your conversation, you haven't achieved much.

Nor should we assume that it is easy to walk into a room full of Chinese officials to take on their battle-scarred leader on his or her home turf. Push too hard and you get an angry exchange and a quick end to the meeting. Too soft, and the Chinese bury you in woolly statements of mutual regard. Success involves having your interlocutor pause and instruct his officials to do something. The rock has just shifted slightly. Now you have to use every means available to consolidate your gain.

High-level Canadian visitors also need to raise broader issues such as the situations in Tibet or Xinjiang, or the continuing cruelty to Falun Gong practitioners. But it helps if even these general concerns can be focused on specific cases and outcomes, such as securing a change in a problematic regulation, or obtaining permission for an individual to travel to Canada for medical treatment. It is also useful to divvy up such cases with like-minded others. Agreeing on a division of labour with partners such as the U.S., the U.K. or our Nordic friends is smart diplomacy, as is regularly sharing insights into problems and possibilities.

As mentioned, my toolbox would also include an official human rights dialogue, even acknowledging its very modest impact. Such dialogues are the place to discuss joint projects in areas like judicial procedure or police work. And they are the working-level window through which we officially raise our cases of concern. Much can also be accomplished through providing smart and careful financial support to progressive organizations working in China. During my time as ambassador, CIDA was winding up its formal assistance programs. But it was still doing good work through a variety of imaginative projects, such as helping young migrant workers seek recourse against unjust employers, protecting Tibetan language and culture, and helping groups on the margins of society gain better access to legal protections. It was hard to argue against a decision to stop providing aid to a country that can finance a space program, commission an aircraft carrier and lavish money of its own on poorer countries (often in ways that undermine our own efforts to link development funds with improvements in governance). But the fact remains that China frequently fails to assist its own people who have been left behind by the country's rapid development.

Sometimes, our very engagement helps to draw out and energize local allies. Our work on behalf of migrant women was ultimately supported by local government officials who were themselves trying to address this problem. Even the railway pitched in, offering to have staff hand out information to young women passengers heading to the big cities. Similarly, we found common cause with local officials in efforts to promote non-controversial themes such as health care and economic development in Tibet and Xinjiang.

While I am very comfortable with CIDA's decision to wrap up its aid program in China, I remain convinced that continuing to assist ethnic and religious minorities, such as Tibetans and Uighurs, and reaching out to support various agents of change in China—lawyers, journalists, environmentalists and other social activists—is in line with our values and interests. We have steadily given up the funding tools we had been using to help marginalized groups in China. Public speeches and behind-the-scenes diplomacy are among our only remaining levers for change. These are important, but you can't have an active and effective human rights program without spending at least some money. Granted, our efforts at encouraging positive change probably shouldn't be part of a now-obsolete program that requires us to channel our assistance via an increasingly prosperous and capable Chinese government.

We should instead go back to the drawing board to design and launch a program that allows us to fund capable Canadian partner organizations, including law schools, religious groups and NGOs, while continuing to support international organizations that have existing China programs. Although CIDA did support many organizations working in China, its agency-wide efforts were scattered and disconnected. We should do this work more purposefully and systematically, as part of a comprehensive China engagement that sets targets and measures progress. And while we shouldn't seek to embarrass, isolate or irritate China, we should no longer be limited to supporting only those causes and projects pre-approved by the government of China.

I did see a continuing role for CIDA in China and pitched the idea, unsuccessfully, to Ottawa. I was convinced that the agency could play a constructive role by advising the Chinese on their own aid program in Africa, a place where Canada, thanks to CIDA, has real connections and credibility. China is criticized for its activities in Africa, at times unfairly. It could use our help in better aligning its efforts with international norms and standards. But by that point, CIDA was so sensitive about appearing to assist a now-wealthy China that its main objective was shutting the door and moving on.

THE OTHER ABSOLUTELY essential lever is direct action and engagement by the embassy itself. I think of this as the pointy end of human rights work in China. By this I mean actually reaching out and connecting with courageous activists who are trying to change the system from within. Sadly, and all too often, it really comes down to helping their families, since the activists themselves have been imprisoned. This involves walking a very fine line. The most important thing is to avoid bringing more problems down on the heads of activists and their families. Sometimes, just making the effort is sufficient, a sign to such people that friends in Canada have not forgotten them. My colleague the German ambassador told me that he had been in the habit of sending cards to one imprisoned activist. It had seemed to him a very small gesture, almost meaningless. But when the activist was released, he told the ambassador that those cards had been like little beacons in the dark during his imprisonment. I thought about this story a lot.

We sent packages of food and toys to the families of imprisoned activists. And we, or colleagues from another embassy, would try to show up at those times, all too infrequent, when the people we were following were granted a court hearing. This was hard to achieve. Notice would be given only at the last minute. And although China was technically willing to allow foreign observers, there was typically no room in the tiny courtroom. Often the best we could do was to show up in the crowd outside.

During much of my time in China, the activist Chen Guangcheng was living in what is euphemistically called "soft detention" at his home in a town in Shandong province. Although he had completed prison time for having had the temerity to bring legal challenges against local authorities for their brutal enforcement of China's one-child policy, he was still effectively a prisoner in his own home. Thugs dressed in plain clothes made sure that nobody could get into his town without permission. We decided to join diplomats from the E.U. and Swiss missions in Beijing in an attempt to go and see Chen. Technically, there was no reason why we couldn't go to see him now that he was a free man. Chinese diplomats are, by the way, free to visit every corner of Canada. David Bostwick, a skilled member of the embassy team with an admirable inclination to get out and see things for himself, was our candidate for the trip. But he and his foreign colleagues got only as far as the edge of town. There they were roughed up by a group of thugs who forced them to turn around without seeing Chen.

When I raised this outrageous incident with the Chinese foreign ministry, I got a shrug and advice to the effect that we should stay away from tough neighbourhoods. We continued to talk about Chen and his deplorable situation, in private conversations and in more public statements, for the remainder of his detention. He eventually eluded his guards and slipped out of town, finding sanctuary in the U.S. embassy. After some negotiation, he was allowed to travel to the U.S., where he was ultimately joined by some of his family. Before Chen left China, David was in regular touch with him via text messages. We were heartened to learn that he had heard about the effort that David and his colleagues had made to see him, and that this had been encouraging to him. That's not a big dramatic outcome, but it counts for something. Simply being able to remind a prisoner that he is not forgotten is a small step forward.

David was a companion on other trips. On one occasion, he introduced Janet and me to the congregation of a small house church in rural China.[3] House churches are Protestant congregations that have chosen not to operate under the jurisdiction (control) of the Chinese state. As a result, many are subject to official harassment. We slipped into a quiet courtyard and sat on tiny benches as elderly people sang hymns and read from their Bibles. I was careful to be very discreet in making my visit. Had I tried to visit one of the much larger and more embattled congregations in Beijing, the repercussions on the community would have been severe. But the visit helped to educate me and inform my own interventions with the authorities.

David and I were joined by Martin Laflamme, another of our activist diplomats, on a visit to Xinjiang in which we called on members of China's Tajik minority. I had become interested in them after reading a speech by the Aga Khan in which he noted that China is home to one of the world's largest communities of his fellow Ismaili Muslims. I had been deeply impressed by the work of the Aga Khan Foundation in Afghanistan, and also knew of the Aga Khan's touching affection for Canada. I wanted to see whether there might be opportunities for the embassy to reach out to the Ismaili community in China, and to help connect them to friends and fellow believers in Canada. Like Tibetan Buddhists and China's Catholics, the Tajik minority can feel cut off from their wider spiritual community.

I decided not to seek official permission for this visit, which involved a four-hour drive along an icy mountain road that connects Kashgar with the more southerly city of Tashkurgan, close to China's border with Pakistan. My final months in China were approaching, and I feared that if I sought permission the authorities would simply stall and let the clock run out. In those cases when I did get permission, I often had to fight to do anything that was even remotely close to my objectives. (On one occasion, I went through the foreign affairs office of a nearby city to organize a call on a Catholic NGO that was doing good work with HIV patients. But when I got to the local train station I was harangued on the platform by a finger-wagging Chinese official who then told me that I was being summoned by the provincial leadership. The waiting priests took this with good humour and gave me an abbreviated fifteen-minute walking tour through their centre. I then set off for downtown, only to find that my call on "the leadership" was a bogus, time-wasting session with a Communist Party nobody.) My visit with the Tajiks wasn't entirely a surprise to the local government. On my final day back in Kashgar, I was followed to every stop on my program by a car carrying the same grim and bulky passengers. I couldn't direct much follow-up work before my posting was over, but I was content that we had made a connection, expanding the embassy's network and its knowledge.

ENGAGING CHINA on human rights is also important because the PRC is increasingly capable of shaping, bending and breaking international norms and standards when it comes to how people relate to their governments. China's elevation of economic progress over political reform is eagerly seized on by lesser dictatorships everywhere. And some of its opportunistic, no-strings-attached lending in Africa sustains corrupt regimes that are willing to trade away resources that might otherwise be the key to national development.

Back in 2005, when he was the U.S. assistant secretary of state, Robert Zoellick famously talked about the importance of China becoming a responsible stakeholder. What he meant was that an increasingly powerful and prosperous China should play a larger and more constructive role in areas such as poverty alleviation, peacekeeping, and the protection and promotion of human rights. While China has moved in some encouraging directions since then, progress has stalled elsewhere, and in some areas China has slid backwards. All too often it is assumed that the best way of securing Chinese compliance is to act as if it already exists. The tendency of officials at CITES to tiptoe around China's role in the illegal trade in wild animals, cited earlier, is an example of this. China encourages this behaviour as being friendly and sensitive to its delicate feelings. But China is simply too important to be given a free pass. While we should always be ready to acknowledge the things that China is doing right, we have to summon the courage to speak honestly about what it is doing wrong.

Canada's approach to human rights in China needs to be coordinated with our like-minded partners, with each taking up specific challenges. In any such division of labour, I can envision Canada staking out three areas of specialization. The first two would build on experience already gained through the CIDA program—namely, protecting the legal rights of migrant workers and supporting China's ethnic minorities. These are worthy activities that China is unlikely to pursue with much enthusiasm or effectiveness itself. Work under these objectives should be pursued through high-level interventions by Canadian political leaders, through training and mentoring by various levels of government in Canada, and through the direct action of the embassy. Canada should also generously support projects delivered by UN agencies and by NGOs from Canada and elsewhere.

By way of example, our main partners in our work to help migrant workers in China were the International Labour Organization, which is part of the UN family, and the All-China Women's Federation. Smart partnerships with such organizations pay added benefits. Some of the most active China-focused NGOs are based in Hong Kong. I discovered that it was highly beneficial to stay in close contact with them, and I learned a great deal thanks to their deep experience on the ground in China and their refreshing candour about conditions.

The third area of focus for Canada on my human rights agenda would be religious freedom. It is clear, with the appointment in 2013 of an ambassador for religious freedom, that this is a priority within the Canadian government's broader human rights agenda. What is not yet clear is the extent to which this will be woven organically into our foreign policy or run separately as a somewhat politicized add-on. Religious freedom should be seen as a human right like any other and championed as such. It *is* a priority because religious freedom is so per-sistently threatened in places such as the Middle East, parts of Africa and China.

Constraints on religious freedom in China are becoming more acute as China's increasingly prosperous citizens look for something extra in their lives. This is clashing with an official view in which reli-gion can be tolerated only so long as it fits neatly within a worldview defined and strictly controlled by the Chinese Communist Party. The Party is notoriously reluctant to provide space to any organization it sees as a rival. This unwillingness can lead in some bizarre directions. Although Amway is now a success in China, at an earlier stage it was viewed with real suspicion and monitored carefully. This was due to the Party's reluctance to countenance revival-style sales meetings that might spin out of control or provide a cover for network-building by organizations such as Falun Gong.[4]

Officials in China tend to divide the world between what they see as domestic faiths, such as Buddhism and Taoism, and foreign faiths, such as Islam and Christianity. One of the most memorable trips I made while living in China was to the city of Dunhuang, on the ancient

Silk Road in far-western Gansu province. Dunhuang is famous for the Mogao Caves, which are grottoes carved from sandstone cliffs by early Silk Road travellers, starting more than 1500 years ago. Magnificent paintings decorate cave walls and ceilings, and wonderful sculptures are carved from the rock itself. These trace the steady progress of Buddhism in China. In the oldest caves, Buddha is Indian in dress and physical appearance. His Chinese nature evolves cave by cave, century by century. The story told by the caves reminds us how much care needs to be taken in assigning a nationality to a particular religion. Faiths, like people, travel. More to the point, the Chinese notion that some beliefs are forever foreign suggests a bias that can only complicate relations between the state, for whom the term *foreign* carries much baggage, and Chinese citizens who are members of such so-called foreign faiths.

This notion that some religions are forever foreign is also encouraged by the state's inability to fit them wholly and completely into the Party's organizational chart. Inside the cover of Bibles in some of China's state-sanctioned Protestant churches are diagrams that show the hierarchy of the church right up to a top box assigned to the State Administration for Religious Affairs, or SARA. This is entirely consistent with the Party's view that it is the ultimate source of authority for all civil society in China. Needless to say, SARA does not reserve a box for the Pope atop their org chart for Catholics in the official Patriotic Church. China's insecurity is intensified when the religious belief is also in some way associated with perceived threats to China's territorial integrity. China's leaders see the intense longing that Tibetans feel for the Dalai Lama as making it harder for Tibet to be wholly incorporated into the PRC. Although China can exert military control, it is frustrated by what it sees as the waywardness and untrustworthiness of ungrateful Tibetans. Similarly, religion is seen as a significant contributor to the great difficulty China faces in pacifying—and assimilating— the Uighurs of Xinjiang. To the leadership, Islam is a worrying link to dangerous and unstable states in Central Asia and the Middle

East. This unease with Islam is widely shared. My tweets about visiting mosques in China almost always elicited suspicious or otherwise
cranky responses. I got used to hearing the same line from Chinese
cabbies whenever we passed through a neighbourhood that was home
to Chinese Muslims. Spotting a bearded man on the street, the cab-
bie would turn and say, "You know who that guy reminds me of?" I
would wait a beat for the inevitable punchline: "Osama bin Laden!"
The result of this general inability to come to terms with Islam as a
current in Chinese life is a degree of official heavy-handedness and
tone-deafness that makes further tension inevitable.

In China, Catholicism and Protestantism are constantly associated
with colonialism. I was often lectured by Chinese officials about the
evils perpetrated by Christians on behalf of Western imperialism. I
normally responded by recalling a trip my daughter Kate and I made
to Xian, China's ancient capital. In addition to visiting the Terracotta
Army, for which the city is famous, we also went to see something
called the Nestorian Stele, a standing stone column on which is carved
a cross, dating from the late eighth century, and text recording even
earlier forays into China by Christians from the Church of the East. In
other words, Christians were visiting China during the Tang dynasty,
only a few hundred years after the arrival of Buddhism. While the tra-
jectories of the two faiths were vastly different, Christianity in China is
much more than a vestige of nineteenth-century Western colonialism.

I became keenly interested in the life and work of Li Madou, or
Matteo Ricci, a Jesuit who arrived in China in 1582. Ricci mastered
Chinese and slowly won access to increasingly senior officials in the
court of the emperor Wanli. Ricci believed that he could have his
greatest impact by winning converts from among these elite ranks.
While his conversion tally was modest, he gained many important
friends and admirers, which in turn enhanced his broader reach and
influence. Whenever I visited Beijing's main cathedral, I used to stop
to admire a bronze statue of Ricci that stands on the grounds of the
original church that Wanli allowed him to build.

Ricci's success was due to his tremendous empathy for China, for its people and, importantly, for their unique outlook on the world. He was convinced that this characteristically Chinese outlook would inevitably condition the terms on which people would accept Christianity. His approach was synergistic, helping his adherents find connecting points between traditional Chinese custom and belief and Christianity. Ultimately, Rome came to believe that Ricci had gone too far in his willingness to accommodate all things Chinese. The Church abandoned his syncretic approach, substituting an evangelism that required candidates to reject their past beliefs and embrace something wholly new and different. Happily, that view has been reconsidered. The Church has come to appreciate Ricci's realism and his rare cultural sensitivity. He is a candidate for sainthood. (A point of historical reference for Canadians: Ricci died in Beijing in 1610, fifteen years before his fellow Jesuit, Jean de Brébeuf, began his work in New France.)

JUST AS DOCTORS FROM CANADA have had a significant impact on the development of modern China, so too have Canadian missionaries. And there is considerable overlap between the two communities. I have already mentioned the Kilborns and Dr. Jessie "Mac" McDonald. They were members of a Canadian Protestant missionary effort that was notable both for its good works and for its thoughtful and generous recognition of the need to build an indigenous church in China. While Chengdu in Sichuan was a centre for this Canadian effort, the Kilborns, Dr. Jessie Mac and others travelled widely, bringing basic education and medical services to many communities throughout the country. I was lucky enough to meet some of the children and grandchildren of these remarkable Canadians when they visited China for the launch of a book of photographs chronicling the early years of the Canadian missionary community in Chengdu.

Some members of the community struggled to balance faithfulness to an evangelizing religious mission with their growing disenchantment in the face of the corruption and social inequality of Republican China. This was particularly true for James Gareth Endicott, probably the most famous of the Canadian missionaries. Endicott was born into a missionary family in Sichuan and educated at the University of Toronto's Victoria College. He was energetic, bright and a tremendously gifted speaker. On his return to China for mission work, he quickly built up a wide network of friends and contacts. By the 1940s, these included Madame Chiang Kai-shek, the American general Joseph Stilwell, and a range of idealistic young Chinese thinkers and activists, some of whom would drift into the growing ranks of the Communist Party. Endicott, disheartened by the corruption and excess around Chiang, was himself steadily radicalized.

By the time of the Korean War, when many Christian missionaries, freshly expelled from China, were speaking out against the draconian, anti-religious programs of the Communists, Endicott was travelling in the opposite direction. He gained notoriety for claims that the United States was using chemical weapons in Korea, statements that resulted in his being censured by both the CCF, forerunner to today's NDP, and the United Church of Canada. The reaction was very different in the communist world, where Endicott was lionized. He was awarded the Stalin Peace Prize in 1952, and stayed committed to leftist causes, navigating the treacherous waters of the Sino-Soviet split of the late 1950s. He received an apology from the United Church a few years before his death in 1982, although not for any change of heart on his part. He remained loyal to the Communist Party of China until the end. Sadly, one of his last public utterances was a chilling defence of the use of force at Tiananmen Square.[5] However you assess Endicott's life and work, he was no colonialist, but was driven instead by a ferocious if, ultimately, uncritical love for China.

Canadian Catholics were also active in mission work in China in the first half of the last century. In his history of Canadians in Shanghai, John Meehan offers a harrowing account of efforts by Canadian and other Jesuits to rescue Chinese victims of some of the first Japanese air raids on the city, and of later efforts to feed some five thousand refugees who had assembled to be close to the priests.[6]

The Scarboro Foreign Mission (SFM) Society, founded in 1918 by a legendarily determined Toronto priest named John Andrew Mary Fraser, also sent priests from Canada to work in China. They were accompanied in this effort by intrepid Grey Nuns from Pembroke, Ontario. Much of their time was spent helping to protect their parishioners in Zhejiang province in East China from the growing violence and chaos of the Japanese invasion. Father John McGoey was one of the Canadian priests serving with the SFM in China. I remember being confused as a small boy when my mother made a reference to McGoey's autobiography, *Nor Scrip Nor Shoes*. I struggled to puzzle out the meaning of the title. It comes, as I would learn, from Christ's instructions to his disciples:

Go: Behold I send you as lambs among wolves.
Carry neither purse, nor scrip, nor shoes; and salute no man by the way.
Into whatsoever house you enter, first say: Peace be to this house.

Luke 10:3–5

The book moves quickly from McGoey's hockey-playing Canadian boyhood to his vocation in the priesthood and on to life as a missionary in an increasingly chaotic China. His work was often interrupted by battles with health problems that were amplified by the rigours of life in a war zone. He was evacuated in 1943,[7] only to return at the end of the war when he and another SFM priest helped coordinate and deliver aid to refugees in Shanghai on behalf of the United Nations Relief and Rehabilitation Administration (UNRRA). Hard-working and pragmatic, McGoey was recognized for his determination in helping to untangle a humanitarian effort that had been hobbled by inefficiencies.[8]

The missionary experience in China is a subject fraught with sensitivities. That missionaries in the nineteenth century at times wittingly or unwittingly furthered the aims of Western governments is undeniable. But by the early twentieth century, when Canadians were becoming active in this work, ideas and approaches were already changing, as was China. Chinese rhetoric can obscure the fact that people like the Kilborns, Dr. Jessie McDonald, James Gareth Endicott and Father McGoey brought to their work a high degree of compassion for the Chinese people and a strong sense of solidarity with them, expressed through typically Canadian pragmatism, practicality and hard work.

ALTHOUGH THE CANADIAN PUBLIC SERVICE is a profoundly secular institution, at its very best it expresses this through inclusiveness and respect for diversity. That diversity is reflected in its membership, which includes many religious believers, myself among them. I am a Catholic. And while, as a senior manager in the public service, I fully respected its secular nature, I didn't stop seeing the world as a Catholic does.

My time in China coincided with a crackdown against the Church, something that had been unleashed despite the best efforts of the Vatican to encourage rapprochement. Priests and bishops were bullied and imprisoned, and the Party moved aggressively to reassert control over Catholic institutions. I would be lying if I didn't admit to feeling real pain at this. I used my sympathy for Chinese Catholics to better appreciate the travails of the Tibetans, the Uighurs and human rights activists of all kinds. And I also worked hard to ensure that this distress didn't prevent me from doing the job I had been sent to China to do—namely, to build the best possible relationship between our two countries.

Early in my time in Beijing, I bumped into an old friend, a priest I had known in Taiwan. He asked if the embassy might open its doors to the international Catholic community, which didn't have a reliable venue for its Sunday Mass. Catholics could and did worship at officially recognized churches, but because the government was taking a harder line against the Vatican, worshippers at official churches were increasingly disconnected from the life of the universal church. Plans to have Mass said in hotels or community centres in the areas where foreigners lived were often cancelled at the last minute with no explanation.

You need to be very careful when you make a decision in an official capacity that also coincides with your own interests. Around this time, Pope Benedict XVI visited the U.K. A theme of his visit was the importance of ensuring that religion has an enduring place in the public square. I reflected on this for some time ... until Janet, as she often does, encouraged me to shift from reflection to practical action. So, I sat down to discuss the idea with fellow Catholics at the embassy. I suggested that we form a group to help support weekly Mass, to which they readily agreed. My good friend Dr. Felix Li immediately volunteered to lead our group. We agreed that anything we did had to be organized by volunteers from within the embassy, that any costs would be recovered from the parish, and that we needed to offer the same option to other faiths, so long as there was a Canadian volunteer group willing to pitch in. As it turned out, most churchgoers in the international community worshipped in officially recognized Protestant congregations that were free of the constraints faced by Catholics.

Our final decision, made with real regret, was that we could only open our doors to foreign-passport holders. I could not break the law of China (even a law I deplored) by allowing Chinese citizens to come to Mass with us. To do so would have meant betraying my role and commitments as a public servant and as an ambassador, and it would have exposed the priest and the Chinese participants to great risk. Still, it pained me when I had to say no to requests to allow Chinese friends, even future spouses of our parishioners, to attend.

The Sunday service, presided over by foreign priests working in Beijing, was a great success. The embassy's main meeting room was filled each Sunday with Catholics from every corner of the world but one. It was particularly popular for families with small children. At Easter, we would throw open the doors to the meeting room and fill the adjacent patio with benches in an effort to seat a portion of our 250-plus attendees. The parish, Our Lady of China, was active in supporting the work done by priests and nuns, foreign and local, in communities in and around Beijing. This included charitable work with migrant workers, with seniors who were isolated and abandoned, and with pregnant women who needed a safe place to stay.

These Sunday mornings were among my happiest memories of Beijing. I thought they sent a good message about Canada's respect for religious freedom and connected us with some of our distinguished Canadian predecessors. But these mornings also gave me, at the end of my career, a sense that my professional life and my personal life were reconnecting, that I was somehow coming home.

WE NEED TO FACE up to the fact that, as China grows in power and confidence, it is increasingly willing and able to challenge our views about human rights not just in China, but in the international arena. This comes at a time when many Canadians are themselves wondering whether it wouldn't make more sense and be more respectful simply to agree to disagree. My own view is that failing to mount an effective challenge to China on this point comes at a real cost to people in China, to people in those countries coming under China's sway and, importantly, to us as Canadians.

The most compelling reason for taking up this challenge is that in doing so, we are standing up for the universal applicability of basic freedoms. We shouldn't be seduced by the argument that this is insensitive to China's unique situation, or that we are somehow forcing China to adopt values specific to the West. Matteo Ricci's abiding empathy provides us with a good example here. We aren't suggesting that China adopt the Canadian Charter of Rights and Freedoms. We should instead support efforts to realize the basic rights outlined in the Universal Declaration in ways that align with Chinese traditions, society and culture. In calling for wider recognition of the right to a fair and public trial, for example, we acknowledge that the trial should be run according to Chinese laws and practice. The first half of the twentieth century provides many good examples of Chinese patriots who were also champions of human freedom, and who dedicated themselves to made-in-China laws and reforms designed to provide their fellow citizens with essential rights and freedoms. Such champions could be found in the second half of the last century, too, although mainly in prisons reserved for enemies of the Communist Party.

While we worry about whether our defence of basic human rights will bruise Beijing's feelings, China is taking a muscular approach to the global dissemination of its own gospel of non-interference. This essentially involves China propping up dictatorial regimes in exchange for access to their resources and the expectation of their sycophantic support. Diplomatic events in Beijing regularly featured embarrassing paeans to China's benevolence from whatever long-serving ambassador from the developing world happened to be the dean, or ceremonial leader, of the Beijing-based diplomatic corps. China foots the bills for many such embassies. At one event in Beijing, I remember being lectured by the ambassador of Fiji, a country whose failure to respect the rights of many of its citizens has led to widespread censure. For him, the rise of a wealthy, powerful and non-judgmental China couldn't be more welcome, allowing him to tune out all those annoying Australians and New Zealanders pressing for the rule of law.

Indeed, Western countries have discovered that their imposition of sanctions on Fiji had an unintended consequence. According to Maya Schmaljohann of the Overseas Development Institute in the U.K., "Sanctions were designed to push Fiji back into democracy, but what they actually did was provide room for China to increase its presence in the Asia-Pacific region."[9] As an indication of how busy China has been in the region, a quarter of Fiji's foreign debt is now denominated in Chinese yuan, up from 2.6 percent in 2008.[10]

Australian academic and China watcher John Fitzgerald writes perceptively about the perils of woolly thinking about so-called "national" values. Pointing to the marriage of convenience arrived at by former Australian prime minister John Howard and the Chinese leadership, he notes, "As prime minister, Howard was fond of saying that Australia valued freedom and equality, and that China did not, but that we could each respect our distinctive national values as long as the two countries focused on shared interests in expanding trade and investment." This dubious trade-off continues to be advantageous in economic terms, although, as Fitzgerald goes on to assert, China appears to have become steadily more confident: "Beijing is taking advantage of more porous national boundaries to monitor, organize and mobilize its far-flung diaspora in order to project China's national values in Australia."[11]

It is not an exaggeration to say that China's behaviour at home and its growing influence abroad constitute a challenge to some of our basic values. So this is a discussion that we cannot ignore. There are, however, two main reasons why people are reluctant to begin the discussion. The first has to do with how people see China itself. Many believe that China is simply too big to be a democracy, too vast and diverse to overcome the poverty and dysfunction of its history through anything other than one-party rule. They argue that trying to introduce more democratic government to 1.3 billion people would undermine China's hard-won stability and set back economic growth. This is not far from the prevailing mindset of China's ruling elite. But in addition to being swayed by the sheer numbers, China's leaders are also influenced by another deeply held conviction. They are convinced that the people they govern are a pretty unreliable lot, prone to criminality and insurrection without firm leadership. So in their view, the only way to preside over such a large and basically ungovernable mass of people is through the iron discipline of the Party.

One of modern China's greatest economic reformers was the brilliant Zhao Ziyang. His exceptional competence ensured him a rapid rise through the leadership ranks in the battered China that emerged from the chaos of the Cultural Revolution. He led efforts to implement Deng Xiaoping's bold economic reforms and ultimately served as general secretary of the Communist Party, making him China's most senior leader next to Deng himself. Zhao held the top Party job in the period leading up to the student protests in Tiananmen Square. He felt tremendous sympathy for the students and was almost overwhelmed by concerns for their safety. As a result, he was viewed with increasing suspicion by Deng and the group of old men, veterans of the Long March and civil war, who made up the rest of the senior leadership. They determined that Zhao bore the ultimate blame for allowing the protests to get out of hand. He was removed from office and placed under house arrest.

Zhao wrote a diary during his long confinement, something that was smuggled out and later published in Hong Kong. It records his life as a senior official and traces his transformation from someone who was wholly focused on economic reform to someone who, through his own tragic experience, became convinced of the need for political reform. Zhao wasn't advocating overnight transformation, but he was increasingly persuaded that the Party needed to embark on a measured, careful and long-term program of political reform, noting, "If we don't move toward this goal, it will be impossible to resolve the abnormal conditions in China's market economy: issues such as an unhealthy market, profiting from power, rampant social corruption and a widening gap between rich and poor. Nor will the rule of law ever materialize."[12]

Unfortunately, the Party took a very different lesson from 1989, shelving any notion of real political reform and focusing instead on economic growth. Deng is reported to have said of Tiananmen, "The gunshots have afforded us 20 years of peace and opportunity for doing business."[13] But China has paid a price for avoiding even modest political reform. Some of Zhao's worst fears about corruption and social inequality have come to pass, which only makes the Party more fearful of departing from an increasingly tenuous status quo.[14]

This leads to the second reason why China's foreign partners are unwilling to engage it on human rights: the real risk of reprisals from a Chinese state that has frightened itself into seeing these overtures as insidious threats. As China has grown, so too has its ability to bully and browbeat other countries in an effort to forestall or cut short unwelcome comments or actions. This is much easier now that it is rich and powerful enough to intimidate most foreign partners in a one-on-one exchange. Over time, for example, China has been able to steadily limit opportunities for the Dalai Lama to meet with foreign leaders in their own capitals. And China's reach is now sufficient to limit the activities of the Falun Gong in other countries, Canada included, despite the fact that the organization's activities are entirely legal and happen to be carried out by people who are citizens, voters and taxpayers in foreign jurisdictions.

When Britain's chancellor of the exchequer visited Beijing in the fall of 2013, deals were signed that would link the City of London more closely to China's banks and investment firms. The visit also improved prospects for Chinese participation in sectors including nuclear power. The *People's Daily* wrote that these moves had been possible because

David Cameron, Britain's prime minister, had admitted previous errors, specifically in relation to having met the Dalai Lama.[15] Although Britain denied the assertion, China's intent was obvious. It was sending a message to other countries about the new terms of trade.

Both of the arguments for treading carefully when it comes to human rights and China have merit. China is big and complicated and, even under the Party's firm hand, subject to a significant degree of violent unrest. So we should have modest expectations about the rate of change. At the same time, China is getting powerful enough to slough off calls for even modest change, and is able to punish, or at least intimidate, those who persist in making them. Managing the dialogue therefore takes patience and listening skills. But abandoning it means failing to contest China's challenge to our most important values. It also plays into one of China's most consistent tactics: getting a thoroughly intimidated opponent to defeat himself, winning without firing a shot.

At this stage we need to remind ourselves again about China not being monolithic. Indeed, even the Communist Party itself isn't monolithic. One of the things that left me feeling most optimistic about China was my exposure to what I call constituencies of change. By this I mean lawyers who want to extend the writ of the law to include the Party, journalists who want to push the envelope when it comes to fearless reporting and members of an emerging civil society who are not afraid to challenge the system. These courageous people are aided and encouraged by support from like-minded friends beyond China's borders. Although they face long odds, they are the people most likely to help China emerge as a more balanced, better governed and increasingly responsible member of the global community. We turn our backs on them at our peril.

We should also do our best to be on the right side of history. Contemporary China works on the basis of a widespread but uneasy complicity in ignoring hard facts about the recent past. The party that currently governs China has, through the history of its rule, perpetrated major crimes against its own people. We are only now beginning to see the emergence of a scholarly debate about just how many millions starved to death in the human-made famine that was the result of Mao's disastrous Great Leap Forward at the end of the 1950s. The Cultural Revolution, which followed it, caused a decade of devastation, and brought almost unimaginable suffering to tens of millions. And in 1989, the only means that China's leadership could come up with for responding to widespread protests by idealistic students in Tiananmen Square was to send in the army with tanks and machine guns.

When I lived in South Korea in the early 1980s, it was still a military dictatorship. People often spoke, quietly but with real passion, about an incident in the southern city of Gwangju. In the spring of 1980, students had gathered in sites around the country to protest against the military government. At Gwangju, paratroops were sent in to quell the protests. Hundreds of students were killed. Many Koreans saw this assault on bright and idealistic young people as a crime so serious that it could not be denied or ignored without doing damage to the country itself. National healing would require an act of contrition at the highest levels. Living as I did in a country that was under complete military control, I found it hard to believe that this desired reconciliation would ever come to pass. Korea was at that point staking its claim as an Asian economic powerhouse, and many visitors, Canadians among them, attributed its success to the unpleasant but "necessary" controls imposed by the ruling party and military.

But discontent continued to rumble beneath the surface. Within a few years, the military dictatorship was gone and the president who had sent in the paratroops was himself in jail. I am not arguing here that China must inevitably follow the pattern that South Korea did. The differences between the two places and times are many. But I don't believe that any society can forever lock away the past. Much of what animates the Chinese Communist Party is a desire to rehabilitate itself, to show a (slightly) kinder and gentler face, to forestall such an accounting. But denial is not a viable long-term strategy.

Writing about that 2013 visit to Beijing by Britain's chancellor of the exchequer, the *Financial Times* observed that China's rise does indeed make some "unpalatable compromises" necessary for Britain. But it went on to say that such concessions could only be countenanced in defence of key British national interests, and not for the sake of making a "fast buck."[16] The frankness of the admission, its very painful starkness, gave me pause. The current discourse about how to get along with a rising China offers many examples of possible compromises, things that might be viewed as unpalatable by some but as pragmatic and necessary by others.

In a thoughtful op-ed titled "Sharing Power with China," the distinguished Australian academic Hugh White outlines a possible new approach to managing China's peaceful rise. It includes the following quid pro quo: "For example, America might accept that China will eventually assert control over Taiwan, and in return China could accept that it cannot make a territorial claim over the whole South China Sea."[17] I was also struck by the furore surrounding troubling allegations that the media company Bloomberg has decided to tone down its previously robust coverage of official corruption in Beijing. The reason suggested is that its feisty reporting threatens Bloomberg's much broader business of selling financial terminals in China, not to mention its ability to market expert advice that depends on access to senior people in China. Both examples point to the difficulty we face in working out a viable relationship with China. You can mount a compelling argument for both compromises. Solving the Taiwan issue *is* key to regional peace. And companies *do* owe it to their shareholders, employees and customers to make prudent business decisions.

But we also need to think more carefully about the long-term effects of such compromises. Ben Richardson, a former Bloomberg editor, recently spoke frankly about the business rationale for "crimped ambitions" when it comes to China reporting. But he also went on to point to the cost of silence: "Lack of transparency and accountability fuel rampant corruption, human rights abuses and environmental crimes. As China goes global, those values and practices are in danger of gaining currency elsewhere."[18]

In his excellent book *The China Choice*, Hugh White carefully lays out the many challenges that China's rise poses for the United States. As far as Taiwan is concerned, the salient new fact for White is that the U.S. can no longer prevent China from seizing the island by force. Although he later expresses the hope that Taiwan's reunification with China will be "peaceful" and "consensual," he clearly believes that the changing power balance in Asia makes it inevitable. Nor, in his view, does the U.S. have any reason for opposing this outcome, so long as it is indeed peaceful and consensual. In fact, he argues that the U.S. should encourage this.[19] But any reading of Taiwanese public opinion over the last decade would argue that a consensual reunion is, if anything, improbable. In a recent study, more than 60 percent of people in Taiwan self-identified as Taiwanese, just under 33 percent self-identified as Taiwanese and Chinese, and "a measly 3.5 percent identified as Chinese."[20] If reunification does happen in the near future, it would far more likely be the result of some form of military or economic coercion by China. This outcome becomes even more likely if U.S. resolve weakens, a change that would fatally undermine Taiwan's own self-confidence and deliver precisely the cost-free outcome that China seeks.

Up until now, Taiwan has been safeguarded within a fog of strategic ambiguity that depends at least as much on U.S. nerve and resolve as it does on Chinese pragmatism and caution. And it has succeeded because the U.S. has been careful to ensure that all parties in Taiwan respect China's red lines relating to any move toward independence for the island. To the extent that there is an objective, it is to buy time sufficient to realize an outcome that would be acceptable to all three parties.

Crimped U.S. ambition would blight the futures of some twenty-five million Taiwanese, and cast a shadow over democratic aspirations in countries that are part of what might come to be considered China's sphere of influence. Nothing is inevitable in foreign policy, nor is very much cost-free. Sheltering and supporting Taiwan will almost certainly be an increasing challenge, but it is a challenge worth facing. Needless to say, the U.S. would welcome the chance to share that burden with like-minded countries, Canada among them.

Moral compromise tends to be infectious. When we cut corners in the defence of core values, we are often among the first casualties. *We* are changed, even diminished when we fail to value the democratic rights of the people of Taiwan, or when financial concerns cause us to turn away from discussing unpleasant facts about China. So I don't fully agree with the *Financial Times*. Accommodating China's rise will indeed require compromises on our part, some of them very difficult. But one of the main objectives of our diplomacy should be to ensure that whatever compromises we face, they can be borne with dignity and are *not* unpalatable.

That's also not to deny the second part of the observation, about not being seduced for a fast buck. We should take some consolation from the fact that, as China opens and embraces market disciplines, its ability to deliver on economic threats decreases. And even if that weren't happening, we need an accounting of our interests that goes beyond the dollars and cents. For some reason, we have recently taken to claiming that Canada's diplomacy is "economic." Asserting that we're only looking to make a buck isn't a particularly warm or enticing message for our partners. And it is exactly the *wrong* message to send to China. Serious countries engage across a wide range of important issues. Lesser nations have smaller ambitions. Edward Luce captured this sentiment in an opinion piece titled "Cameron's Britain Has Lost America's Respect." He quoted a dismayed U.S. official who said in the wake of Cameron's Beijing visit, "Who would have thought that a

British prime minister would go to China with no agenda other than selling things?"[21] We need to have more than sales on our agenda, too.

China fiercely resists efforts to change the way it governs internally. And it is increasingly successful in making its resistance extra-territorial, challenging other countries on their own turf about any of the many issues it considers sensitive. Engaging China on the subject of human rights takes confidence and courage. Just as it is unwise to take too confrontational an approach, it is also not a good idea to appear too soft. Long before President Obama made his first visit to China, the then secretary of state, Hillary Clinton, announced that the United States would not allow conversations about subjects like human rights to derail important discussions about things like the economy. And the president decided to defer a meeting with the Dalai Lama until after he had made his first trip to Beijing. Far from getting the relationship off to a good start, it served to undermine it. The Chinese, sensing a degree of weakness that could be exploited, stage-managed the 2009 Obama visit so as to leave the president with little to show for it.

Anson Chan, who was the second-most-senior official in British Hong Kong at the time of its handover to China in 1997 and carried on in a similar role under Chinese rule until 2001, argues that a firm backbone is necessary in dealing with Beijing: "If you roll over and pull your punches, it just encourages Beijing to be even more demanding the next time round."[22] She was referring to the general disinclination among Western countries to challenge Beijing's "crimped ambitions" when it comes to Hong Kong. The specific issue was whether the city's citizens would be free to elect their leader, the chief executive, via universal suffrage. This is something China promised in the "Basic Law" it enacted for its governance of Hong Kong after the handover. But officials in Beijing ultimately offered only a highly constrained and unambitious form of universal suffrage, something that seemed to run counter to the spirit of the 1997 agreement between Britain and China, when Hong Kong was viewed by both sides as a valuable incubator of reform. While the people of Hong Kong will get to vote for their chief executive in 2017, the choice will be limited to candidates who have been pre-qualified by a nominating committee drawn mainly from pro-China elites. Candidates are also required to display a "love of country," which many interpret to mean love of the Communist Party.

What is happening to Hong Kong's democratic aspirations represents an important skirmish in a larger, global debate about the relationship between people and the state that presides over them. Unfortunately, many in the West have taken the view that it is unwise to challenge China's preference for rigid state control. Britain, which, having failed to implement democracy in Hong Kong, secured China's agreement that the city would largely be left to pursue its own course, has been conspicuously absent from the debate. Nor have Canada and other democracies said much. I am afraid that we will look back on this broad silence as enabling a damaging precedent, a step back in the cause of human freedom.

We need to be tolerant and understanding when it comes to acknowledging the challenges China faces. And we need to be fair and generous in pointing to its remarkable accomplishments. But in doing so, we must keep a tight hold on our own basic values, rooted as they are in some fundamental notions about the nature and worth of every human person.

MY CHINA LIFE

THIRTEEN

From Kabul to Beijing

B efore taking up my job as ambassador to China, I spent more than two years as the Canadian government's coordinator for our mission in Afghanistan. The assignment was professionally challenging, and physically and emotionally draining. It also had a powerful influence on my thinking and professional development. Although I hadn't anticipated this, I came to see my work on Afghanistan and my work in China as being linked, with my experiences in Ottawa, Kabul and Kandahar on the Afghanistan file serving as a prelude to my work in Beijing. My experience working to coordinate Canada's engagement in Afghanistan helped me to better understand some of the obstacles I would encounter in China. Both assignments pointed to more fundamental challenges we need to overcome if we are to design and deliver effective Canadian foreign policy.

My job as Afghanistan coordinator, which began in 2007, was far from my first exposure to the place. Janet and I had visited the country twice during the peaceful 1970s, just before it was plunged into more than thirty years of violence and extremism. So, when I took up my Afghanistan assignment, I had the opportunity to reconnect with a country I had known long before. But I was also, although I didn't know it then, preparing for my China assignment.

I had been asked to bring greater coordination to a Canadian mission in Afghanistan that was uneasily and unevenly divided between the Canadian Forces on the one side and civilians led by Foreign Affairs and CIDA on the other. We were faced with two big problems. The first was that we had allowed ourselves to be drawn into a violent and almost unimaginably complicated mission in Kandahar without having a clearly defined set of Canadian objectives. As a result, different parts of the Canadian government pursued their own, more self-interested, organizational goals.

For the military, Kandahar was a classic counter-insurgency campaign in which Canada's civilian contributions such as diplomatic engagement, the training of local officials and massive development spending were tools to support what the military saw as a far more important combat mission. For the Canadian Forces, the Kandahar mission was a long-awaited opportunity to re-equip and repurpose a military that was anxious to prove itself as something more than a peacekeeping force.

The civilians at Foreign Affairs and CIDA believed that they were engaged in classic reconstruction work. Their efforts to rebuild a war-torn region would be supported by the security presence of the Canadian Forces. And for the civilians, Afghanistan was only one of a number of priorities, a list that also included commitments in Haiti and Darfur. As a result, the civilian mission to Kandahar was not adequately resourced with people, becoming instead largely a matter of cheque-book diplomacy. Asked to define the mission, civilians would rattle off the long list of UN-sponsored projects they were helping to fund.

A second and related problem was that nobody had thought about how to provide the leadership necessary to ensure that the Canadian Forces and Canada's public servants worked together to achieve truly national objectives. It was as if all that was necessary was to deploy these very disparate national assets to far-off Kandahar and they would figure out how to assemble themselves into a tightly integrated whole. Except that they didn't. And as our casualties mounted in and around Kandahar, the government struggled, and failed, to explain to Canadians just why we were there. It took the extraordinary intervention of a group of deeply experienced and eminent Canadians led by former deputy prime minister John Manley to turn this around. In addition to my other duties, I was lucky enough to serve as secretary to Manley and his panel, and was later tasked with implementing their recommendations as the head of a special task force based in Ottawa. I travelled to Kandahar, Kabul and other parts of Afghanistan regularly.

Over the coming months, I became part of an effort to refocus the government's attention on an issue of national importance. It wasn't easy, but thanks to some tremendously dedicated soldiers and civilians, we achieved most of the goals that we had set for ourselves in Kandahar—no small accomplishment given that these individuals were working in the teeth of a ferocious insurgency. And we rose to a level of civilian–military cooperation that was quite simply the best among the NATO countries operating in Afghanistan.

During the course of my work, I learned a lot about management. Thanks to some distinguished colleagues and mentors, I learned even more about leadership. I saw first-hand what happens when a government isn't particularly clear about what it's trying to achieve. But I also learned what's possible when it is. And I came to appreciate the difference between government as simply the sum of its self-interested parts and government in which the parts are coordinated and skilfully deployed to achieve larger, truly national objectives. The lessons of Afghanistan were hard learned and deeply felt. By the time I turned my attentions to very different challenges in Beijing, my Afghanistan experience had shaped my approach to leadership and public service.

IN JULY 2009, I wrapped up my work on the Afghanistan task force and travelled to China to serve as Canada's ambassador. This was another return journey for me. In 1985, I began studying Chinese at the Canadian Forces Language School in Ottawa. I thought I'd be heading to Beijing, but I was asked to finish my studies early in order to become part of a three-person team being sent to Shanghai to open a consulate general, thus re-establishing a presence we had given up when the Communists came to power.[1]

In early 1986, the Canadian government had rented four small houses in a development near Shanghai's airport. Three were assigned to the newly arrived trio of Canadian staff, and a fourth was turned into a makeshift office. Diplomatic mailbags were stored in a bathtub. An antiquated telex machine, our only reliable link to the outside world, was housed in a back bedroom. Canadians needing consular assistance would often show up at my front door rather than at the house designated as the consulate general. And our local Chinese staff, former factory employees who had never worked with foreigners before, had a hard time understanding the fussy distinction we made between the office and our homes. At first, they entered both at will.

It was a very different city then. Shanghai was still viewed with suspicion by Chinese who remembered its old decadence and its raffish international character. Shanghainese have never been popular in China. They are resented for being too clever in negotiations, and are notorious for their brash urban contempt for their country cousins, a category that includes all other Chinese. The city I brought my family to live in (our children Aidan and Kate were infants, and Sean was born during our posting) was virtually identical to the one that fell to the Communists in 1949. The central government milked it for revenues without reinvesting in its infrastructure. Smoke-belching factories shared downtown streets with once-elegant apartment blocks.

The apartments themselves were now subdivided into tiny units into which crowded the tide of families that had surged in to reclaim the city after 1949. Conveniences such as bathrooms and telephones were few in these vast tenements, and all life passed under the watchful eyes of elderly snoops who were paid by the Party to indulge their natural inclination to pry into the lives of their neighbours.

Today, Shanghai is a city of elegant people hurrying from sleek automobiles into expensive clubs and shops, China's version of what Tokyo, New York and London have become. Back then, Shanghai was much more connected to the traditional rhythms of Chinese life. During watermelon season, families would crowd on stoops and sidewalks in the relative cool of the evenings. Fathers, wearing white singlets rolled up over ample tummies (to enhance the cooling effect), hacked melons expertly and doled out the dripping chunks. This was such a widespread phenomenon that the city government posted notices warning people of the hazards of slipping on seeds and rinds.

In 1987, Steven Spielberg came to town with a large crew to film *Empire of the Sun*, which is set in the Japanese-occupied Shanghai of World War II. The city was so unchanged that he only had to put up a few vintage billboards and place some 1940s-era cars on the street to create a very realistic version of 1942. Janet, along with much of the rest of the small expat community, was hired as an extra. Each time the film airs on TV she gathers us to watch for the scene, about twenty minutes in, where she utters the futile cry of "Taxi, taxi!" in a crowd of panicky foreigners fleeing the doomed city.

The movie deal had been worked out with the support of China's ambitious mayor, Jiang Zemin. He was intent on returning Shanghai to its old role as an economic engine for East Asia. I wish I could claim to be a visionary, but I remember scoffing at the first plans I saw for the redevelopment of Pudong, then a dowdy jumble of wharves and warehouses across the river from the old downtown. Today, its futuristic skyline is often used to symbolize China's dynamic rise. Jiang's rapid elevation to China's presidency and Party chairmanship in the wake of Tiananmen helped make this transformation possible. By the time I left Shanghai in the summer of 1988, we had a well-equipped office in a downtown district that was showing signs of new life. We had also begun to build an experienced team of local Chinese support staff who were wise to the ways of Canadians. And we were growing a network of contacts in and around Shanghai, which was quickly returning to its traditional role as China's most international city.

I returned to a job on the China desk back at Foreign Affairs in Ottawa. The late 1980s was a period of rising optimism, rapid change and growing political ferment in China. It ended in tragedy on the early morning of June 4, 1989, when the People's Liberation Army fired on unarmed students protesting in Tiananmen Square. A large part of my work after that involved helping to shape Canada's response to the massacre. We scaled back what had been a rapidly growing and multi-faceted relationship, and put its high-level component on hold for a period that would effectively last five years, ending with Prime Minister Chrétien's massive Team Canada mission to China in 1994. But even during those years of frozen high-level relations, we maintained programs that would support reform and change in China, and we kept our embassy open.[2]

It was the right response, and it taught me two lessons. The first is that some partners are so important that, whatever the disagreement, it is essential to leave at least some lines of communication open, if only to understand developments that might have an impact on Canada. And keeping even a low-level dialogue going can be a way of ensuring that a powerful country isn't pushed into a dangerous sense of isolation. The second lesson is that, in the public fury to repudiate all aspects of the now-damaged relationship, you have to be careful that you don't end up punishing people who are part of the solution rather than part of the problem. Freezing contact with progressive Chinese university professors, reformist local politicians or visionary

entrepreneurs isn't a particularly smart way of responding to problems
that have their origins elsewhere in the Chinese system.

I took leave from government in 1995 and spent the next three years
as executive director of the Canada China Business Council (CCBC),
a role that put me in close touch with the heads of nearly two hundred
Canadian companies then active in China. The CCBC is one of the
best-known and most respected Canadian brands in China. Among
the useful things that it does is to promote networks among Canadian
firms, allowing China-savvy business people to mentor those new to the
market, and introducing Canadian specialists in Chinese law, banking
and accounting to neophyte exporters in need of such expertise. It also
functions as a voice for Canadian business, identifying issues—such
as tax or regulatory problems faced by foreign firms in China—that
inform government policy. The CCBC's isn't the only voice that the
Canadian government should listen to, but it is central in determining how our relationship with China can contribute to our long-term
prosperity. And, at its best, it highlights issues, such as the fundamental
importance of the rule of law, that have a far broader importance.

MY NEXT ASSIGNMENT saw me spend three years running
Canada's unofficial office in Taiwan. With trade, political, consular
and immigration sections, the Canadian Trade Office in Taipei is an
embassy in all but name. Its existence is a legacy of the flexibility gained
when we established diplomatic relations with China. At the time, we
were careful not to preclude future non-official relations with Taiwan.
We have many shared interests in areas such as trade and investment, education and culture. While I was there, we also launched a
set of exchanges between Canada's First Nations and their Taiwanese
counterparts. Taiwan was peopled thousands of years before the first
Chinese ventured across from the mainland about eight hundred years
ago. The descendants of those original inhabitants face many of the

same problems encountered by indigenous peoples everywhere, and they responded eagerly to outreach by delegations from Canada.

I got to know many of Taiwan's political figures, including Taipei's mayor (and Taiwan's future president), Ma Ying-jeou. Ma was an avid runner who eagerly accepted the invitation to serve as chair of the Taipei version of the Terry Fox Run. This was organized by our office and attracted thousands of participants. I served as Ma's vice-chair. He was something of a heartthrob, and although we would start the run together, he would quickly be engulfed by thousands of excited young women. I learned to pose my questions to him before we reached the 500-metre mark.

My recollections of Taiwan are shaped by two powerful memories. The first is of witnessing the rising tide of Taiwanese self-confidence and political courage that swept the KMT government from power. The KMT leaders were the political heirs to Chiang Kai-shek and had, for much of the previous fifty years, run Taiwan as a province of China. A strong new spirit of local identity swept the land, resonating powerfully among Taiwanese people in Canada, many of whom came back for the election. The vote, which brought to power a party with a much stronger sense of Taiwanese distinctiveness, was conducted with impressive civility despite the high political drama.

The second vivid memory is of living through the powerful earthquake that struck Taiwan in September 1999, killing more than 2400 people. Although our own office was shaken up, we were able to deploy staff to the quake zone to find and assist hundreds of young Canadians who had moved there to teach English. And we worked with Canadian NGOs and Taiwanese expatriates in Canada to deliver assistance to the remote communities most affected. That event is also, strangely enough, associated with one of my happiest memories of Taiwan. A full year after the earthquake, and long after almost all the assistance projects had been wrapped up, we partnered with Matthew Lien, a Yukon musician who is hugely popular in Taiwan, to organize an open-air concert in the most affected zone. We used the event to celebrate the opening of a school library that had been repaired and restocked with help from Canada. Most of the people at the concert were from Taiwanese aboriginal communities. Many brought their children. It was a chance to relax under the stars, listen to good music and feel connected to other people.

Following my return to Ottawa in 2001, I spent much of my time working on Asia Pacific issues, meaning that I continued to spend a great deal of time on Canada–China relations. I travelled to Beijing on visits by prime ministers Chrétien, Martin and Harper, and sat in on their meetings with China's leaders. In fact, when I was assigned to the Afghanistan file in 2007, it was one of the very few times in my career that I was not in some way connected to China.

MY 2009 TRANSITION from working on Afghanistan to taking up my job in Beijing was purposely brief. I left the Afghanistan file quickly and quietly, without properly saying thank you and goodbye to the members of my team. It had been a long, hard slog, and for the first time in my career I felt that I was running on empty. But I wasn't worried about doing my job in China. Indeed, plans and ideas were already crowding my mind. The prospect of returning to the Canada– China file gave me a much-needed lift. I did a three-week refresher course at a Chinese-language school, happily holing up in the library to struggle through texts and hunt down Chinese characters. I felt foolish when I showed up for class carrying my heavy dictionary. Things had changed in the twenty-five years since I first studied, starting with the availability of online dictionaries that are much easier to use and far richer in terms of content.

I didn't have a lot of free time during my studies, but I relaxed at the end of my day by reading *Two Innocents in Red China*, which recounts the experiences of Pierre Trudeau and Jacques Hébert on their visit to China in 1960. It was written at a time when relatively few Western visitors and even fewer Canadians had direct experience of the country. The book displays considerable sympathy for a China that was then struggling to stand on its own after its decisive split with the Soviet Union. Just when you think that the authors are beginning to take the sympathy a bit too far, the tone shifts to gentle irony, exposing the foibles and excesses of the true believers among whom the two "innocents" are travelling.

I was reading the 1968 English edition of the book, which begins with a note written by Trudeau as prime minister. He laughs off inevitable criticism: "If there are any statements in the book which can be used to prove that the authors are agents of the international Communist conspiracy, or alternatively fascist exploiters of the working classes, I am sure that my co-author, Jacques Hébert, who remains a private citizen, will be willing to accept entire responsibility for them."[3] It is easy to forget that there was a time when a political leader felt free enough to be anything other than drearily safe and earnest, or when a leader could talk seriously about topics that were considered controversial (and still are). In his 1968 note, Trudeau returns to the idea that had animated the 1960 visit: "There is at least one comment in the book which I believe to be as true today as it was when we left for Peking: '... it seemed to us imperative that the citizens of our democracy should know more about China.'"[4]

So here you have a new prime minister reflecting in print about a politically controversial trip made eight years earlier, and reminding us that with citizenship comes the responsibility of taking an informed interest in important parts of the wider world. In 1968, Trudeau was convinced that China needed to be brought in from its isolation, and that Canada's own foreign policy was incomplete without a formal relationship with the PRC. By 1970, Canada and China had established diplomatic relations. It was a development that provided the formula and momentum for China's re-emergence on the broader international scene, including the resumption, in 1979, of full diplomatic relations with the United States.

There is a lot in this to think about. We had in Trudeau a prime minister who was convinced of the importance of a controversial foreign policy decision, one that had as much to do with his reading of long-term Canadian interests as it did with his desire to contribute to the peaceful unfolding of world affairs. And all of this is based on his own direct experience. He led rather than followed the conventional wisdom, including that component of it emanating from Washington. Recognition of China is a good example of our middle power energies flowing through a smart connection with a rising power.

TRUDEAU'S BOOK was an inspirational read at the outset of my term as ambassador, an opportunity to reconnect with someone whose bold thinking and confident style had inspired my generation. Although my professional career began in 1981 in the twilight of the Trudeau era, his energy and vision still animated our lively and ambitious partnership with China. It is hard to believe now, but in the 1970s and 1980s Canada was one of the most influential of China's partners. That was largely thanks to a generous and well-crafted development assistance program that included food aid, support for key sectors such as agriculture and power generation, and a highly innovative exchange program that helped rebuild China's universities. At that time, it was possible to believe that China would bring to political reform at least some of the creative energy that was helping to open its economy. But that hope was crushed in Tiananmen Square in 1989.

The years immediately following Tiananmen were of necessity a period during which the official relationship was essentially dormant. As mentioned, most high-level exchanges were curtailed, as were most high-profile events. Officials meanwhile carefully tended those programs that were most likely to keep China open to the outside world.

Two things were notable about the resumption of the relationship in the early 1990s. The first is that we were among the last of China's traditional partners to re-engage, a questionable tactic for a country of our size. It's much better for us to be among the first movers, as we were on recognition of China. Once the major players have made their move, nobody really notices who comes next. Second, when we did resume relations, we found ourselves in the midst of a much more crowded field. We couldn't simply rest on the laurels that Trudeau had won for us.

Canadian policy in the 1990s was officially built around a four-pillar strategy that included promoting trade and investment; encouraging sustainable development; advancing human rights, good governance and rule of law; and connecting more closely with China on peace and security issues. But our main emphasis was on the first pillar. This was the era of the huge Team Canada trade missions. While these were important in helping Canadian companies enter the Chinese market, the care and feeding of such beasts—involving the prime minister, multiple ministers and premiers, and hundreds of companies—occupied a good part of the China resources in Foreign Affairs. They also created a narrative in which Canada was the visiting petitioner (or supplicant) and an increasingly confident China was the decider.

Meanwhile, the Ottawa bureaucracy was becoming so large and complex that it was difficult to step back and see all four priorities in perspective. As the trade and investment pillar gained prominence, CIDA, which managed the development work and a significant portion of what we did on human rights and governance, was increasingly disconnected and aloof. Years later, as ambassador, I found it hard to get a handle on everything CIDA was doing, and even harder to connect that to a larger Canadian agenda. The fourth pillar, which focused on peace and security, was, depending on your perspective, either in the earliest stages of gestation or empty.

The Chrétien era was notable for its energy and its optimism in relation to China. And both were repaid by the Chinese. We were delighted to be described by the then premier, Zhu Rongji, as China's "best friend." Much of this positive energy carried on into the brief Martin era. Indeed, during their 2005 meeting in Ottawa, Prime Minister Martin and President Hu Jintao agreed that the relationship qualified as a "strategic partnership." Definitions like this are important signals to the Chinese bureaucracy about what is possible with other countries. We were being offered the chance to establish even more high-level links and agreements, and to begin work on an agenda for moving forward.

Martin's unique contribution to the development of the relationship was his vision for bringing a rising China closer to what he saw as the centre of global governance. He played a significant role in the creation of the G20, an institution that has provided China and other major developing nations with a more powerful voice on the global stage. But as timely, generous and visionary as this was, it was also tinged with a degree of naïveté. It was a bit like Dr. Johnson's definition of second marriage: the triumph of hope over experience. Because the G20's focus is primarily economic, its proponents tend to view member countries entirely through an economic lens. While this is an important perspective, it can lead to wishful thinking about the degree to which participating countries actually do share the same outlook and approach to world affairs.

Speaking in Beijing in early 2005, Martin envisioned the new organization as something that would "build on the success of the G8." His more inclusive forum would involve "regional powers, such as South Africa, Brazil and India—and of course the new global power, China." He went on to describe a dialogue covering "such pressing global issues as terrorism, public health and the degradation of the environment." It would operate on an entirely new basis, he said: "No speeches, no scripted sessions, just a new, efficient way to devise concerted, multilateral action that produces real results."[5]

I was struck by how eager the new proponents of the G20 in Ottawa were to write the obituary of the G8, the one forum in which leaders actually *do* manage to do away with scripts and speeches. (With Russia absent, the G7 answers even more closely to this description.) Frank and unscripted talk among like-minded leaders is exactly what *doesn't* happen in the G20. China, most of all, sticks to scripts, talking points and carefully devised strategy. That's not a reason *not* to engage China and other developing countries, but we shouldn't allow our fondest hopes for the format to delude us into thinking that everybody approaches such high-level diplomacy the same way. Not surprisingly, the G20 was most successful at tackling the global economic crisis. But it's worth noting that the early years of the G20 also coincided with a period of renewed Chinese truculence in its region and beyond.

Meanwhile, it was difficult to get anybody in Ottawa to think creatively about the opportunities implicit in the term "strategic partnership," a mechanism that actually *does* allow officials in countries so designated—such as Australia, which is particularly good at this—to cooperate with China on health, security and the environment. Although the idea was to bring senior officials from Canada and China together to work on a shared agenda, it was impossible to generate much enthusiasm on the Canadian side. We had to settle for a very unsatisfying teleconference in which senior Canadian officials read overlong prepared texts at their increasingly bored and frustrated Chinese counterparts. It was as if Ottawa was so transfixed by shiny new ideas, like the G20, that it couldn't be bothered with old-fashioned, one-on-one diplomacy.

THE CHRÉTIEN–MARTIN YEARS have a golden lustre for many in Canada's small China-watching community. The shine is enhanced by the supposed gloom of the Harper years that followed. I share the view that the new Harper government took too much time to get its

China policy in place or, worse, even to understand that it needed one. I was part of those debates. But I also believe that our China policy was, by 2006, very much in need of an overhaul. For one thing, the Team Canada brand of trade promotion needed to be packed away. As novel as it had been in its day, we needed to move on from being a one-note petitioner in Beijing. I also think it is highly likely that the prevailing optimistic consensus on China would have been tested had the Martin government not been defeated. China's growing assertiveness in its region and beyond was just one of many signals that the Communist Party was not becoming a like-minded institution.

But instead, the new Harper government was excoriated for daring to depart from what had been a bipartisan consensus on the importance of engaging China. This was portrayed as a lack of sophistication, something akin to the know-nothingism of the Tea Party in the United States. Paul Evans, an academic veteran of the China-policy skirmishes of that era, describes the views of many in the Harper government as follows: "A significant number of the caucus and Cabinet, especially those from the Reform/Alliance side of the party, continue to see China as godless, totalitarian, a security threat, and ruled by an illegitimate and morally unacceptable government."[6]

To be fair, Evans is absolutely correct in pointing out that although at least some of the government's more influential ministers and MPs hold these beliefs about China, there hasn't been much inclination to address them in terms of actual foreign policy, beyond generally avoiding the perception of being too close to the leadership in Beijing. But Evans is even more concerned about the extreme nature of the views themselves. Later, for example, he worries about the tendency to see China "as international outlier, supporter of odious regimes, assertive irredentist intent on recovering lost territory, and full-throttle challenger of a liberal international order," which, he says, "misrepresents a much more complicated picture."[7] What's most interesting about these views is that, while they appear extreme and dogmatic, they aren't entirely wrong. China *does* support odious regimes, and it *is* a challenger of the liberal international order. That the Communist Party of China is godless, while true, is perhaps less noteworthy than is its deplorable treatment of the many in China who are not.

If there is much to criticize in the standoffish approach that the Conservatives first adopted, the tendency of the Liberals to see China as Canada's new best friend was also off base. Indeed, you could argue that in the Chrétien–Martin era—which in its final stages even saw an effort to link the Liberal Party with the Communist Party of China, much as the Liberals affiliated with other political parties in the democratic world[8]—the assessment was equally unbalanced on the side of unwarranted optimism and uncritical acceptance. Like many others, I was worried by the over-lengthy Harper-era re-evaluation of the relationship. But I also understood that the new government needed to think through some difficult issues. The prime minister was deeply concerned by what he saw as China's deplorable record on human rights. This was brought into sharp relief by the case of a Canadian citizen named Huseyincan Celil, who had been spirited into China and was being held beyond the reach of Canadian consular officials. The prime minister was dug in on this case, driving the system to focus its energies, somewhat belatedly, on an imprisoned Canadian.

My own view is that, as serious as they are, consular disputes need to be addressed on a level other than that of leaders, which represents the main line of the relationship. The trouble is that if you get a no on that level, there is no other court of appeal. And the main line of the relationship is then blocked. Officials need to use every possible means to keep the conversation open. While their ultimate objective is securing freedom, near-term goals include securing better treatment and access to the imprisoned Canadian and his or her family. The main thing, particularly in China, is to avoid a confrontation that yields a decisive no. Prime ministers are driven to get involved in consular cases when they believe that officials aren't doing their jobs on behalf of distressed Canadians, often because of undue deference to foreign sensitivities.

High-level intervention can generate more problems than it solves, but activism on behalf of a fellow Canadian is not the worst thing a prime minister can be accused of.[9] I was also struck by how readily many of the prime minister's critics used lines that were right out of China's playbook. He was, for example, widely criticized for not meekly turning up in Beijing for the opening of the Olympics, when China, fresh from cracking down in Tibet, basked in near-universal praise, something that echoed the tradition of lesser states hurrying to Beijing to pay tribute.

But the reality is that the China policy rethink, while necessary, was sufficiently leaky, messy and drawn out to roil relations and make rapprochement more difficult. Those in the public service who argued for a speedy return to the comfortable, pre-election status quo were seen as the modern equivalent of Diefenbaker's "Pearsonalities," public service holdovers from the Liberal years. But they contributed to this caricature through their own inability to fully respect the concerns that motivated the newly elected government.

It was getting harder to figure out just where we wanted to go. That's because there was no longer any place to have a larger, strategic discussion. This should have happened in the regular meetings of the Cabinet committee responsible for looking at foreign affairs issues. Unfortunately, unlike the Manley panel, which provided hard-nosed but pragmatic advice to the government, official Ottawa, when left to its own devices, was unable to produce a foreign policy plan that survived much beyond its discussion at Cabinet. Every participating department—and there were far too many—had to add its own wish list to the discussion. What emerged were long inventories of what every department wanted to achieve. Far from having a tough discussion about the four or five things that we absolutely needed to get right with China, officials would simply serve up a laundry list of disparate activities, ministers would sign off on the "strategy," and absolutely nothing would change.

I was more than once struck by the fact that on Afghanistan, the government sought and accepted blunt criticism and hard truths from outside experts. They told the prime minister that he had to "own" the file, to which he readily agreed. Then, after consulting Parliament, the government distilled the Manley panel's advice into a new and readily understandable action plan and put in place a mechanism to ensure that it was delivered in a coordinated way by the soldiers and civilians on the ground. As significant as Afghanistan was, China is of vastly more strategic importance to us. Yet we are content to muddle along.

Foreign Affairs was itself unable to do much. The idea of a feisty collaboration between ministers and their officials was dying, if not dead. The department was mainly seen by the new government as a collection of incompetent and politically unreliable people, useful only for carrying out very specific and carefully monitored tasks. Ministers were themselves shielded by vigilant political staffers, the non-public servants who serve as a minister's political antennae. At least one of their number was attached to the Prime Minister's Office and enforced orthodoxy in terms of policy and messages.

What was most bizarre was that while political staffers were suspicious and dismissive when it came to relying on professional advice from Foreign Affairs, they invested the Chinese ambassador in Ottawa with oracular status, even visiting the Chinese embassy on St. Patrick Street to seek his views. He would even accompany our foreign minister on trips to China.

On these visits, meetings would conclude with Canada's foreign minister summing things up with his travelling companion, China's ambassador to Ottawa. Meanwhile, the accompanying officials from Canada's foreign affairs department watched, unconsulted and in silence, as the minister and ambassador worked out follow-up steps.

Typically, the Canadian minister was disarmingly frank in laying out our position, a degree of candour that was never reciprocated. It was as if it was more damning to be suspected of having liberal sympathies than it was to actually be a Communist, and as if the Canadian government was intent on conducting foreign policy without its public service. The exception to this trend was the political staffers in the office of the minister for International Trade, for whom the only consideration was whatever it was they believed, at times wrongly, they had just been instructed to do by the prime minister's office. The result was that they brought to their dealings with Chinese officials the same degree of high-handedness, contradiction and confusion that marked their relations with Canadian officials.

There are reasons why the public service is an essential partner in delivering foreign policy. Quite apart from the fact that public servants provide highly useful expertise and experience, and that so explicitly *not* respecting them causes them to be sidelined and rendered useless, they also provide a degree of distance in dealing with foreign officials. This allows issues to develop, and provides Canadian ministers time to reflect, consider all options, and intervene at a much higher and more decisive level. Throughout my time in China, I was carefully managed by the foreign ministry in Beijing. My access to senior people was strictly rationed and only provided to achieve specific ends, such as the communication of a special request or the delivery of a particularly harsh scolding. And every person I dealt with, at every level, was clearly following the same playbook for dealing with Canada.

Canada's performance wasn't any better coordinated at the Beijing end. When I arrived at the embassy, I was struck almost immediately by the sense that we needed to relearn almost everything we had struggled to get right in Afghanistan. The embassy was little more than convenient office space for a broad range of actors from multiple departments working in almost complete isolation from one another. More than sixty Canadians worked at the embassy in Beijing, drawn from departments including Foreign Affairs, CIDA (which has since been consolidated with Foreign Affairs), National Defence, Agriculture Canada, Natural Resources Canada, the RCMP, the Public Health Agency and the provinces of Alberta, Ontario and Quebec. Many departments that weren't represented at the embassy frequently sent staff to China to pursue projects. Each department jealously guarded its individual China plan. Those departments that had representatives at the embassy expected that they would be completely autonomous, working in isolation on whatever it was that the department saw as a priority. That made it almost impossible for me to promote teamwork in support of larger and more comprehensive Canadian objectives. By way of example, I argued, without much success, that close and careful coordination among a range of departments would be necessary if we were to increase flows of Chinese tourists and students to Canada while at the same time screening out corrupt officials and other unwelcome fugitives. I spent a lot of time on the phone with senior people at a range of departments in Ottawa, explaining how and where we could make greater progress by sharing information and working together.

Within Foreign Affairs itself, the deep divide between the foreign policy people and the trade people (a remnant of a misguided Martin-era divorce) was a huge obstacle. Even among the trade people, individual officers worked directly for highly compartmentalized parts of the headquarters bureaucracy, with budgets that were tightly controlled from the other side of the world.[10]

I quickly came to the conclusion that it was futile for me to try to orchestrate, from my perch in Beijing, the careful thinking about objectives and how to achieve them that had so characterized our work in Afghanistan post-Manley. There wasn't any evident appetite for this, nor was there even a venue for such a conversation. Nobody in Ottawa was playing the coordinating role on China that I had played on Afghanistan. Fortunately, having the prime minister visit just a few months after my arrival in Beijing offered me the focusing lens I needed. The very discipline of preparing for the prime minister's exchanges with China's leaders, of distilling a broad inventory of interests down to our highest priorities, offered a chance for a much-needed reset of the embassy's hitherto incoherent work plan.

My first opportunity came in the form of a lunch with the senior Chinese diplomat He Yafei in the fall of 2009, an event that I described back in Chapter 4. He and his staff had proposed the event to get started on planning Prime Minister Harper's first visit to Beijing. I wanted to get his agreement to the idea of building the visit around a joint statement that Prime Minister Harper and Premier Wen Jiabao could sign. This document would formalize with the Chinese our agreement on four priorities: trade and investment, energy and environment, health, and governance, a category that for us included human rights. Although we had been talking about these topics since the strategic partnership had been mooted in the Martin era, there had been little to no pickup until now. A fifth priority, covering education, would be added during the prime minister's second visit in early 2012.

I had been thinking a lot about just what it was that the Chinese intended when, back in the Martin years, they had described their relationship with Canada as a "strategic partnership." What I came to see is that China needs to define its relationships with other countries. Strategic partners are important countries with which China establishes an agenda for cooperation. That sends a signal to its vast bureaucracy. Chinese officials are expected to meet regularly with their counterparts in countries that have been designated as strategic partners to ensure that the shared agenda gets delivered. Even more important, leaders from both sides meet once a year to update the agenda and add leader-like ambition. I was enthusiastic about this arrangement because it offered me the chance to get through the Ottawa muddle and focus our work with China on a limited number of agreed priorities. The Chinese clearly wanted to use Harper's 2009 visit to get this going.

In my many messages back to Ottawa, I made the point that our evolving agenda with the Chinese needed to be managed in a way that was entirely new to us. We needed to bring energy and ambition to the bilateral agenda, while at the same time remaining realistic about China's capacity and inclination to challenge us. In one meeting with deputy ministers back in Ottawa, I observed that they seemed divided between those who saw China as an opportunity and those who saw it as a threat. I told them that we need to understand that China is both. Closing our doors to China is no more an option than is opening them heedlessly, without safeguards. We need to see China as it is: neither as the sum of all fears nor as a like-minded and benevolent partner. We aren't China's best friend, nor is it ours. But it *is* a vitally important partner that we can't afford to ignore.

Interestingly, the Australians were working on the same track. In 2013, after two years of careful planning and deft diplomatic work, they announced a new strategic partnership with China that built in an annual meeting of leaders along with Cabinet-level consultations on political and economic issues. Unfortunately, we never got that far.

I CAME TO THINK of my time as ambassador as a play in three acts:

Act One consisted of the prime minister's 2009 visit and the follow-up work that we did in its wake. I made it clear that focusing on the unfinished business of the joint statement was the embassy's top priority. There was plenty of work to do. Among other things, we now had to negotiate the implementation of the big tourism agreement that Harper and Wen had announced. I called on the RCMP when I was back in Ottawa to reinforce the importance of our ongoing cooperation in police work. I saw this as critical in reassuring people on both sides that we could safely ramp up the flow of tourists and students from China while preventing Chinese fraudsters from entering Canada.

Duane McMullen, the very talented head of our commercial section, brought new thinking to managing the trade relationship. He argued that we needed to move beyond an approach that was largely passive, lumbering along with little intensity until a Canadian product or producer was unfairly treated by China, at which point we would go into crisis mode. In his view, it was clearly the intent of the prime minister and the premier that we see our trade relationship not as a series of one-off negotiations but as a partnership. He worked with Agriculture Canada and Canadian industry to develop a more patient and consistent process for obtaining market access. Instead of pushing for dramatic home-run announcements, he encouraged the Canadians to advance by hitting singles, moving forward, month by month, with small gains. And, as mentioned previously, we worked much harder at listening respectfully to China's own agenda and doing what we could that was consistent with our own standards. All of this translated into improved access for a range of Canadian products, such as beef, pork and canola.

We also began to lay the groundwork for new and more substantial exchanges in areas such as the environment, as promised in the joint statement. This was relatively easy, given that we could call on the talents of the then environment minister, Jim Prentice, who was keenly interested in China, and whose forthright approach, which included showing interest in the good things that the Chinese were doing, went down well in Beijing.

It was harder to make progress on energy. The Chinese were actually open to having an expanded dialogue that would involve governments, the private sector and academic researchers. They were aware that they didn't know as much about Canada as they needed to. They also understood that addressing this deficit required improving communications between a range of players on both sides. With admirable pragmatism and ambition, they suggested an annual policy conference at which experts from both countries would discuss new technologies, infrastructure plans and constraints, and environmental issues. They were also interested in learning more about the political process—how decisions get made in Canada.

I am convinced that this kind of dialogue could have taken us a long way in building trust and confidence.

It would also have allowed us to signal, early on, where the red lines were for us. But when it came to canvassing for interest, there was little enthusiasm from officials in Natural Resources Canada or from Canadian industry. Not responding creatively at a time when the Chinese were keenly interested would soon cost us. Later, when the government outlined somewhat opaque new regulations relating to investment in the oil sands by state-owned entities, the Chinese were understandably confused. Unfortunately, we had passed up a chance to help them to better understand our concerns.

I was also struck by the degree of interest that China brought to ministerial-level exchanges on health issues. But I thought we needed more creative thinking on the Canadian side about our own interests. In my view, these include identifying emerging health threats in China; developing an inventory of areas where Chinese research might be of interest to us; encouraging links between Canadian and Chinese medical schools; and helping to promote commercial collaboration. My sense is that here, as elsewhere, the Chinese are better at zeroing in on what they want than we are.

The embassy became much more active on human rights, seeing this as the Canadian contribution to the fourth priority, governance. A big part of my job involved connecting CIDA's programs supporting migrants and minority groups, hitherto mostly invisible to Canadians, to the human rights program run out of Foreign Affairs. I wanted to be able to tell a coherent story to people in China and in Canada about *all* the good things Canada was doing and why we were doing them. But for the story to sound coherent, it first had to *be* coherent, which is why I spent so much time trying to encourage people at the embassy to share information and work more closely together. In my own speeches and media interviews, I talked about the actions we were taking on behalf of migrant workers, and made the point that we were doing this in partnership with similarly motivated Chinese agencies. Highlighting such partnerships became a regular part of the narrative we shared with our followers on weibo.

ACT TWO BEGAN for me in the second half of 2010, an auspicious moment in the Canada–China relationship, and a great time to be ambassador. We were marking the fortieth anniversary of the re-establishment of diplomatic relations. It was also the year in which Shanghai held its world's fair, an event at which Canada's pavilion was a must-see for Chinese visitors. And it brought the back-to-back visits of China's President Hu Jintao to Canada and Governor General Michaëlle Jean to China.

Part of the reason for Hu's visit was his participation in the G20 summit in Toronto. But the size and stature of the delegation was intended to send us a message. The Chinese made it clear that they wanted to advance the strategic partnership that the visit of the prime minister had effectively revived the year before. It was an invitation to do the kind of careful, year-to-year planning that the Australians were already engaging in. This was timely. We had made real progress on the agenda that leaders had set, but we hadn't yet put in place a mechanism for managing the process consistently on the Canadian side.

President Hu and the prime minister launched a number of the initiatives that had been promised in the joint statement. Most notably, the technical details underpinning the big tourism agreement having been wrapped up before the visit, our door was now open to mass tourism from China. And they also helped set a forward agenda. The most important part of this came when, in their working meeting, Hu and Harper tasked officials to work together to come up with ideas for deepening the economic relationship. This was widely seen as code for determining whether conditions were right for exploring a free trade agreement, something about which the Chinese had begun to send out cautious feelers.

The visit was also notable for the fact that Hu made explicit China's willingness to negotiate a loan to Canada of two pandas. This was perhaps the most misunderstood of the announcements. It certainly meant that we were formally back in China's good books. Indeed, China engages in what amounts to panda diplomacy, using the promise of a panda deal as means of rewarding friendly countries or wooing countries that it wants to become friendly. Pandas are one of the few soft power cards China has to play, one of the few things that absolutely everybody, everywhere likes about the country. Since pandas are only found in China, and since it insists that any babies that happen to be born in foreign zoos remain Chinese property, this isn't going to change anytime soon. But what the offer meant in practical terms was that officials on the Chinese and Canadian sides were now free to work out the appropriate details necessary to secure the loan. Barring an almost unimaginable screw-up (something that became all too imaginable), a pair of Canada-bound pandas would emerge from this process.

This agreement was, not surprisingly, seen by the political people in Ottawa as a major coup, but it also generated enormous confusion. Over the next eighteen months, I would do my best, often unsuccessfully, to discourage visiting ministers from asking the increasingly confused Chinese to agree to the loan. I would explain that the Chinese already *had* agreed to begin discussions, but that, like the tourism agreement of 2009, we would have months of tough technical negotiations—about questions such as where and how the pandas would be housed, what would happen to any offspring born during the Canadian sojourn (as noted, they belong to China) and, importantly, what the financial terms would be—before the final deal was signed. The main thing was to ensure that the Canadian zoos could put together a package that would satisfy those Chinese officials charged with sending pandas overseas and, most important, getting them back again.

The main complication on the Canadian side was that we had not one but three zoos in the negotiations, resulting in a multi-year, multi-zoo proposal that was entirely new to the Chinese. The discussions got a bit easier when one of the three zoos, the one in Granby, Quebec, dropped out, leaving Toronto and Calgary negotiating two back-to-back five-year terms. That worked better for the Chinese, who were concerned about moving the pandas around so much, and who generally worked on the basis of a ten-year agreement. It was also a smart move for the Canadians. While pandas are a huge draw, they are also very expensive to acquire and maintain. The finance manager at the Toronto Zoo estimates that the pandas are costing the zoo $1.8 million per year.[11] That includes an annual payment to China, which is normally set at $1 million. The Canadian zoos figured that the pandas would more than pay for their keep over five years. But they were less sure about the economics of a longer stay as the novelty wore off.

The embassy worked hard at helping the Canadian zoos understand which officials were central to getting a final yes from the Chinese government and which ones were simply along for the ride as a perk for some past service. We were dealing with a confusing array of Chinese organizations, so this advice was important. We also helped to reassure the Chinese as the nature of the Canadian proposal shifted over time. While the Chinese did not feel particularly constrained about changing details on their side, any change on our side (and to be fair, there were quite a few changes, most frustratingly around when the project would actually commence) created opportunities for the Chinese to appear perplexed, pause and make the most of our apparent vulnerability. Fortunately, one of the most senior Chinese officials had done some of her professional training in Canada, and served as a calm and reliable court of final appeal.

At one point, visiting minister Jim Prentice gave an optimistic update about the project to a travelling reporter from the *Calgary Herald*. During his time in Beijing, Prentice had actually enabled us to advance on some technical issues and, by visiting one of China's struggling national parks, win some important new friends. But the article once again confused an Ottawa that was all too easily confused. I returned to Canada for meetings only hours after the minister had himself departed. That meant that I touched down in Vancouver just as his interview was being digested in Ottawa. I turned on my BlackBerry to find dozens of "urgent" messages about pandas. Had the deal been signed? Were the pandas already being crated for their journey? Why hadn't I prepared anybody for this major development? I explained that absolutely nothing had changed. The Chinese had simply (and patiently) once again confirmed that, pending successful completion of technical negotiations, they would approve the loan.

While I was frustrated about how much prominence the project had for Ottawa—and I kept a plastic panda on my desk as a reminder of this—I wasn't completely unsympathetic. On one occasion, I bumped into a Beijing-based correspondent for a Canadian TV network at a local airport in far-off Sichuan province. Since he was always complaining about how tight-fisted his network was with travel funds, I asked him why his bosses had relented. He told me that he was covering a panda event, which was just about the only China story that could be counted on to attract large numbers of viewers in panda-crazy Canada. His editors had let him know that he had carte blanche to travel anywhere to cover any story in China—as long as it had a panda in it.

FOR A FEW memorable minutes during the Ottawa visit, President Hu's impassive poker face gave way to animation. It came during the call by the president on his actual host, the governor general. Hu, as president, is China's head of state. That means that his official counterpart in Canada is the governor general (who is delegated to act in this capacity by the queen). The prime minister's official counterpart is China's premier, although Canadian PMs typically call on both the president and the premier during their visits to China. The Chinese can actually be quite fussy about this distinction now, although this was not always the case.

As a young foreign service officer in Shanghai, I was a bit player in the negotiations around the 1986 visit of the then governor general, Jeanne Sauvé. It was the first trip to China by someone holding that office, and the Chinese were genuinely confused. They seemed to understand that there was a person delegated to represent the queen in Canada (although the very fact of our continuing ties to the Crown was itself amazing to them), but what authority did this person have *outside* Canada? That's actually a good question, but we asked the Chinese to forego the constitutional Q&A and simply take our word for it. They did, but allowed themselves the quiet pleasure of appearing mystified from time to time, just to alarm us.

The Chinese were used to our peculiar ways by 2010, and Hu and his delegation duly accepted the invitation to join Governor General Michaëlle Jean for lunch at her residence, Rideau Hall, in Ottawa. Pomp and ceremony Canadian-style is impressive but is offered on a much more human scale than in Beijing. After the welcome, guests went in to a lunch that was enlivened with songs and dances by artists from Canadian Aboriginal communities. It was evident that the governor general was giving Hu a spirited play-by-play explanation. And it was equally evident that he was enjoying it. As dessert was being served, Hu got up and delivered an impromptu (a word never previously associated with him) thank you, complete with his promise of a warm welcome for Jean and her delegation on the return visit to China that they would be making in the next week.

He stayed true to his word. When I rushed back to China to zero in on the final preparations for the visit, my embassy colleagues told me that the Chinese organizers had already promised that we could have *anything* we wanted. So we used the trip, and Jean's impressive skills as a communicator, to highlight the human side of the relationship. The governor general amazed students at Shanghai's elite Fudan University with her frank comments about her early struggles as an immigrant in Canada. In the southern city of Guangzhou, her meeting with young migrant workers, all women, featured more of the same. The young women were nervous and tongue-tied until Jean built a bridge to them by speaking of her own experience. They ended up sharing their stories and speaking frankly about their ambitions for a better life. It was necessarily a private session, but the fact that it happened enabled us to talk publicly about our efforts to improve the lives of China's migrant workers, something that CIDA had until then been strangely reluctant to do. And we travelled to a town that was only beginning to recover from the devastating 2008 Sichuan earthquake. The governor general met with children, parents and teachers in an attractive new school built with lumber donated by Canada.

That we were operating under new and unfamiliar rules was evident to me more than once. Chinese protocol officers, like their counterparts the world over, are sticklers for punctuality. This was not the governor general's strong suit. At the end of a long and busy day at the Shanghai Expo, I waved off calls for the delegation to get moving because I could see that Jean and her husband were finally enjoying a private conversation. Protocol cut me some slack and moved away. About five minutes later, my colleague Owen Teo, the main organizer of the visit, pulled me aside to explain that some five hundred police had for some time been blocking off Shanghai's famous Bund, the waterfront thoroughfare at the heart of the city, for our return trip. I got the wagons rolling.

The last event of the visit was a small dinner with President Hu. I had become confident enough to assume that this was the only event for which we absolutely had to be on time. Even the most senior

Chinese officials lose their cool if you fail to appear within fifteen minutes of the start of a meeting with state leaders, including people several ranks below Hu. Guests are parked in elegant holding rooms so that the event can begin at precisely the appointed time. The closing dinner was only steps away from where the governor general was staying, but it was evident that she was again running late. The fifteen-minute mark passed, then ten, then five as I paced in the lobby. The people I had sent up to knock on the door of the vice-regal suite all returned unaccompanied. Visits fail because of less than this. I looked over nervously at the Chinese chief of protocol. But, to my amazement, he appeared to be completely relaxed, contemplating the sunset. Sensing my growing despair, he turned to me and said, "Don't worry, he *likes* her."

ACT THREE of my China posting opened over the next months. I used the afterglow of the two big visits to maintain momentum and ambition. I was starting a campaign to have education listed as a bilateral priority. This would see it added to the priority topics that leaders discuss in their precious and limited time together. While education is a provincial responsibility in Canada, the steady flow of incoming students from China is having a national, coast-to-coast impact. I wanted to develop this trend, but I was even more interested in encouraging a flow in the opposite direction. I wanted to see if we could aspire to something like President Obama's 2009 call for a hundred thousand young Americans to travel to China to study over the next four years. This seemed to me a wonderful example of government leadership, of helping to prepare a country for its future.

I was also encouraged by the fact that the Chinese were now sending subtle signals about being open to discussing free trade. I thought the best way of testing their seriousness was by pushing for a conclusion to our negotiation of a Foreign Investment Promotion and Protection

Agreement (FIPA), something that had been languishing for more than a decade. We try to put a FIPA in place with our most important investment partners. Given the deficiencies of the investment environment in China, this was clearly a Canadian objective, something that would provide a modest but useful levelling of the playing field.

Any aspirations for regularizing an annual exchange of high-level visits were set back by the election of May 2, 2011, in Canada. A pause during and immediately after an election is completely understandable. Once an election is called, the normal business of government stops. Official travel by the prime minister and Cabinet ministers comes to a standstill. But for us, the pause lasted long after the ballots were counted. The prime minister didn't return to China until early 2012.

I WAS WRAPPING UP my Christmas holidays in the last days of 2011 when I got word that the prime minister had been invited to visit China in early February. Not only was that a perilously short period within which to pull things together but also our planning time was further reduced by the fact that Chinese New Year, when all of China shuts down completely for more than a week, would fall just before the visit. And although we had been assured that Ottawa would keep the visit as simple as possible given the limited planning time available, it quickly morphed into a hugely ambitious undertaking. Multiple ministers were to accompany the prime minister, and each would lead delegations that would link up with the official party at various stops on the agenda.

When I sat down to discuss preparations with my Chinese counterparts, they made it clear that we should again be ambitious in thinking about the forward agenda. But I also wanted to be sure that we had completed some important unfinished business, things that would help guide our ambition. I went back to Ottawa to request a special effort on two files. The first involved covering the remaining ground on our negotiation of a FIPA. Although the working-level Chinese negotiators were still dug in, I believed that we could overcome these obstacles if we deployed a senior negotiating team in the days before Chinese New Year.

I was similarly confident about efforts to negotiate amendments to the Canada–China Nuclear Cooperation Agreement. This would allow for sales of Canadian uranium, a development of major importance to suppliers in Saskatchewan and an important new element in our growing energy relationship with China. But we first needed to ensure that the Chinese agreed to safeguards sufficient to confirm that Canadian-origin uranium was restricted to civil (rather than military) use. We still had some ground to cover, but here again I felt that an eleventh-hour push would enable us to get a deal. The teams were deployed, and when the Chinese New Year break arrived, we were within striking range of success on both agreements. But the Chinese were unable to give us the green light until several days after they had emerged from their New Year's break. As it turned out, it wasn't until I greeted the deplaning prime minister that I could confirm that we had secured both deals.

The visit was to include a stop in Chongqing, where the prime minister would announce the successful conclusion of our panda negotiations in the presence of one of the two Canada-bound animals. This deal, too, had only been concluded on the eve of the PM's arrival. And by the time of the visit, both governments had agreed to elevate education as a priority focus of the relationship. The Chinese had also begun to step up a campaign for moving quickly to free trade negotiations. They noted that since leaders would be presented with the report, commissioned during President Hu's 2010 visit, on prospects for deepening economic relations, we now had an ideal opportunity to move forward. I was surprised by the intensity of Chinese interest and the uncharacteristic openness of their top negotiators in playing this card.

It was highly likely that interest in Canada had risen considerably because of Chinese concerns about the Trans-Pacific Partnership (TPP), the U.S.-led effort to build a trans-Pacific free trade agreement on the foundations of existing deals among smaller players. Significantly, the agreement did not include China,[12] an omission that stoked Chinese fears of being marginalized by the United States and its allies. Opening negotiations with Canada (and concluding long-standing negotiations with Australia[13]) would, in Chinese thinking, provide a defence against being isolated.

IN 1241, A MONGOL ARMY reached the gates of Vienna. But instead of pressing their advantage, the hitherto all-conquering horde mysteriously turned their horses around and rode back to Asia. For some reason this scene comes to mind when I think back to the prime minister's 2012 visit. It represented something of a high-water mark in our multi-year re-engagement with China. But instead of boldly carrying on through gates that were opening before us, we turned around and left the field. The Mongols made their decision on learning of the death of the great Khan. We lacked a similarly dramatic rationale. Instead of outlining an ambitious agenda with China for the months ahead, we simply downed tools and moved on to other projects and partnerships in Asia and beyond. China's expression of interest in pursuing free trade negotiations was left hanging in the air. It was almost as if the effort to re-engage had never happened.

Nothing was said to me about this, but it was immediately evident that Ottawa's enthusiasm for the relationship had decreased dramatically. There was little response from the system when it came to following up on the opportunities the visit had created. It was quickly clear that China was not the priority that it had been only weeks before. My guess—and a guess it remains—is that the politicians in Ottawa felt that our effort to engage China was taking us beyond the comfort zones of many Canadians. China's eagerness to push toward free trade spooked people. That concern only increased with the announcement of the bid by China National Offshore Oil Corporation to acquire ownership of Nexen of Calgary. For every Canadian who visited China and felt he or she had seen a golden future, there were many more at home who, already worried about the implications of China's rise, had no desire to see Canada more closely linked to the PRC.

Much of my time was spent trying to ensure that no bridges were burned or lasting damage done. Because nothing had been communicated to Canadian officials, much less to the Chinese, it was difficult to get the message right. At the best of times, only a portion of what is decided by ministers and their political advisors is clearly transmitted to public servants. But when all transmissions cease, safe navigation becomes far more difficult. Of course, if my suspicions are correct, it would have been a very difficult message to communicate. Chinese officials rarely understand, much less sympathize with, the idiosyncrasies of our political system. Suggesting to the Chinese that we needed to take a break would have simply meant that we would forfeit our favourable position among China's partners. Which is what happened in any event.

The Chinese, like most people, set more store by actions (or, in our case, a lack of action) than words. They duly noted our cold shoulder on free trade and our decision, made in the context of the Nexen takeover, to limit future investments from their state-owned enterprises. They waited patiently while the FIPA languished in legislative limbo in Canada. And they filled their dance card with visits from other, more clearly interested leaders. Canadian ministers still visited China and made polite statements about the strength of the relationship, but the reality is that we had opted out, stepped back and recommenced our flavour-of-the-month diplomacy. In 2013, the government's crowning economic success was a free trade agreement with the E.U., no small achievement. In 2014, we signed a deal with South Korea. No one seemed to notice that there was a China-sized hole in our trade policy.

This is not to suggest that if we had been more attentive to the relationship with China, the way ahead would have been smooth and problem free. On the contrary, my strong sense is that most democracies tend to have cyclical relationships with China, in which friendly and positive periods alternate with unfriendly and difficult times. This is due to the fundamental differences between China and the West and the inevitability of conflict on important issues. The likelihood of friction is increasing as China becomes more globally active and as more people travel back and forth between our societies.

Britain and France were recently in China's bad books following high-profile visits to both countries by the Dalai Lama. Australia had to endure the troubling prosecution by China of an Australian business person accused of stealing state secrets. As previously noted, Norway continues to be the subject of Chinese ire because a committee nominated by the Norwegian parliament awarded the Nobel Peace Prize to Chinese dissident Liu Xiaobo. Given the inevitability of conflicts and periods of discord with China, it is even more important to use the good times as periods of construction during which we put in place the infrastructure of agreements and exchanges on which relationships between countries depend. Such infrastructure can't prevent the bad periods, but by providing more opportunities for communication and negotiation, it can make the dips shorter and less steep.

The idea is not to ignore fundamental differences or to acquiesce in the face of Chinese bad behaviour, but to find the means to manage through the difficulty. The summer of 2014 brought allegations that Chinese hackers had attacked computers at National Research Council Canada. This was followed within days by the deeply troubling detention of a Canadian couple living near China's border with North Korea. These were very clear signals that the latest positive phase in the relationship—that long period of upward momentum that began in the year or so before Prime Minister Harper's 2009 visit to Beijing—was over.

I am not at all sure that any action on our part would have made the Chinese less likely to spy on us, or any less inclined to take such an inexplicably cruel step against the two Canadians. The inescapable conclusion is that we need to work harder at creating opportunities to address these and other problems that will inevitably emerge in our relationship with such a complicated and often intensely frustrating partner. That process appears to be underway. Finally getting around to ratifying the FIPA in September 2014, two and a half years after the agreement was signed, probably didn't win us much goodwill in Beijing. But at least it got us talking to the Chinese, and it made it easier to schedule the official visit to China that Prime Minister Harper made in advance of the APEC meeting in Beijing in November 2014.

The November 2014 trip to Beijing went some way toward reanimating the Canada–China relationship at the highest level. It brought agreements that point to the resumption, after two and a half years of inactivity, of work on building the infrastructure for a more sophisticated and durable relationship. Leaders announced that Canada would be home to one of the first banking operations in the Americas for clearing commercial contracts in China's currency, the renminbi (RMB). Previously, Canadian companies active in China had been required to go through a costly, two-step process, converting their contracts first into U.S. dollars and then into RMB. In addition to being more convenient and economical for Canadian business, the agreement also advances a Chinese agenda for internationalizing its currency, part of the larger process of Chinese economic reform.

In addition, Prime Minister Harper and Premier Li Keqiang also agreed to what they termed the Foreign Affairs Ministers Dialogue and the Canada–China Economic and Financial Strategic Dialogue. These will be launched in 2015 and will alternate on a regular basis between China and Canada. This picks up on the notion of strategic partnership that the Chinese have consistently offered to us.

While these are indeed welcome developments, it remains to be seen whether they signal a complete resumption of the upward momentum in the relationship that was evident until early 2012, or simply the minimum in terms of ambition in a year in which China's hosting APEC made it necessary for the prime minister to visit Beijing. One thing is clear: although it is gratifying to have re-engaged China after more than two years of inactivity, we have in that time fallen even further behind Australia, which concluded negotiations with China on a free trade agreement—in time for Xi Jinping's November 2014 visit to Canberra.

Another way of assessing the impact of the recent visit is to ask whether Canada now truly intends to manage its relationship with China at the strategic level. This is something that would be evident from the following: First, the prime minister would need to make it clear that he "owns" the relationship, or, in other words, that he takes responsibility for leading it. High-level leadership is necessary if we are to achieve clarity around the key objectives Canada absolutely needs to get right in its relationship with China. And while the relationship should necessarily have an array of important working parts—mechanisms such as the regular foreign policy and economic dialogues agreed to during the prime minister's 2014 visit to Beijing—overall direction and coordination should be left to leaders on both sides, much as China's relationship with Australia is.

Second, Canada's public service should be deployed creatively and extensively to advance our objectives, under the direction of the ministers most central to the relationship. Public servants would be expected and encouraged to share with their political masters their best professional advice about how to make progress toward key objectives, as well as how to deal with the inevitable challenges that come with closer links with China.

Third, a truly strategic policy approach would also be characterized by serious investment in our military assets to ensure that we can be more active in Asia when it comes to such matters as combatting piracy, responding to humanitarian disasters, and training. We would also continue to invest in the people and technology needed to enhance cyber-security and discourage Chinese interference in Canadian society.

Finally, a strategic engagement of China would also be distinguished by efforts to inform and engage Canadians. This would involve regular messages from the prime minister and key ministers as to why such a policy approach is necessary and in our interest. It would also involve efforts to engage the provinces, municipalities, the private sector, academics and NGOs in the difficult process of getting this right.

However you look at it, it is hard to argue against a policy that encourages far greater attention to China, much more regular communications with its leaders, a deeper and richer network of exchanges and agreements, and a far more sophisticated ability to identify and mitigate the risks that come with closer engagement. This will require a level of sophistication in terms of foreign policy development and delivery that is rare for Canada. We will need to think much more clearly about what we want from the relationship and what we don't want. We will also have to lift our game when it comes to deploying all the foreign policy assets and instruments available to us intelligently and purposefully. In other words, we need to bring to the management of our relationship with China the kind of urgency and intensity that we ultimately brought to our mission in Afghanistan. The stakes are far, far higher with China, given how central it is to our security, prosperity and well-being. There is no excuse for not bringing a similar level of focus to what amounts to *the* major foreign policy challenge on our horizon.

Connecting the Dots

The rise of China represents a wake-up call for Canada. As citizens of a globally engaged middle power, we need to understand that no country other than the United States is now more important to us than China in determining whether, to borrow the words of Gareth Evans, "the world is to be safer, saner, more just and more prosperous."[1] And even when we focus more narrowly on our own, Canadian future, China is second only to the U.S. in terms of its impact on our prosperity, security and well-being.

The first and possibly the biggest challenge we face is in seeing China as it is, and not through the prism of our wildest fears or fondest hopes. We shouldn't demonize China, nor should we naively confer on it the status of being just like us. We should certainly acknowledge China's economic dynamism, and its growing political power and influence. But we should also be aware of its many problems, from demographic decline to environmental degradation. And we need to think clearly about the extent to which a culture of corruption, impunity and self-interest has eroded the Communist Party's hold on power.

We need to be alive to positive change in China: small but encouraging trends in governance at the grassroots level, modest but discernible improvements in the tolerance of dissent, and efforts to improve

China's performance as a development donor and as a partner in global climate talks. But at the same time, we need to remain concerned about China's backsliding on human rights cases, about its assertiveness in its East Asian region and about its interference in our own affairs. We need to acknowledge that it is a rising but insecure China, and not an increasingly feeble Russia, that poses the greatest challenge to global security over the long term. And we need to banish the tendency to believe that China will become a responsible stakeholder if we simply pretend it is one already. Above all, we need to be willing to stand up for values that China is now challenging. Our sympathy for China's very different culture and history should not lead us to abandon belief in the universality of basic human rights. We need to remind ourselves that such belief isn't simply a by-product of consensus at the UN, that it flows from deeply held convictions about the dignity of every human being.

We also need to think clearly about future scenarios for China. We need not accept that its continuing rise is inevitable or that it can or will continue to grow at the pace that it has over the last three decades. But we do need to understand that China is already so big that even its stumbles or missteps will have an impact on us. We can't afford not to pay attention. My sense is that China will face a growing array of challenges because it has for too long put off any real effort to embrace political reform. But I also think that, despite these challenges, China will muddle through, and that we will continue to feel the effects of its exciting, exuberant, chaotic and messy evolution.

Canadians tend to fall into three broad categories when it comes to thinking about China. The first comprises people who either aren't aware of or aren't particularly concerned about what's happening. The second group is aware of China's growing significance, but wishes it wasn't happening. For these people, denial or avoidance is the preferred option. And then there are some who are aware, and who believe that things are all for the good. They are confident that just as our American bus seems to be breaking down, we can hop on a speedy and comfortable Chinese vehicle instead. We should be wary of such undue optimism. Canada has grown and prospered in a largely American world. Despite many differences across the 49th parallel, people in both countries share a faith in democratic governance, rule of law and, if only as a longer-term objective, the universality of basic human rights. Canadians also continue to be sheltered and protected by American power and influence, a fact that should engender our gratitude and remind us that our success and prosperity have been enabled thanks to an American-influenced world order. Even if China never becomes the dominant global actor, a world in which it is steadily more influential and powerful will almost inevitably be more challenging and, at times, uncomfortable for us.

We need to encourage an entirely different school of thought, what I call "China realism." We need to acknowledge China's growing importance to us, and accept the fact that this creates both opportunities and challenges. We should see China neither as the sum of all fears nor as the answer to all our prayers. We need to see China steadily and see it whole, its dynamism and innovation, its aggressiveness and insecurity. And we need to craft an intelligently self-interested, thoughtful and long-term approach to the relationship.

While it would be nice to think that a more pragmatic, long-term and realistic approach to engaging China will emerge from grassroots thinking and activism, the indications are that this simply isn't happening. Polling suggests that we are increasingly anxious about Asia in general and China in particular, and are as a result more inclined to favour non-engagement with both.[2] Governments are picking up on this. If the past is anything to go by, foreign policy innovation in Canada requires leadership from the top down as well as activism from the bottom up. Pierre Trudeau was not alone in seeing the importance of having a full, official relationship with mainland China, but it would not have happened when it did without him. Similarly Brian Mulroney wasn't the only person in Canada to be concerned about apartheid, nor was he even the first. But his leadership, including his formidable powers of persuasion, animated and energized our outreach to the forces of change in South Africa. For John Manley and his colleagues, the *sine qua non* of getting to a clear, achievable and worthy Canadian engagement in Kandahar was ensuring that the prime minister ultimately owned the strategy. That Stephen Harper readily accepted this role made a huge difference.

We could use some of the leadership that Pierre Trudeau displayed in inspiring Canadians to engage a China whose Mao-era ideology was justifiably feared. Trudeau understood that we simply had to get on with the task of navigating a world in which China was becoming more influential. Prime ministerial leadership on China has two principal objectives. The first and most important is to encourage a conversation among Canadians about the opportunities, the risks and the options available to us. Far from being a one-off, this requires ongoing dialogue. We can wait until a coming economic or security crisis makes this conversation urgent and inevitable. Or we can embark on it now, when options are more numerous and when we can play a greater role in influencing outcomes.

The second objective of prime ministerial leadership involves ensuring that we have the ability to engage China effectively, to aspire to the kind of purposeful and sophisticated foreign policy required of serious countries. No small task, this involves changing government itself, encouraging a degree of focus and coordination that is rarely otherwise achieved. We need to bring to our engagement of China the competent resolve that we eventually brought to the mission in Afghanistan, a country of far less strategic importance to us.

Job one in this respect is to bring clarity around a very short list of priorities. This is a challenge, given the propensity of large bureaucracies to complicate rather than simplify. Why not focus on achieving a limited number of important objectives under the headings that we have already agreed on with China—trade and investment, energy and environment, health, governance and education? This would mean that a limited number of ministers are key to moving the agenda forward. And nothing motivates ministers more than the instructions embedded in the "mandate" letters that they receive from the prime minister. Ideally, these should be focused on key objectives and should bring needed clarity to the division of labour on shared files.

This collective work would be organized under a single China committee of Cabinet chaired by the foreign minister under the ever-watchful eye of the prime minister.[3] While the committee's objectives would at times include measurable achievements, such as opening the Chinese market to a particular product or securing China's agreement on an issue of importance to Canada, they would also include building the infrastructure of agreements and exchanges that a successful relationship with China requires. At the APEC meetings of November 2014, we took the first step in this process, agreeing to schedule regular meetings of Chinese and Canadian ministers responsible for foreign and economic affairs. But we should also strive, like Australia, to make such exchanges add-ons to annual meetings at the level of leaders, people who have the perspective to see the big picture and who have the authority to ensure that the right connections get made.

This includes thinking about the essential connections between our relationship with an increasingly powerful China and our middle-power aspirations for a better world. Our diplomacy should, for example, include much smarter engagement with China on broader, global issues, such as climate change. We have a big stake in ensuring that China continues to add ambition to its goals for combatting growth in greenhouse gas emissions. It would help, of course, if our own record on the environment were more commendable. But simply being more aware of China's huge and growing impact on the planet's air and water would be a start. It doesn't make much sense for Canada to crusade at the UN to protect the world's oceans when our ocean-related conversation with a hugely influential global player like China is largely about persuading them to buy seal meat.

We should also be approaching China with ideas for development assistance in Africa. And we could go much further than we have in working with China to curb illegal financial flows, many of which now originate in China. We need to work closely with China on issues relating to global health, food safety and the protection of endangered species. And we need the courage and confidence to challenge China when it comes to a growing global debate about respect for free speech, rule of law and religious freedom.

While we should support China's inclusion and participation at the heart of global governance, meaning in institutions such as the G20 and the UN, we should not delude ourselves into thinking that China will play by the same rules that we do or work to achieve the same objectives. We should also have clearer expectations about the responsibilities that come with China's larger role. We need to treat China with respect, but not with deference. Effective diplomacy does not preclude being willing and able to challenge and disagree. If anything, our experience with the G20 should lead us to value the G7 (meaning the G8 without Russia) more, not less. The G7 offers a rare and welcome opportunity for dialogue among democratically elected leaders. It is always a bad idea to appear to be conspiring against China, something that only fuels its insecurity. But it is also wrong to look on passively as China methodically limits the international space available to the Dalai Lama, as it bullies the Vatican and the Nobel Committee, and as it pushes a highly selective and self-interested gospel of non-interference. The G7 is an effective place for thinking more carefully about what the international community owes China and what it has the right to expect of China. (At the very least, we might want to use it to stiffen our collective spines and resist competing with one another to curry favour in Beijing.) In their recent book *Brave New Canada*, authors Derek H. Burney and Fen Osler Hampson take this thinking a step further, encouraging Canadians to bypass the G7/G8 entirely. They advocate the formation of a "D10," an idea originally developed by the U.S. State Department. The D10 would be a new global grouping with a membership restricted to the largest and most capable democracies.[4]

We also need to be willing and able to contest the challenge to some of our basic values that a confident, activist China, eager to reshape the existing international order, is beginning to mount. We should be particularly vocal in countering the argument, attractive to dictators everywhere, that economic development, however long it takes, is an alternative to the emergence of fundamental democratic rights. This is not to suggest that we ignore natural differences of emphasis and approach, or that we advocate destabilizing revolutionary change. But we need to combat the notion that even the first steps in terms of political reform should be put off for a tomorrow that never comes. Of course, we need to do this carefully and respectfully, particularly in relation to China itself. Hugh White offers a useful reminder about the difference between "criticising a government's policies and actions and contesting that government's essential authority."[5]

Most of all, we should remain conscious of the fact that China is not monolithic, that it is home to a diversity of views and beliefs and an encouraging variety of what I call constituencies for change. Offering generous scholarships and exchanges to lawyers and judges, journalists, activists, police and other government officials is a smart investment in the future, and much closer to what China's true "best friends" would do.

A previous Australian government wisely endowed academic research into the economic consequences for Australia of China's rise. We could certainly benefit from research that helps us better understand how China's global assertiveness influences Canadian security. We also need to better understand the implications of China's global quest for energy, its growing influence on global food markets and prices, and its influence on global health and the environment. And we should focus much more intently on the extent to which China's exuberant and footloose citizens are shaping trends in tourism, education and residential real estate. It would be interesting to create a virtual institute, funding research at universities across Canada. A big part of this would include welcoming the top international specialists for each topic to come to Canada to share their ideas, with a particular focus on welcoming China's own academic stars.

NOT ALL OF OUR DELIBERATIONS in Canada about managing the relationship should be shared with the Chinese. We need to have a sophisticated understanding of possible security threats emanating from China, whether they be an increase in Chinese military assertiveness, or a lengthening of China's reach into Canada to appropriate technology or intimidate Canadians. We can contribute to our own security, and to the security of our region, by being part of broader efforts to manage China's peaceful rise on terms that are acceptable to us and our allies. But that is going to take a larger investment in our navy than is currently on the books. Being able to deploy ships to the Pacific is central to Canada's aspiration to play a more significant role in Asia. It also effectively pushes out the defence of our own coastline to the places where many of the threats originate. But most important, our naval presence in the region, alongside allies such as Australia, can contribute to defusing what is now a tense Sino-American standoff. We need to make it clear that many countries, and not just the United States, have a stake in promoting a safe, cooperative and rules-based Asia Pacific region. To do this, we need to communicate (and truly believe) that we are prepared to accommodate China's growing presence, so long as this is managed cooperatively.

Taking such a step will require a high degree of political courage, because we also need to be aware of very real threats to our domestic security emanating from China. But this needs to be combined with a heavy infusion of realism. Having our security agencies simply warn Canadians about hacking or espionage isn't sufficient, nor is advising us to close our doors particularly practical. We need to be able to deter as well as detect. That's a lot harder to do, but simply making the effort, and making it clear that we are both vigilant and willing to act, raises the cost and risk to China of mounting operations against us. Our recent decision to call China on its aggressive cyber-espionage was a step in the right direction.

There will be many other times when we need to manage and mitigate. Being clear with Chinese technology companies about our security concerns and requiring them to cover the cost of confidence-building procedures before approving their investment proposals is one approach that the British are already applying. But we also need to do much more sophisticated risk analysis. This includes thinking more carefully about the cost of barriers to people-to-people exchanges, and eliminating impediments that don't actually make us any safer. If the people promoting greater tourist and student flows from China need to make their case, so do the border guardians who often make this more difficult.

AUSTRALIA RECENTLY CONDUCTED extensive consultations across the country that resulted in an impressive white paper titled *Australia in the Asian Century*. It was a blueprint for helping Australia become more capable of cooperating—and competing—with its Asian neighbours. Much of the report dealt with education and included ambitious new targets for training in Asian languages and creating opportunities for young Australians to study and work in Asia. It also pointed to the importance of ensuring that more senior public servants and corporate board members have significant Asia experience. Not too long after the document was issued, Australia had an election that brought the opposition to power. One of the first casualties was the white paper. That's how democracy works. But whether it worked in the best interests of Australian foreign policy is another question. Consensus and continuity are important.

Well before the election, I heard one of the architects of the white paper talk about the project. What he said that caught my attention was that in the earliest days of planning, people agreed on the need to mount a "whole of government" effort. But over time, they began to see this as only part of the solution. They actually needed a "whole of country" effort. That phrase stuck with me as I thought about how we manage our future with China. The federal government is an essential player because of how China works. It can help open doors into an otherwise bewildering Chinese system. Government is also important because a relationship with China needs to be *managed* far more than do relationships with countries that are more like us. Professional advice is needed on big questions of strategy and tactics. But because communications are difficult, and the cultural divide is still wide, getting the small stuff of diplomacy right—matters of tone, gesture and approach—is also essential. We cannot afford to overlook or ignore a capable and deeply experienced foreign service if we are to navigate safely and effectively.

Acknowledging the importance of more truly managing the relationship, and then actually doing just that, will mean reversing a worrying trend. Canada seems to be quietly abandoning the notion that a professional, non-partisan public service is an essential part of our highly successful model of governance. We no longer attach sufficient value to "fearless advice" from highly competent people whose perspective stretches beyond the next election. Let me put it bluntly: we can't get the China relationship right if we leave public servants on the bench and assign the day-to-day management of our diplomacy to non-accountable and intensely partisan political staffers. At the same time, Canadian public servants need to muster both the ability and the courage to deliver fearless advice; they need to be able to see beyond their own organizations to advance larger, Canadian objectives; and they need to display at all times the non-partisan professionalism that inspires trust from their political masters and from the Canadian public they serve.

But the China relationship isn't just the business of Canada's federal government. Provincial and municipal diplomacy matter a great deal. As China struggles with new challenges in health care and the environment, and as demand for safe food products continues to grow, there is scope for far more activism by provincial and municipal leaders from across Canada. Communities everywhere need to think carefully about being open to investment from China and being clear about our expectations. We shouldn't be worried about having high standards for all investors, wherever they come from. Being open and welcoming to Chinese investors doesn't mean pretending that Canada operates like China. Rules and regulations matter and should be clearly communicated and rigorously enforced through inspection and monitoring. Ensuring that local levels of government have an important say on major investment projects encourages investors to do their homework. Smart and evolving Chinese companies will build these higher standards into their business plan. Those who don't do so will, and should, fail.

Likewise, communities need to think about the transformative impact of inflows of Chinese students and tourists. We should indeed acknowledge that education is in many ways a business, but we also need to remember that it is far more than that. We need to pay more attention to quality than quantity, ensuring that the end result is a better educational experience for all students. That is made easier if we are committed to helping foreign students, wherever they come from, acclimatize to Canada in every sense of the word.

We also need to think more carefully about where Canada fits in an exciting new world of Chinese mass tourism. By that I mean being much more attuned to what Chinese travellers actually want. This starts with the obvious: basic services in their own language and at least a few menu options that are familiar. Thinking more creatively about the more rarified tastes of the growing ranks of high-net-worth solo travellers represents the difference between being ahead of the curve as opposed to forever following it.

It's hard to argue that investment from China isn't having at least some impact on real estate markets in our biggest cities. Wealthy Chinese are not the only investors looking to park some money in real estate in destinations that are seen as both secure and desirable. But because of its size, China's impact is almost certainly far greater. This fact should encourage us to have a discussion, either nationally or in our largest cities, about how we get the balance right between providing high-quality affordable housing and encouraging the economic boost that comes from a lively and open real estate market. If such a discussion in turn encourages us to compare notes with other jurisdictions, so that we find creative new ways to keep our cities dynamic and welcoming, prosperous but also affordable, that's even better. And making the effort to get at the actual facts, rather than being guided by anecdotes and urban myths, would be a big improvement.

THAT'S NOT A BAD NOTE on which to end. Looking back, it is striking to see how much of what passes for a national discussion about the implications of China's rise is based on anecdote and emotion. Fear and hope are natural and necessary human responses, but they are not a good basis for policy-making. Deng Xiaoping used to exhort fellow reformers with an aphorism about crossing the river by feeling for the stones. We should be similarly deliberate, ensuring that we have a sound footing on facts. Our foreign policy needs to be founded on a more confident national understanding of China and what its rise means for Canada.

I became even more convinced of this need in the wake of some recent work I did for the Asia Pacific Foundation of Canada, when I co-chaired the study that examined the extent to which we are preparing the next generation of Canadians for a future in which Asia will be steadily more important.[6] We looked at the extent to which training in Asian languages is available across the country. We also considered whether we are offering opportunities for young Canadians to pursue studies, work terms or internships in Asia. And we examined whether we are building Asia into the curriculum, so that all educated Canadians will have at least some exposure to Asia's history, culture and current affairs, and how this relates to Canada.

In doing this, we looked at what's happening in the United States, and further afield in Australia, New Zealand, Germany and France. While we found Canadian islands of progress in places such as Edmonton, Vancouver and Toronto, we found nothing like the sustained and serious efforts mounted in those other countries. Worse, as mentioned above, polling shows that while Canadians agree about the growing importance of Asia, they are not yet willing to see Asia claim much share of the curriculum. We have yet to be convinced that a changing future requires change from us, too. My sense is that this has a lot to do with our ambivalence about the rise of Asia in general and China in particular. It's as if making an effort to better understand China somehow equates to acquiescing in everything China does. On the contrary, making the effort to understand China enables us to manage our side of the relationship more effectively, and gives us more say in shaping our own future.

If we work at understanding China better, we are also likely to have an even more profound respect for its people, a deeper sympathy for what they've been through and a greater admiration for what they are accomplishing now. Such an understanding will also help us to grasp the extent of the problems that China still faces and the tragic inadequacy of some of the solutions that the ruling Communist

Party continues to propose. Here again, we need leadership from the top to connect with determined grassroots commitment and activism. Students, parents and teachers need to hear from federal and provincial leaders that investing in the skills and experience necessary to better understand China is central to managing our Canadian future.[7]

Growing our "China competence" will enable us to respond positively and confidently to the opportunities that are being generated by China's remarkable rise. It will also allow us to better meet and mitigate the challenges that come with this. That's an approach entirely worthy of a skilled partner and a capable middle power.

Epilogue

A s our time in Beijing was drawing to a close, I was busy writing final reports, preparing for the handover of official duties and making farewell calls. After hours, Janet and I were consumed with inventories, travel preparations and goodbyes. But we also rushed out to see a few of the places that we hadn't got around to visiting during the previous three years. At the top of our list was the village of Zhoukoudian, which sits just beyond the sprawl of Beijing. The change is abrupt. You leave behind congested highways and ragged suburbs and enter a cool and leafy park. The place owes its tranquility to the fact that it is a protected cultural site. Here, almost one hundred years ago, scientists found bone fragments that led to the identification of the early human who would be called Peking Man.

A tree-lined avenue leads to the museum. Neatly spaced along the way are signs introducing the most important scientists, Chinese and foreign, from the team that discovered and researched the find. Although we were driving at a good pace, my well-trained ambassadorial eye caught sight of a reference to Canada on one of the signs as we sped by. I went back for a look. The sign introduced me to Dr. Davidson Black, a paleoanthropologist from Toronto. Born in 1884, he grew up with a keen interest in a natural world that was still close at hand. A chilly, late-fall exploration of the wetlands around Toronto's Ashbridges Bay (a pleasant walk from where I write) resulted in a case of rheumatic fever that almost killed him. He survived to pursue a brilliant academic career at the University of Toronto. After graduation, he used his background in anatomy to gain entry into an international community of scientists who were developing the field of comparative anthropology.

Black accepted a position at the relatively new Peking Union Medical College in 1919. At least part of the attraction of the new job for him was being close to the expeditions and fieldwork then being conducted to look for evidence of early human society in Asia. He did not have to go far afield. Black played a key role in identifying a fossil fragment found at a site in nearby Zhoukoudian as being part of the jaw of an early human. He succeeded in obtaining funding from the Rockefeller Foundation to conduct detailed research, and fought hard to maintain that support through the precarious early years of the project. His dedication was rewarded in late 1929 when a virtually complete skull was found at the site, a discovery that generated global interest in the project and a willingness to revise existing thinking about the origins of the human species.

What I found most interesting about the references to Black in China is that he is remembered as much for his efforts to promote the development of Chinese scholarship and research capacity as he is for his own work. He was a generous colleague and took pains to ensure that work on the fossils was conducted in China rather than entirely in the West. Describing Black's collaboration with his local team, a Chinese colleague paid him a tribute that was even rarer then than it is today: "He [Black] forgot altogether about their nationality or race because he realized that science was above such artificial and accidental things."[1] His Chinese colleagues also admired his amazing work ethic and rare dedication. Black died at his desk in Beijing in the spring of 1934.

There is no escaping the fact that China's rise will have an impact on Canada. We can't choose to opt out or to evade our share of what is a global phenomenon. But we can decide to respond calmly and intelligently, and with generosity and openness rather than with fear or suspicion. This will challenge us, but we should remember that we have some history with China. Despite our modest size, we've made a real difference there. Canada has produced heroic doctors such as Omar and Retta Kilborn, Norman Bethune and Jessie McDonald; dedicated missionaries spanning the spectrum of orthodoxy from Father John McGoey to James Gareth Endicott; and, albeit not often enough, political leaders such as Pierre Trudeau, who have helped us to see that our foreign policy is incomplete without a thoughtful engagement of China. At our very best, we've brought to the relationship the tolerance, respect and sense of shared purpose of a Davidson Black. These qualities aren't consigned to history. They are quintessentially Canadian. We need to call on them again.

Notes

Preface

1. Hennessy, Peter. *Whitehall*. New York: Free Press, 1989. 5.
2. From Conrad, Joseph. Epigraph. *The Shadow-Line*. 1917. Toronto: Vintage, 2007. 13.
3. Leys, Simon. *Chinese Shadows*. New York: Viking, 1977. 103.

Prologue

1. "Room for Growth." *Financial Times*. 23 July 2013. www.ft.com/intl/cms/s/0/ 5c0f6f74-f3ab-11e2-942f-00144feabdc0.html#slide3.

ONE: A Middle Power in Middle Age

1. Evans, Gareth. "Middle Power Diplomacy." Chile Pacific Foundation. Santiago, Chile. 29 June 2011. Inaugural Edgardo Boeninger Memorial Lecture. www .gevans.org/speeches/speech441.html.
2. Andrew, Arthur. *The Rise and Fall of a Middle Power*. Toronto: James Lorimer & Company, 1993. 41.
3. Slater, Joanna. "Canada Abandons UN Bid in Embarrassing Turn for Harper." *Globe and Mail*. 12 Oct. 2010. www.theglobeandmail.com/news/politics/canada -abandons-un-bid-in-embarrassing-turn-for-harper/article4262871.

TWO: Blue Lobster Tweets

1. Terazono, Emiko. "Global Fish Prices Leap to All-Time High." *Financial Times*. 18 June 2013. www.ft.com/intl/cms/s/0/af42937a-d811-11e2-9495-00144feab7de .html#axzz3L7yPanEZ.
2. Fisheries and Oceans Canada. "Statistics, Canadian Trade Exports, by Major Market and Country." www.dfo-mpo.gc.ca/stats/trade-commerce/can/export/ export-eng.htm.

3. By the time I left China, our site was second only to the U.S. embassy's in terms of popularity.

4. Vanderklippe, Nathan. "Canadian Embassy's Social Media 'Fans' in China Mostly Zombies." *Globe and Mail*. 10 Sep. 2014. www.theglobeandmail.com/news/world/canadian-embassys-social-media-fans-in-china-mostly-zombies/article20506692.

5. Bundalet, Brett. "Cultural Savvy Essential for Success in New Food Markets." *Chronicle Herald* [Halifax]. 28 May 2012. http://thechronicleherald.ca/business/101381-cultural-savvy-essential-for-success-in-new-food-markets.

6. "Clearwater Branding Lobsters to Curb Counterfeit Crustaceans." CTV News Atlantic. 22 July 2011. http://atlantic.ctvnews.ca/clearwater-branding-lobsters-to-curb-counterfeit-crustaceans-1.673644.

7. Figures provided by Clearwater Seafoods. Email to author from Clearwater CEO Ian Smith, 12 July 2014.

8. "Report: China Starts Stockpiling Metals Again." Mining.com. 2 June 2013. www.mining.com/report-china-starts-stockpiling-metals-again-90612.

9. Jordan, Pav, and Brent Jang. "Investors Look to Teck for Clues to China's Path." *Globe and Mail*. 3 Feb. 2013. www.theglobeandmail.com/report-on-business/industry-news/energy-and-resources/investors-look-to-teck-for-clues-to-chinas-path/article8154667.

10. "B.C. Lumber Exports to China Soar." CBC News. 17 July 2011. www.cbc.ca/news/canada/british-columbia/b-c-lumber-exports-to-china-soar-1.1073899.

11. "Merchandise Imports and Exports between Canada and [Country Selected] by Harmonized System Section, Customs Basis." Canadian International Merchandise Trade Database, Statistics Canada. www5.statcan.gc.ca/cimt-cicm/home-accueil?lang=eng.

12. CIBC. "In Focus." 16 Apr. 2013. www.cibc.com/ca/pdf/canada-needs-to-accelerate-exports-to-emerging-markets-en.pdf.

13. Batty, Neil, and Frank Bingham. "Australia's Exports to China 2001–2011." Department of Foreign Affairs and Trade, Australia. Dec. 2012. www.dfat.gov.au/publications/stats-pubs/australias-exports-to-china-2001-2011.pdf.

14. Humel, Neil. "China, Australia and a Very Hard Landing." *Financial Times*. 4 July 2013. http://ftalphaville.ft.com/2013/07/04/1556362/china-australia-and-a-hard-landing.

15. "Merchandise Imports and Exports Between Canada and China, by Harmonized Section, Customs Basis." Statistics Canada. 2001, 2011. www5.statcan.gc.ca/cimt-cicm/home-accueil?lang=eng.

16. Kauth, Glenn. "IMAX Wins $7-million Victory against Ex-employee Who Stole Technology." *Canadian Lawyer*. 14 July 2014. www.canadianlawyermag.com/legalfeeds/2181/imax-wins-7-million-victory-against-ex-employee-whole-stole-technology.html.

17. Harkinson, Josh. "The Solar Industry's New Dirty Secret." *Mother Jones*. 19 Aug. 2013. www.motherjones.com/blue-marble/2013/08/solar-industrys-new-dirty-secret.

18. Fallows, James. Introduction. *China Airborne*. New York: Pantheon, 2012. 7.

19. Aronson, Susan Ariel. "How Disciplining China Could Save the WTO." *Vox*. 9 Feb. 2010. www.voxeu.org/article/how-disciplining-china-could-save-wto.

20. In an effort to get back in China's good books, Norway's leaders did not meet with the Dalai Lama when he visited Oslo in the spring of 2014.

21. Stephens, Philip. "A Painful Lesson in How Not to Deal with China." *Financial Times*. 5 Dec. 2013. www.ft.com/intl/cms/s/0/cb01954e-5d12-11e3-a558 -00144feabdc0.html#axzz3L7yPanEZ.

22. "Study Opens Up Opportunities for Canadian Canola in China." Canola Council of Canada. 1 Aug. 2013. www.canolacouncil.org/news/study-opens-up -opportunities-for-canadian-canola-in-china.

23. Artuso, Antonella. "Premier Kathleen Wynne Defends Trade Mission to China." *Toronto Sun*. 1 Oct. 2014. www.torontosun.com/2014/10/01/premier -kathleen-wynne-defends-trade-mission-to-china.

24. Bergeron, Patrice. "Quebec Premier Says He Won't Lecture Communist Leaders on Human Rights during Trade Mission to China." *National Post*. 26 Oct. 2014. http://news.nationalpost.com/2014/10/26/quebec-premier-says-he-wont -lecture-communist-leaders-on-human-rights-during-trade-mission-to-china.

THREE: Cold Feet and Mixed Signals

1. Cornish, Margaret. "Behaviour of Chinese SOEs: Implications for Investment and Cooperation in Canada." Canadian International Council, Canadian Council of Chief Executives. Feb. 2012. www.ceocouncil.ca/wp-content/uploads/2012/02/ Margaret-Cornish-Chinese-SOEs-February-2012.pdf.

2. McGregor, Richard. Prologue. *The Party*. By McGregor. New York: HarperCollins, 2010. xiii.

3. Nianzu, Shen. "The Revolving Door of Chinese Politics." *Economic Observer*. 3 July 2013. www.eeo.com.cn/ens/2013/0703/246090.shtml.

4. Sorkin, Andrew Ross. *Too Big to Fail*. New York: Viking, 2009. 452–4.

5. Fallows, James. "Be Nice to the Countries That Lend You Money." *Atlantic*. 1 Dec. 2008. www.theatlantic.com/magazine/archive/2008/12/be-nice-to-the-countries -that-lend-you-money/307148.

6. Something that had a lot to do with the fact that Toronto was the home base of Felix Chee, CIC's highly trusted Canadian advisor.

7. Statistics provided by Canadian embassy, Beijing.

8. "China's CNOOC Offers $15B for Calgary Oil Firm Nexen." CBC News. 23 July 2012. www.cbc.ca/news/business/china-s-cnooc-offers-15b-for-calgary-oil-firm -nexen-1.1142570.

9. Cornish, op. cit., 11.

10. "2012 National Opinion Poll: Canadian Views on Asia." Asia Pacific Foundation of Canada. 23 April 2012. www.asiapacific.ca/surveys/national-opinion-polls/2012-national-opinion-poll-canadian-views-asia.

11. Lewis, Jeff, and Claudia Cattaneo. "Life after CNOOC's Nexen Deal: Is China's Honeymoon with Canada's Oil Patch Over?" *Financial Post*. 7 Dec. 2013. http://business.financialpost.com/2013/12/07/life-after-cnoocs-nexen-deal-is-chinas-honeymoon-with-canadas-oil-patch-over/?__lsa=05a0-11b9.

12. Prentice, Jim. "North American Energy at a Crossroads." Alberta Chamber of Resources, Edmonton. 7 Feb. 2014. Speech. www.cibc.com/ca/pdf/investor/edmonton-final-en.pdf.

13. Lardy, Nicholas R. *Markets over Mao*. Washington, DC: Peterson Institute for International Economics, 2014. This book decisively challenges the notion that the state dominates the Chinese economy.

14. Ivison, John. "Foreign Investment in the Oil Sands Have Dropped off a Cliff since the Nexen Takeover." *Financial Post*. 1 Oct. 2013. www.cibc.com/ca/pdf/investor/edmonton-final-en.pdf.

15. Roberts, Dexter. "Almost Half of China's Rich Want to Emigrate." *Bloomberg Businessweek*. 15 Sep. 2014. www.businessweek.com/articles/2014-09-15/almost-half-of-chinas-rich-want-to-emigrate.

16. Garst, William Daniel. "China's Footloose Rich on the Move." *China Daily Online*. 12 May 2012. http://usa.chinadaily.com.cn/opinion/2012-12/05/content_15986322.htm.

17. Roberts, Dexter, and Jasmine Zhao. "China's Super-Rich Buy a Better Life Abroad." *Bloomberg Businessweek*. 22 Nov. 2011. www.businessweek.com/magazine/chinas-superrich-buy-a-better-life-abroad-11222011.html.

18. Zoellick, Robert. "International Treaties Can Once Again Help China Advance." *Financial Times*. 10 Mar. 2014. www.ft.com/intl/cms/s/0/b8b391ec-a634-11e3-8a2a-00144feab7de.html#axzz3L7yPanEZ.

19. Snelder, Julian. "Foreign Direct Investment: Ten Simple Questions." *The Interpreter*. 12 June 2014. www.lowyinterpreter.org/post/2014/06/12/foreign-direct-investment-ten-questions.aspx?COLLCC=1580063501&.

FOUR: Breaking the Breakfast Barrier

1. Arita, Shawn, Sumner La Croix and James Mak. "How China's Approved Destination Status Policy Spurs and Hinders Chinese Travel Abroad." *Working Paper No. 2012-6R*. The Economic Research Organization at the University of Hawai'i. 19 Oct. 2012. www.uhero.hawaii.edu/assets/WP_2012-6R.pdf.

2. Ibid.

3. Kar, Dev, and Brian LeBlanc. "Illicit Financial Flows from Developing Countries:

2002–2011." Global Financial Integrity. Dec. 2013. www.gfintegrity.org/report/2013-global-report-illicit-financial-flows-from-developing-countries-2002-2011.

4. "Flood of Money Leaving China." CBC News. 26 Oct. 2012. www.cbc.ca/news/business/flood-of-money-leaving-china-1.1158402.

5. Arita, La Croix and Mak, op. cit.

6. We ultimately did secure ADS before the Lai judgment was delivered.

7. "Statistics and Figures, International Visitor Arrivals." Canadian Tourism Commission. http://en-corporate.canada.travel/research/statistics-figures/international-visitor-arrivals#international.

8. Table: "Individual Traveller Spending (Euro)." *The Chinese Luxury Traveler 2013*: 23. The Hurun Report and International Luxury Travel Market/Asia. June 2013. http://up.hurun.net/Humaz/201312/20131218145843792.pdf.

9. Luke, Paul. "Chinese Tourist Dollars Are Big Attraction in BC." *Province*. 11 Aug. 2012. www2.canada.com/theprovince/news/story.html?id=f38fabbf-cd32-4133-bd46-9886c7498744&p=3.

10. "'Walking Wallets': Chinese Tourists the World's Biggest Travelers." *Sydney Morning Herald*. 10 Jan. 2014. www.smh.com.au/it-pro/walking-wallets-chinese-tourists-the-worlds-biggest-travellers-20140110-30lce.html.

11. Day, Emma. "Harrods Welcomes Unionpay." Harrods. 12 Apr. 2012. www.harrods.com/content/the-store/news-events/2011/harrods-welcomes-unionpay.

12. Wells, Jane. "Chinese Tourists Fuel Beverly Hills Economy." *NBC News*. 25 Apr. 2014. www.nbcnews.com/business/economy/chinese-tourists-fuel-beverly-hills-economy-n90211.

13. Ibid.

14. "New Zealand Hotel Chain Launches China Optimum Service Standards." *Xinhuanet*. 15 May 2013. http://news.xinhuanet.com/english/business/2013-05/15/c_132382372.htm.

15. Statistics are from China Travel Guide. "Outbound Tourism in 2013." www.travelchinaguide.com/tourism/2013statistics/outbound.htm; from the website of the U.S. National Tourism Office. http://travel.trade.gov/view/m-2013-I-001/index.html; and from the 2013 annual report of the Canadian Tourism Commission. https://en-corporate.canada.travel/sites/default/files/pdf/Corporate_reports/final_2013_annual_report_en.pdf.

FIVE: The University of Beautiful Cars

1. "Facts and Figures: Canada's Performance in International Education, 2012." Canadian Bureau for International Education. www.cbie.ca/about-ie/facts-and-figures

2. Fee schedules for both school districts are (Coquitlam's for 2014; TDSB's for 2013–14) posted online. www.internationaled.com/forms/Price_Sheet.pdf; www.tdsb.on.ca/Portals/0/aboutus/international/docs/tuition%20fee%20and%20refund%20policy%20english%2014-15.pdf.

3. McDonald, Moira. "Toronto School Board Opens Beijing Office in Attempt to Lure More Foreign Students." *National Post.* 17 July 2013. http://news.nationalpost.com/2013/07/17/toronto-school-board-opens-beijing-office-in-attempt-to-lure-more-foreign-students.

4. "University of Beautiful Cars, FAQs." Tumblr.com. http://universityofbeautifulcars.tumblr.com/about.

5. Weiss, Elizabeth. "Can International Students Save U.S. Public Schools?" *New Yorker.* 3 Apr. 2014. www.newyorker.com/business/currency/can-international-students-save-u-s-public-schools.

6. Lowe, Sophia J. "Learning from Australia's Export Education Model." *World Education News & Reviews.* 1 Aug. 2009. http://wenr.wes.org/2009/08/wenr-julyaugust-2009-practical-information.

7. McNeilage, Amy, and Lisa Visentin. "Academics Accuse Universities of 'Addiction' to International Students and their Cheating." *Sydney Morning Herald.* 12 Nov. 2014. www.smh.com.au/national/education/academics-accuse-universities-of-addiction-to-international-students-and-their-cheating-20141112-11lbdi.html.

8. In the wake of criticism, the title of the article changed from "Too Asian" to "Too Asian?" to "The Enrollment Controversy."

9. Seo, Eunkyung, and Heesu Lee. "China Beats US for Korean Students Seeking Career Ticket." *Bloomberg.* 5 Sep. 2013. www.bloomberg.com/news/2013-09-04/china-beats-u-s-for-korean-students-seeing-career-ticket.html.

10. Waldmeir, Patti. "Chinese Parents Count Cost of Sending Children to Overseas Universities." *Financial Times.* 29 Dec. 2013. www.ft.com/intl/cms/s/0/98c4a5ac-63c1-11e3-b70d-00144feabdc0.html#axzz3L7yPanEZ.

11. Link, Perry. "The Long Shadow of Chinese Blacklists on American Academe." *Chronicle of Higher Education.* 22 Nov. 2013. http://chronicle.com/blogs/worldwise/the-long-shadow-of-chinese-blacklists-on-american-academe/33359.

12. Lewin, Tamar. "US Colleges Finding Ideals Tested Abroad." *New York Times.* 11 Dec. 2013. www.nytimes.com/2013/12/12/education/american-colleges-finding-ideals-are-tested-abroad.html?pagewanted=all.

13. Buckley, Chris. "China Takes Aim at Western Ideas." *New York Times.* 19 Aug. 2013. www.nytimes.com/2013/08/20/world/asia/chinas-new-leadership-takes-hard-line-in-secret-memo.html?pagewanted=all.

14. McGiffert, Carola (president of the 100,000 Strong Foundation). "U.S. Reaches Major Milestone: 100,000 American Students Study in China." *Huffington Post.*

7 July 2014. www.huffingtonpost.com/carola-mcgiffert/us-reaches-major-mileston_b_5571793.html.

15. Sponsored by the Asia Pacific Foundation of Canada and the Munk School of Global Affairs at the University of Toronto.

16. Bradshaw, James, and Colin Freeze. "McMaster Closes Confucius Institute over Hiring Issues." *Globe and Mail*. 7 Feb. 2013. www.theglobeandmail.com/news/national/education/mcmaster-closing-confucius-institute-over-hiring-issues/article8372894.

17. Alphonso, Caroline, and Karen Howlett. "Toronto School Board's Qualms over Chinese Partnership Prompt Backlash." *Globe and Mail*. 22 Aug. 2014. www.theglobeandmail.com/news/national/education/toronto-school-boards-qualms-over-chinese-partnership-cause-backlash/article20166438.

18. Rushowy, Kristin. "China Seeks to End Confucius Deal with Toronto School Board." *Toronto Star*. 23 Oct. 2014. www.thestar.com/yourtoronto/education/2014/10/23/china_seeks_to_end_confucius_deal_with_toronto_school_board.html.

SIX: Buying a Piece of Canada

1. Marr, Garry. "CMHC Leaves Out Question of Foreign Condo Investors, but Economist Says It's Only 5%." *Financial Post*. 8 Aug. 2014. http://business.financialpost.com/2014/08/08/cmhc-leaves-out-question-of-foreign-condo-investors-on-major-survey. Figures released by CMHC in December, 2014, suggesting that foreign investors accounted for just 2.4 percent of the condo market in Toronto and 2.3 percent in Vancouver, were met with scepticism, pointing to the great difficulty in determining where funds and investors actually originate. Marr, Gerry. "CMHC Finally Releases Foreign Ownership Data on Housing—Too Bad Few Believe It." *National Post*. 16 Dec. 2014. http://business.financialpost.com/2014/12/16/cmhc-finally-releases-foreign-ownership-data-on-housing-too-bad-few-believe-it.

2. Bell, Stewart. "Would-be Canadians to Wait Longer for Citizenship as Tories Toughen Language and Knowledge Rules." *National Post*. 6 Feb. 2014. http://news.nationalpost.com/2014/02/06/immigration-changes-mean-would-be-canadians-will-have-to-wait-four-years-not-three-to-apply-for-citizenship.

3. O'Neil, Peter. "Ottawa Blasts Quebec for 'Fraud' Program That 'Takes Money' from Rich Immigrants Who Move to Other Provinces." *National Post*. 1 Aug. 2013. http://news.nationalpost.com/2013/08/01/ottawa-blasts-quebec-for-fraud-program-that-takes-money-from-rich-immigrants-who-move-to-other-provinces.

4. Carman, Tara, and Peter O'Neil. "Ottawa Scraps Investor Immigrant Program." *Vancouver Sun*. 3 Oct. 2014. www.vancouversun.com/news/Ottawa+scraps+investor+immigrant+program/9496380/story.html.

5. Vanderklippe, Nathan. "To Many Chinese, Buying Entry to Canada Was 'Paradise for the Corrupt.'" *Globe and Mail.* 14 Feb. 2014. www.theglobeandmail .com/news/world/world-insider/to-many-chinese-buying-entry-to-canada-was -paradise-for-the-corrupt/article16893249.

6. "The Fight against Corruption Goes International." *Caixin Online.* 3 Dec. 2014. http://english.caixin.com/2014-12-03/100758479.html.

7. Young, Ian. "Sister Act: Fake Chinese Buyers Distract from Reality of Vancouver's Housing Market." *South China Morning Post.* 2 July 2014. www.scmp .com/comment/blogs/article/1544921/sister-act-fake-chinese-buyers-distract -reality-vancouvers-housing.

8. Young, Ian. "The Rule of Thirds: New Evidence of the Chinese Role in Vancouver's Housing Market." *South China Morning Post.* 27 Aug. 2014. www.scmp.com/ comment/blogs/article/1581034/rule-thirds-new-evidence-mainland-chinese -role-vancouvers-housing.

9. Chunyan, Zhang. "China Pouring Billions into London Real Estate." *China Daily.* 14 Jan. 2014. http://europe.chinadaily.com.cn/business/2014-01/14/content _17233448.htm.

10. Condon, Turi, and Scott Murdoch. "Chinese New Wave Rocks Property Market." *Australian.* 26 Oct. 2013. www.theaustralian.com.au/business/property/ chinese-new-wave-rocks-property-market/story-fn9656lz-1226747147870.

11. "Australians Priced out of Housing, Report Says." BBC News. 5 Mar. 2014. www .bbc.com/news/business-26445106.

12. Christie, Lee. "Chinese Buyers Flood U.S. Housing Market." *CNN Money.* 8 July 2013. http://money.cnn.com/2013/07/08/real_estate/chinese-homebuyers.

13. Balkissoon, Denise. "Penthouse International: How Rich Foreign Buyers Are Fuelling the Condo Explosion." *Toronto Life.* 6 Nov. 2012. www.torontolife.com/ informer/features/2012/11/06/toronto-condos-foreign-buyers.

14. "The B.C. Bolthole." *The Economist.* 17 June 2014. www.economist.com/blogs/ americasview/2014/06/housing-vancouver.

15. Todd, Douglas. "Vancouver Planner Andy Yan Fights to Prevent a 'Zombie City.'" *Vancouver Sun.* 20 Apr. 2013. http://blogs.vancouversun.com/2013/04/20/ vancouver-planner-andy-yan-fights-to-prevent-a-zombie-city.

16. SFU's Vancity Office of Community Engagement organized a March 21, 2013, panel discussion on "Foreign Investment in Vancouver's Real Estate Market." http://youtube/rR_z4q2hFzs.

17. Francis, Diane. "To Tame Toronto's Housing 'Bubble,' Ban Foreign Buying." *Financial Post.* 13 Apr. 2012. http://opinion.financialpost.com/2012/04/13/to -tame-torontos-housing-bubble-ban-foreign-buying.

18. MacDonald, Alistair, Paul Vieira and Will Connors. "Chinese Fly Cash West,

by the Suitcase." *Wall Street Journal*. 1 Jan. 2013. http://online.wsj.com/articles/ SB10001424127887323635504578213933647167020.

19. Weise, Karen. "Why Are Chinese Millionaires Buying Mansions in an L.A. Suburb?" *Bloomberg Businessweek*. 15 Oct. 2014. www.businessweek.com/articles/2014-10-15/ chinese-home-buying-binge-transforms-california-suburb-arcadia.

20. Hongyuran, Wu, and Liu Caiping. "Money Transfer Service CCTV Criticized Was Approved by Regulator, BOC Says." *Caixin Online*. 10 July 2014. http://english .caixin.com/2014-07-10/100702352.html.

21. "How Chinese Fortunes Are Hidden in Australia." *Financial Review*. 25 Oct. 2014. www.afr.com/p/national/how_chinese_fortunes_are_hidden _EQ7mBdl8pJh7Hy3q9aw6qO.

22. Roberts, Dexter. "'Operation Fox Hunt' Nabs Dirty Chinese Officials Abroad." *Bloomberg Businessweek*. 22 Sep. 2014. www.businessweek.com/articles/2014-09-22/ china-hunts-down-corrupt-officials-who-fled-abroad.

23. Goldman, Henry, and Allyson Versprille. "Real-Estate Pros Fight NYC Tax on Wealthy Absentee Owners." *Bloomberg*. 15 Oct. 2014. www.bloomberg.com/ news/2014-10-15/real-estate-pros-fight-nyc-tax-on-wealthy-absentee-owners.html.

24. "Luxury Home Sales Surge in Vancouver, Calgary, Toronto." *CTV News*. 28 Jan. 2014. www.ctvnews.ca/canada/luxury-home-sales-surge-in-vancouver-calgary -toronto-1.1659333.

25. Jordan, Miriam. "Investor Visas Soaked Up by Chinese." *Wall Street Journal*. 27 Aug. 2014. http://online.wsj.com/articles/investor-visas-soaked-up-by-chinese -1409095982.

26. Vieira, Paul, and Wei Gu. "Canada Unveils New Plan to Attract Wealthy Immigrants" *Wall Street Journal*. 16 Dec. 2014. www.wsj.com/articles/canada-unveils -new-immigrant-investor-plan-1418784959.

27. SCMP's Ian Young believes that, despite the federal government's interest in ending the practice of Vancouver-bound immigrants circumventing the system by using Quebec's investor program, this significant flow of people will continue: Young, Ian. "Blame Quebec: Why Halting the Immigrant Investor Programme Hasn't Halted Flow of Immigrant Investors to Vancouver." *South China Morning Post*. 31 Dec. 2014. www.scmp.com/comment/blogs/article/1671607/ blame-quebec-why-halting-immigrant-investor-programme-cant-halt-flow.

SEVEN: The Unfinished Empire

1. Levin, Dan. "China Remodels an Ancient Silk Road City, and an Ethnic Rift Widens." *New York Times*. 5 Mar. 2014. www.nytimes.com/2014/03/06/world/ asia/china-remodels-an-ancient-silk-road-city-and-an-ethnic-rift-widens.html.

2. Rashid, Ahmed. "China Takes a Leaf out of Stalin in Central Asia." *Financial*

Times. 30 Dec. 2012. http://blogs.ft.com/the-a-list/2013/12/30/china-takes-a
-leaf-out-of-stalin-in-central-asia.

3. Norbu, Dawa. *Red Star over Tibet*. New York: Envoy, 1987. 261.

4. Erickson, Andrew. "Watch This Space: China's New Air Defense Zone." *Wall
Street Journal*. 25 Nov. 2013. http://blogs.wsj.com/chinarealtime/2013/11/25/
watch-this-space-chinas-new-air-defense-zone.

5. Reunification isn't quite the correct term since the PRC, which was created in
1949, has never exercised authority over Taiwan.

6. Scobell, Andrew, and Scott W. Harold. "An 'Assertive' China? Insights from
Interviews." *Asian Security* 9.2 (2013).

7. Ibid.

8. Keck, Zachary. "U.S., China Trade Barbs over Surveillance Flights." *Diplomat*.
10 Sep. 2014. http://thediplomat.com/2014/09/us-china-trade-barbs-over
-surveillance-flights.

9. Steele, Jeanette. "Navy Opens Its Hatches to China." U-T San Diego. 13 Sep. 2013.
www.utsandiego.com/news/2013/sep/13/top-chinese-admiral-gets-tour-of
-sd-bases.

10. "China Ship Sent to Spy on RIMPAC Naval Exercises." Voice of America.
21 July 2014. www.voanews.com/content/china-ship-sent-to-spy-on-rimpac
-naval-exercises/1961652.html.

EIGHT: China's Long Reach

1. Chase, Steven, and Colin Freeze. "Chinese Government Hacked Computers,
Ottawa Says." *Globe and Mail*. 29 July 2014. www.theglobeandmail.com/news/
national/chinese-hacked-government-computers-ottawa-says/article19818728.

2. Vanderklippe, Nathan, and Mark Mackinnon. "China Probes Two Canadians for
Alleged Theft of State Secrets." *Globe and Mail*. 4 Aug. 2014. www.theglobeandmail
.com/news/world/china-probes-two-canadians-for-alleged-theft-of-state-secrets/
article19908947.

3. Lilley, James, former U.S. ambassador to China and CIA veteran. Interview on
PBS's *Frontline* ("From China with Love"). Jan. 2004. www.pbs.org/wgbh/pages/
frontline/shows/spy/interviews/lilley.html.

4. Wilson, Duff, and John Shiffman. "Special Report: Hunting for US Arms
Tech, China Taps Legion of Amateurs." *Reuters*. 18 Dec. 2013. http://in
.reuters.com/article/2013/12/18/us-breakout-smugglers-special-report
-idINBRE9BH0MV20131218.

5. Fyfe, Robert. "China Spying on Us: CSIS." *National Post*. 29 Dec. 2004. www.
primetimecrime.com/Articles/Media%20Articles/NP%20China_files/NP%20
China.htm.

6. de Pierrebourg, Fabrice, and Michel Juneau-Katsuya. *Nest of Spies*. Toronto: HarperCollins, 2009. 147.

7. Bell, Stewart. "Ontario's Qing Quentin Huang, Accused of Spying for China, Was 'against Capitalism,' Former Employer Says." *National Post*. 3 Dec. 2013. http://news.nationalpost.com/2013/12/03/ontarios-qing-quentin-huang -accused-of-spying-for-china-was-against-capitalism-former-employer-says.

8. Hamilton, Graeme. "Montreal Man, Wang Hongwei, Wanted by FBI for Alleged Plot to Export Agricultural Trade Secrets." *National Post*. 5 May 2014. http://news.nationalpost.com/2014/05/05/montreal-man-wang-hongwei -wanted-by-fbi-for-alleged-plot-to-export-agricultural-trade-secrets-to-china.

9. Apuzzo, Matt. "Chinese Businessman Is Charged in Plot to Steal US Military Data." *New York Times*. 11 July 2014. www.nytimes.com/2014/07/12/business/ chinese-businessman-is-charged-in-plot-to-steal-us-military-data.html.

10. Nakashima, Ellen. "U.S. Said to Be Target of Massive Cyber-Espionage Campaign." *Washington Post*. 10 Feb. 2013. www.washingtonpost.com/world/ national-security/us-said-to-be-target-of-massive-cyber-espionage-campaign/ 2013/02/10/7b4687d8-6fc1-11e2-aa58-243de81040ba_story.html.

11. "Nortel Collapse Linked to Chinese Hackers." *CBC News*. 15 Feb. 2012. www.cbc .ca/news/business/nortel-collapse-linked-to-chinese-hackers-1.1260591.

12. Sanger, David E., David Barboza and Nicole Perlroth. "Chinese Army Unit Is Seen as Tied to Hacking against US." *New York Times*. 18 Feb. 2013. www.nytimes .com/2013/02/19/technology/chinas-army-is-seen-as-tied-to-hacking-against -us.html?pagewanted=all.

13. Ibid.

14. Anderlini, James. "China Clamps down on US Consulting Groups." *Financial Times*. 25 May 2014. www.ft.com/intl/cms/s/0/310d29ea-e263-11e3-89fd -00144feabdc0.html#axzz3L7yPanEZ.

15. Culpan, Tim, Ian King and Dina Bass. "China Raids Microsoft Offices in Anti-monopoly Investigation." *Bloomberg*. 29 July 2014. www.bloomberg.com/news/ 2014-07-29/microsoft-probed-by-regulators-in-china-amid-u-s-tension.html.

16. "China Targets Own Operating System to Take on Likes of Microsoft, Google." *Reuters*. 24 Aug. 2014. www.reuters.com/article/2014/08/24/us-china -technology-idUSKBN0GO08H20140824.

17. Payton, Laura. "Former Nortel Exec Warns against Working with Huawei." *CBC News*. 11 Oct. 2012. www.cbc.ca/news/politics/former-nortel-exec-warns -against-working-with-huawei-1.1137006.

18. See "Why Did Kodak, Motorola and Nortel Fail?" *Information Week*. 1 Dec. 2012. www.informationweek.com/it-leadership/why-did-kodak-motorola-and-nortel-fail/d/d-id/1102245?. Also: McFarland, Janet. "'Culture of Arrogance' Felled Telecom Giant Nortel, Study Finds." *Globe and Mail*. 17 Mar. 2014. http://

www.theglobeandmail.com/report-on-business/culture-of-arrogance-doomed
-nortel-analysis-concludes/article17521736.

19. Chase, Steven. "Ottawa Set to Ban Chinese Firm from Telecommunications Bid." *Globe and Mail.* 10 Oct. 2012. www.theglobeandmail.com/news/politics/ottawa-set-to-ban-chinese-firm-from-telecommunications-bid/article4600199.

20. "UK to Probe Huawei Staff's Role at Cybersecurity Centre." BBC News. 18 July 2013. www.bbc.com/news/technology-23355950.

21. Beeby, Dean. "Phishing Scam Ensnares Almost 2000 Justice Department Staff." *Huffington Post.* 22 June 2014. www.huffingtonpost.ca/2014/06/22/mock-email -scam-justice-department_n_5519549.html.

22. "Some Politicians under Foreign Sway: CSIS." *CBC News.* 22 June 2010. www .cbc.ca/news/politics/some-politicians-under-foreign-sway-csis-1.909345.

23. Fitzgerald, John. "Why Values Matter in Australia's Relations with China." *The Asan Forum.* 13 June 2014. www.theasanforum.org/why-values-matter-in -australias-relations-with-china.

24. Garnaut, John. "Chinese Spies at Sydney University." *Sydney Morning Herald.* 21 Apr. 2014. www.smh.com.au/national/chinese-spies-at-sydney-university -20140420-36ywk.html.

25. Jacobs, Josh. "'Take China Seriously without Being Afraid of It': A Conversation on Manufacturing, Aerospace and China with James Fallows." MIT LGO. 12 Dec. 2012.http://lgo.mit.edu/news/articles/fallows-manufacturing-china-aerospace/fallows-manufacturing-china-aerospace.html.

NINE: Saving Little Fatty

1. Hensman, Bertha. "The Kilborn Family: A Record of a Canadian Family's Service to Medical Work and Education in China and Hong Kong." *Canadian Medical Association Journal* 27. 26 Aug. 1967. www.ncbi.nlm.nih.gov/pmc/articles/PMC1923254/pdf/canmedaj01230-0041.pdf.

2. "'Jessie Mac': A Missionary Doctor in China." *Georgina Kelman: Works on Paper.* 11 June 2012. http://georginakelman.blogspot.ca/2012/06/jessie-mac-missionary -doctor-in-china.html. Also: Tomes, Nigel. "The Last to Leave—'Jessie Mac,' Canada's Medical Missionary to China." *Church in Toronto.* 10 Jan. 2012. http:// churchintoronto.blogspot.ca/2012/01/last-to-leave-jessie-mac-canadas.html.

3. "SARS Outbreak in Canada." Canadian Environmental Health Atlas. www.ehatlas. ca/sars-severe-acute-respiratory-syndrome/case-study/sars-outbreak-canada.

4. Ramzy, Austin. "China Cuts Tuberculosis Cases by More than Half since 1990." *New York Times.* 21 Mar. 2014. http://sinosphere.blogs.nytimes.com/2014/03/21/china-cuts-tuberculosis-cases-by-more-than-half-since-1990.

5. Ibid.

6. Jiaying, Liu. "China's Cancer Survival Rates 'Trail Those in Developed Countries.'" *Caixin Online.* 6 Nov. 2014. http://english.caixin.com/2014-11-06/100747693.html.

7. Vanham, Peter. "China Enters Vaccine Premier League." *Financial Times.* 9 Oct. 2013. http://blogs.ft.com/beyond-brics/2013/10/09/china-enters-vaccine-premier-league.

8. Waldmeir, Patti. "Chinese Medical Demand Fuels Private Hospital Takeovers." *Financial Times.* 13 Aug. 2014. www.ft.com/intl/cms/s/0/5dbcf898-db11-11e3-9a27-00144feabdc0.html#axzz3L7yPanEZ.

9. Chiose, Simona. "Norman Bethune's Legacy Endures as Canadian, Chinese Medical Schools Partner Up." *Globe and Mail.* 15 Oct. 2014. www.theglobeandmail.com/news/national/education/norman-bethunes-legacy-endures-as-ottawa-china-medical-schools-tie-up/article21119802.

10. Fang, Lan. "Marketizing China's Elder Care Conundrum." *Caixin Online.* 20 Sep. 2013. http://english.caixin.com/2013-09-20/100584390.html.

11. Woodhead, Michael. "China's Rural Timebomb: Half a Billion Elderly People with Chronic Diseases and No Care." *China Medical News.* 6 Aug. 2014. www.chinesemedicalnews.com/2014/08/chinas-rural-timebomb-half-billion.html.

12. Waldmeir, Patti. "The Changing Face of Growing Old in China." *Financial Times.* 17 June 2014. www.ft.com/intl/cms/s/0/72e45ef6-bfcc-11e3-b6e8-00144feabdc0.html#axzz3L7yPanEZ.

13. "Rick Hansen to Collaborate with China Rehabilitation Research Center, Peking Third Hospital, and China Disabled Persons' Federation." Rick Hansen Foundation. 14 Apr. 2011. www.rickhansen.com/Media-Room/Media-Article-View/Article/23/rick-hansen-to-collaborate-with-china-rehabilitation-research-center-peking-thi.

TEN: Air, Water and Animals

1. Wong, Edward. "Air Pollution Linked to 1.2 Million Premature Deaths in China." *New York Times.* 1 Apr. 2013. www.nytimes.com/2013/04/02/world/asia/air-pollution-linked-to-1-2-million-deaths-in-china.html.

2. "Officials Admit 'Cancer Villages' Exist in China." *Caijing.* 21 Feb. 2013. http://english.caijing.com.cn/2013-02-21/112520130.html.

3. Jian, Yang. "China's River Pollution 'a Threat to People's Lives.'" *People's Daily Online.* 17 Feb. 2012. http://en.people.cn/90882/7732438.html.

4. Lin, Luna. "Beijing Water Shortage Worse than the Middle East." *Chinadialogue.* 29 Aug. 2013. www.chinadialogue.net/article/show/single/en/6319-Beijing-water-shortage-worse-than-the-Middle-East.

5. Kuo, Lily. "China Has Launched the Largest Water-Pipeline Project in History." *Atlantic*. 7 Mar. 2014. www.theatlantic.com/international/archive/2014/03/china-has-launched-the-largest-water-pipeline-project-in-history/284300.

6. Ontario Ministry of the Environment. "Fine Particulate Matter." Air Quality Ontario. 2010. www.airqualityontario.com/science/pollutants/particulates.php.

7. Demick, Barbara. "U.S. Embassy Air Quality Data Undercut China's Own Assessments." *Los Angeles Times*. 29 Oct. 2011. http://articles.latimes.com/2011/oct/29/world/la-fg-china-air-quality-20111030.

8. Ibid.

9. Yuchen, Zhang. "Beijing Needs 2.5M More Parking Lots." *China Daily USA*. 2 July 2013. http://usa.chinadaily.com.cn/china/2013-07/02/content_16710775.htm.

10. Wong, Edward. "China's Plan to Curb Air Pollution Sets Limits on Coal Use and Vehicles." *New York Times*. 12 Sep. 2013. www.nytimes.com/2013/09/13/world/asia/china-releases-plan-to-reduce-air-pollution.html.

11. Osnos, Evan. "One Nation under Smog: The Rules for Beijing Living." *New Yorker*. 14 Jan. 2013. www.newyorker.com/news/evan-osnos/one-nation-under-smog-the-rules-for-beijing-living.

12. Brill, Emily. "Is the Air Quality in Beijing Worse than Ground Zero's after 9/11?" *Atlantic*. 11 Sep. 2013. www.theatlantic.com/china/archive/2013/09/is-the-air-quality-in-beijing-worse-than-ground-zeros-after-9-11/279589.

13. Luo, Chris. "Smog? It Bolsters Military Defence, Says China Nationalist Newspaper." *South China Morning Post*. 9 Dec. 2013. www.scmp.com/news/china/article/1376804/smog-it-bolsters-military-defence-says-chinese-nationalist-newspaper?page=all.

14. "Environmental Concerns on the Rise in China." Pew Research Center's Global Attitudes Project. 19 Sep. 2013. www.pewglobal.org/2013/09/19/environmental-concerns-on-the-rise-in-china.

15. "Chinese Anger over Pollution Becomes Main Cause of Social Unrest." *Bloomberg*. 6 Mar. 2013. www.bloomberg.com/news/2013-03-06/pollution-passes-land-grievances-as-main-spark-of-china-protests.html.

16. Shen, Samuel, and Kazunori Takada. "Car Makers Shrug off New China Sale Restrictions." *Reuters*. 16 July 2013. www.reuters.com/article/2013/07/16/us-china-autos-idUSBRE96F09P20130716.

17. Wong, Edward. "China's Plan to Curb Air Pollution Sets Limits on Coal Use and Vehicles." *New York Times*. 9 Sep. 2013. www.nytimes.com/2013/09/13/world/asia/china-releases-plan-to-reduce-air-pollution.html.

18. Vidal, John, and David Adam. "China Overtakes US as World's Biggest CO_2 Emitter." *Guardian*. 19 June 2007. www.theguardian.com/environment/2007/jun/19/china.usnews.

19. Smith, Noah. "The 10 Stealth Economic Trends That Rule the World Today." *Atlantic*. 30 Sep. 2013. www.theatlantic.com/business/archive/2013/09/the-10-stealth-economic-trends-that-rule-the-world-today/280107.

20. Clark, Pilita. "China's Emissions Outstrip those of E.U. and U.S." *Financial Times*. 22 Sep. 2014. www.ft.com/intl/cms/s/0/51d2dd20-4170-11e4-b98f-00144feabdc0.html#slide0.

21. Clark, Pilita, and Lucy Hornby. "Chinese Pollution: A Shift in the Wind." *Financial Times*. 27 Apr. 2014. www.ft.com/intl/cms/s/0/9ea031fe-cc5c-11e3-9b5f-00144feabdc0.html#axzz3LDWEtVI1.

22. Seligsohn, Deborah. "China at Durban: First Steps toward a New Climate Agreement." ChinaFAQs. 16 Dec. 2011. www.chinafaqs.org/blog-posts/china-durban-first-steps-toward-new-climate-agreement.

23. York, Geoffrey. "China Emerges as Rock Star at Durban Climate Summit." *Globe and Mail*. 5 Dec. 2011. www.theglobeandmail.com/news/world/china-emerges-as-rock-star-at-durban-climate-summit/article4180299.

24. Clark, Campbell. "China and India Lead Condemnation of Canada's Kyoto Withdrawal." *Globe and Mail*. 13 Dec. 2011. www.theglobeandmail.com/news/politics/china-and-india-lead-condemnation-of-canadas-kyoto-withdrawal/article4180991.

25. Wong, Edward. "China's Climate Change Plan Raises Questions." *New York Times*. 12 Nov. 2014. www.nytimes.com/2014/11/13/world/asia/climate-change-china-xi-jinping-obama-apec.html. And John Cassidy. "Is China Really Going Green?" *New Yorker*. 15 Nov. 2014. www.newyorker.com/news/john-cassidy/can-china-really-go-green.

26. Ramzy, Austin, and Chris Buckley. "Politicians and Climate Experts React to U.S.–China Emissions Pact." *New York Times*. 12 Nov. 2014. sinosphere.blogs.nytimes.com/2014/11/12/politicians-and-climate-experts-react-to-u-s-china-emissions-deal.

27. Bailey, Ronald. "The Inconvenient Truth about the U.S.–China Emissions Deal: It's Meaningless." *Time*. 13 Nov. 2014. http://time.com/3583621/the-inconvenient-truth-about-the-u-s-china-emissions-deal-its-meaningless.

28. The Chinese point out, with some justification, that this is because so many polluting industries have been outsourced to China by companies in the developed world.

29. Vaughan, Adam. "Pangolins Being Eaten to Extinction, Conservationists Warn." *Guardian*. 29 July 2014. www.theguardian.com/environment/2014/jul/29/pangolins-being-eaten-to-extinction-conservationists-warn-anteaters.

30. Hennessy, Michelle. "Stolen Rhino Horns Were Removed from Exhibition 'Due to Risk of Theft.'" *thejournal.ie*. 19 Apr. 2013. www.thejournal.ie/rhino-horns-museum-874936-Apr2013.

31. Wassener, Bettina. "China Destroys 6 Tons of Ivory." *New York Times*. 6 Jan. 2014. http://sinosphere.blogs.nytimes.com/2014/01/06/china-destroys-6-tons-of-ivory.

32. "Vanishing Point: Criminality, Corruption and the Devastation of Tanzania's Elephants." Environmental Investigation Agency. Nov. 2014. http://eia -international.org/wp-content/uploads/EIA-Vanishing-Point-lo-res1.pdf.

33. Cardenal, Juan Pablo, and Heriberto Araújo. *China's Silent Army*. Toronto: Allen Lane, 2013. 202–3.

34. Pilling, David. "China Is the Key to Saving Endangered Species." *Financial Times*. 14 Aug. 2013. www.ft.com/intl/cms/s/0/49e7516c-0423-11e3-a8d6 -00144feab7de.html#axzz3LDWEtVI1.

35. Pauly, Daniel. "Time to End Secrecy over Chinese Overseas Fishing." *Chinadialogue*. 30 Apr. 2013. www.chinadialogue.net/article/show/single/en/ 5958-Time-to-end-secrecy-over-Chinese-overseas-fishing.

36. Thompson, Leah. "Why Defenders of Killer Whales Are Worried about China." *ChinaFile*. 29 May 2014. www.chinafile.com/Why-Defenders-Killer-Whales-Are -Worried-About-China.

37. Smith, Jeremy. "Chinese Mining Fuels Trade in Guinea's Apes." *Chinadialogue*. 22 Mar. 2013. www.chinadialogue.net/article/show/single/en/5813-Chinese -mining-fuels-trade-in-Guinea-s-apes.

38. Ibid.

39. Ibid.

40. Fisher, Lorraine. "'I Cried Every Day': British Vet's Harrowing Mission to Give Sight Back to Bears Blinded in China's Cruel 'Farms' That Harvest Their Bile for Medicine." *MailOnline*. 16 Aug. 2014. www.dailymail.co.uk/news/article-2726593/ British-vet-giving-sight-bears-rescued-Chinas-unspeakably-cruel-bile-trade.html.

41. Guynup, Sharon. "China's Threat to Wild Tigers." *New York Times*. 28 June 2014. www.nytimes.com/2014/06/29/opinion/sunday/chinas-threat-to-wild-tigers .html.

42. "100 Million Sharks Killed Each Year, Say Scientists." *Guardian*. 1 Mar. 2013. www .theguardian.com/environment/2013/mar/01/100-million-sharks-killed-each -year.

43. Coonan, Clifford. "Shark Fin Soup off the Menu: China's Crackdown on Extravagant Banquets Gives Sharks a Second Chance." *Independent*. 2 Sep. 2013. www.independent.co.uk/news/world/asia/shark-fin-soup-off-the-menu-chinas -crackdown-on-extravagant-banquets-gives-sharks-a-second-chance-8795235.html.

44. *The Guardian* reported in March 2014 that a pair of Tibetan Mastiffs, status dogs for China's wealthiest people, were sold for more than $3 million. www.theguardian .com/world/2014/mar/20/china-dog-breeder-sells-tibetan-mastiff-twins.

45. "Photos: Truckload of 520 Dogs Rescued from Slaughter near Beijing." *Shanghaiist*. 19 Apr. 2011. http://shanghaiist.com/2011/04/19/photos_truckload_of_520 _dogs_rescue.php#photo-1.

46. "Yulin Dog Meat Festival Goes Ahead, but in Subdued Fashion." Humane Society

International. 3 July 2013. www.hsi.org/news/news/2013/07/yulin_dog_meat _festival_qa_060313.html.

47. Anderlini, Jamil. "China Acts over Poisoned Dog Meat and Chicken Feet." *Financial Times*. 27 Aug. 2014. www.ft.com/intl/cms/s/0/9a32baf2-2dd6-11e4 -b330-00144feabdc0.html#axzz3LDWEtVI1.

48. Huifeng, He. "Dog-Eating Festival Loses Its Bite as Animal Rights Activists Step In." *South China Morning Post*. 22 June 2014. www.scmp.com/news/china/article/ 1537990/yulin-festival-dog-meat-sales-down-activists-take-fight-tradition?page=all.

49. "Tibetan Monks and Endangered Cats." *Economist*. 16 Sep. 2013. www.economist .com/blogs/analects/2013/09/secret-weapon-battle-save-snow-leopard.

50. Schaller figures in Peter Matthiessen's wonderful 1978 book, *The Snow Leopard*. New York: Penguin, 1978.

51. "Tibetan Monasteries Serve as Critical Allies for Snow Leopards." Panthera. 5 Sep. 2013. www.panthera.org/node/4117.

52. Ibid.

ELEVEN: The Food We Eat

1. "Environmental Concerns on the Rise in China." Pew Research Center's Global Attitudes Project. 19 Sep. 2013. www.pewglobal.org/2013/09/19/environmental -concerns-on-the-rise-in-china.

2. McGregor, Richard. *The Party*. New York: HarperCollins, 2010. 181–91.

3. Philpott, Tom. "Why China's Farms Are Failing." *Atlantic*. 21 Aug. 2013. www .theatlantic.com/china/archive/2013/08/why-chinas-farms-are-failing/278906.

4. "China's Farmers, Consumers Feeling the Effects of Widespread Soil Pollution." *CBC News*. 25 Aug. 2014. www.cbc.ca/news/world/china-s-farmers-consumers -feeling-the-effects-of-widespread-soil-pollution-1.2745183.

5. Wenting, Zhou. "Probes Show Dangerous Straws on Sale." *China Daily*. 16 July 2013. http://usa.chinadaily.com.cn/epaper/2013-07/16/content_16782345.htm.

6. Moore, Malcolm. "China Goes Organic after Scandal of Cooking Oil from Sewers." *Telegraph*. 30 Aug. 2010. www.telegraph.co.uk/news/worldnews/asia/china/ 7971983/China-goes-organic-after-scandal-of-cooking-oil-from-sewers.html.

7. Timmons, Heather. "Can High-Tech Chopsticks Improve Food Safety in China?" *Atlantic*. 4 Sep. 2014. www.theatlantic.com/international/archive/2014/09/can -high-tech-chopsticks-improve-food-safety-in-china/379613.

8. Moore, op. cit.

9. "Canadian Dairy Trade Bulletin." Agriculture and Agri-Food Canada. May 2013. www.dairyinfo.gc.ca/pdf/tradebulletin_e.pdf.

10. "Baby Milk Rationed in the U.K. over China Export Fear." BBC News. 8 Apr. 2013. www.bbc.com/news/business-22066243.

11. Smyth, Jamie. "'White Gold' Turns New Zealand into the 'Saudi Arabia of Milk.'" *Financial Times*. 3 Mar. 2014. www.ft.com/intl/cms/s/0/552bb834-a1c5 -11e3-953b-00144feab7de.html#slide0.

12. Ivison, John. "Groundwork Finally Paying Off for Canadians Who Invested in China Long-Term." *National Post*. 4 Feb. 2013. http://fullcomment.nationalpost .com/2013/02/04/john-ivison-groundwork-finally-paying-off-for-canadians -who-invested-in-china-long-term.

13. Ibid.

14. Van Praet, Nicolas. "Saputo Inc Eyeing More Acquisitions beyond Australia's Warrnambool, CEO Says." *Financial Post*. 6 Feb. 2014. http://business.financialpost .com/2014/02/06/saputo-earnings-acquisition. Also: McKenna, Barrie. "As the Dairy Industry Goes Global, Canada Is Being Left Behind." *Globe and Mail*. 15 Dec. 2013. www.theglobeandmail.com/report-on-business/economy/as-the -dairy-industry-goes-global-canada-is-being-left-behind/article15977477.

15. Mitchell, Tom, and Neil Hume. "China Fines Milk Formula Makers in Pricing Probe." *Financial Times*. 7 Aug. 2013. www.ft.com/intl/cms/s/0/d40bda56-ff06 -11e2-97dc-00144feabdc0.html?siteedition=intl#axzz3LDg1169c.

16. Mitchell, Tom. "Milk Powder Groups Rethink High Prices in China amid Crackdown." *Financial Times*. 9 Aug. 2013. www.ft.com/intl/cms/s/0/2f122908 -00d5-11e3-8918-00144feab7de.html#axzz3LDg1169c.

17. Chin, Josh. "Xi Jinping Gets Mocked Going after New Zealand on Food Safety." *Wall Street Journal*. 7 Oct. 2013. http://blogs.wsj.com/chinarealtime/2013/10/07/ xi-jinping-gets-mocked-going-after-new-zealand-on-food-safety.

18. Adams, Christopher. "Fonterra's Botulism Scandal 'Gift' to China Govt." *New Zealand Herald*. 18 Oct. 2013. www.nzherald.co.nz/business/news/article .cfm?c_id=3&objectid=11141873.

19. "Fonterra Announces Tie-up with Big China Dairy Firm." BBC News. 27 Aug. 2014. www.bbc.com/news/business-28948102. With analysis from John Sudworth, BBC News, Shanghai.

20. "Buyers and Brands Beware in China." *Wall Street Journal*. 24 July 2014. http:// online.wsj.com/articles/buyers-and-brands-beware-in-china-1406220037.

21. Smyth, Jamie. "Australia: From Mining to Dining." *Financial Times*. 2 June 2014. www.ft.com/intl/cms/s/0/4161f052-e586-11e3-8b90-00144feabdc0.html# axzz3LDg1169c.

22. Shufelt, Tim. "The Next Frontier of Branding." *National Post*. 27 Jan. 2011. http://business.financialpost.com/2011/01/27/the-next-frontier-of-branding -2.

23. Ma, Damien, and William Adams. *In Line behind a Billion People*. Upper Saddle River, NJ: FT Press, 2013. 49–74.

24. Twilley, Nicola. "What Do Chinese Dumplings Have to Do with Global Warming?"

New York Times. 25 July 2014. www.nytimes.com/2014/07/27/magazine/what-do
-chinese-dumplings-have-to-do-with-global-warming.html.

25. Hornby, Lucy, and Gregory Meyer. "China's Cofco Takes on Global Trading Houses." *Financial Times*. 5 Mar. 2014. www.ft.com/intl/cms/s/0/978dae32-a452
-11e3-b915-00144feab7de.html#slide0.

26. Minter, Adam. "Coming Your Way: China's Rotten Apples." *Bloomberg*. 30 Sep. 2013. www.bloombergview.com/articles/2013-09-30/coming-your-way-china-s
-rotten-apples.

27. Lee, Jolie. "PetSmart, Petco to Stop Selling Dog and Cat Treats Made in China." *USA Today*. 21 May 2014. www.usatoday.com/story/news/nation-now/2014/05/
21/petco-dog-treats-china/9367449.

TWELVE: The Buddha of Compassion

1. Moore, Greg. "China's Cautious Participation in the UN Human Rights Regime." *Human Rights & Human Welfare* 1.1 (Jan. 2001). www.du.edu/korbel/hrhw/volumes/
2001/1-1/kent.pdf.

2. Ibid.

3. I was inspired to make this trip after reading Liao Yiwu's thought-provoking book about Christianity in China, *God Is Red*. New York: HarperCollins, 2011.

4. McGregor, Richard. *The Party*. New York: HarperCollins, 2010. 210–12.

5. Romalis, Coleman. "A Marxist Revolutionary Marches On." *Globe and Mail*. 16 July 1990.

6. Meehan, John D. *Chasing the Dragon in Shanghai*. Vancouver: UBC Press, 2011. 135.

7. McGoey, John H. *Nor Scrip Nor Shoes*. Boston: Atlantic/Little, Brown, 1958. 140–52.

8. Ibid., 159.

9. Craymer, Lucy. "Fiji Attracts Old Friends as China's Clout Grows." *Wall Street Journal*. 30 Oct. 2014. http://online.wsj.com/articles/fiji-attracts-old-friends-as
-chinas-clout-grows-1414678386.

10. Ibid.

11. Fitzgerald, John. "Why Values Matter in Australia's Relations with China." *The Asan Forum*. 13 June 2014. www.theasanforum.org/why-values-matter-in-australias
-relations-with-china.

12. Zhao, Ziyang. *Prisoner of the State: The Secret Journal of Zhao Ziyang*. Translated and edited by Bao Pu, Renee Chiang and Adi Ignatius. New York: Simon & Schuster, 2009. 271.

13. Lam, Willy. "Forgetting Tiananmen, and What Came before It." The Jamestown Foundation. 4 June 2014. www.jamestown.org/single/?tx_ttnews%

5Btt_news%5D=42467&tx_ttnews%5BbackPid%5D=7&cHash=
98f4dcc55ef666c8a4920d4c7b0891ce#.VIRgN410zIU.

14. This dilemma is carefully chronicled in Professor David Shambaugh's book *China's Communist Party: Atrophy and Adaptation*, a book I turned to frequently during my time in Beijing.

15. Espino, Nathaniel, and Stephen Tan. "U.K. Tibet Pledge Fostered China Deals, People's Daily Says." *Bloomberg*. 17 Oct. 2013. www.bloomberg.com/news/2013 -10-17/u-k-pledge-on-tibet-fostered-china-deals-people-s-daily-says.html.

16. "Osborne Offers a Red Carpet to China." *Financial Times*. 14 Oct. 2013. www.ft.com/ intl/cms/s/0/439d56a2-34c6-11e3-8148-00144feab7de.html#axzz3LDn6MAZ9.

17. White, Hugh. "Sharing Power with China." *New York Times*. 19 Mar. 2014. www .nytimes.com/2014/03/20/opinion/sharing-power-with-china.html.

18. Fallows, James. "Another Bloomberg Editor Explains Why He Has Resigned, over Its China Coverage." *Atlantic*. 25 Mar. 2014. www.theatlantic.com/international/ archive/2014/03/another-bloomberg-editor-explains-why-he-has-resigned-over -its-china-coverage/359565.

19. White, Hugh. *The China Choice*. Oxford, U.K.: Oxford University Press, 2013. 94–7.

20. Lowther, William. "Taiwanese, Hong Kongers Identify Less with China." *Taipei Times*. 23 Oct. 2014. www.taipeitimes.com/News/front/archives/2014/10/23/ 2003602704.

21. Luce, Edward. "Cameron's Britain Has Lost America's Respect." *Financial Times*. 16 Mar. 2014. www.ft.com/intl/cms/s/0/0356eb86-ab67-11e3-8cae -00144feab7de.html#axzz3LDn6MAZ9.

22. Sevastopulo, Demetri. "Former Hong Kong Official Says UK Failing to Defend Democracy." *Financial Times*. 22 June 2014. www.ft.com/intl/cms/s/0/e5501f1a -fa06-11e3-bb9d-00144feab7de.html#axzz3LDn6MAZ9.

THIRTEEN: From Kabul to Beijing

1. Christian Sarrazin, a dynamic and very engaging diplomat, was the new consul general, my boss. Deana Brynildsen helped build up our presence and was a steady hand at providing consular services to a growing Canadian population.

2. We were lucky to have as our ambassador in Beijing the deeply experienced Earl Drake. He worked closely with Howard Balloch, who ran the China desk in Ottawa and was one of the brightest policy minds in the department.

3. Hébert, Jacques, and Pierre Elliott Trudeau. *Two Innocents in Red China*. Toronto: Oxford University Press, 1968.

4. Ibid, ix.

5. Martin, Paul. Canada–China Business Council Dinner. Beijing, China. 21 Jan. 2005. Prime Minister's Address. www.l20.org/news/GE47_AddressbyPMPaulMartin.pdf.

6. Evans, Paul. *Engaging China*. Toronto: University of Toronto Press, 2014. 75.

7. Ibid., 90.

8. Ibid., 54.

9. The only solution is patient and persistent advocacy pitched at a level high enough and forceful enough to command attention but not so high and forceful as to back people into a corner or trigger a petulant response.

10. In Afghanistan, this kind of micromanagement was described as wielding the 10,000-kilometre screwdriver.

11. Deschamps, Tara. "Pricey Pandas Can't Turn Zoo's Year Around." *Toronto Star*. 24 June 2014. www.thestar.com/news/gta/2014/06/24/pricey_pandas_cant_turn_zoos_year_around.html.

12. China continues to promote its own separate plan for Asia Pacific free trade.

13. China and Australia signed their free trade agreement in November 2014.

CONCLUSION: Connecting the Dots

1. Evans, Gareth. "Middle Power Diplomacy." Chile Pacific Foundation. Santiago, Chile. 29 June 2011. Inaugural Edgardo Boeninger Memorial Lecture. www.gevans.org/speeches/speech441.htm.

2. This is evident in polling conducted by the Asia Pacific Foundation of Canada. See their "2014 National Opinion Poll: Canadian Views on Asia." 10 June 2014. www.asiapacific.ca/sites/default/files/filefield/national_opinion_poll_2014_final_0.pdf.

3. Australia established something similar, but at the level of deputy ministers.

4. Burney, Derek H., and Fen Osler Hampson. *Brave New Canada*. Montreal and Kingston: McGill-Queen's University Press. 2014. 16–17.

5. White, Hugh. *The China Choice*. New York: Oxford University Press, 2013. 145.

6. Mulroney, David, and Janet De Silva. "Canada's Asia Challenge: Creating Competence for the Next Generation of Canadians." Asia Pacific Foundation of Canada. 4 Nov. 2013. www.asiapacific.ca/sites/default/files/filefield/asia_competence_tf_-_final_revised_report.pdf.

7. A little encouragement from CEOs and business councils would also help!

Epilogue

1. Hood, Dora. *Davidson Black*. Toronto: University of Toronto Press, 1964. 60.

Acknowledgments

I owe many thanks to Janice Stein and the Munk School of Global Affairs for generously providing me with a perch from which to do my thinking and reading, and from which to launch my cross-Canada conversations. I have also benefitted greatly from my reconnecting, through the Munk School, with my alma mater, the University of Toronto. No other Canadian institution is so closely linked with the past, present and future of our relationship with China. U of T friends such as Joe Wong, Wendy Dobson, Rick Halpern, Ariana Bradford and Kai Xing have provided wise and generous advice.

I am also tremendously grateful to the Asia Pacific Foundation of Canada (APFC) for allowing me to join in their work of exploring how to prepare the next generation of Canadians for our Asian future. The APFC's former CEO, Yuen Pau Woo, has been a source of inspiration and advice for decades. I have since come to know and benefit from the collective wisdom of APFC colleagues such as Kasi Rao, Doug Goold, Eva Busza and Jordan Dupuis. And Erin Williams, faithful quarterback at the APFC for the "Asia competence" project, deserves special thanks for her patience, perseverance and great good sense.

Sarah Kutulakos, executive director of the Canada China Business Council, has thoughtfully explored a range of tough China issues with me, as has her boss, my long-time friend and mentor Peter Harder. I have sparred passionately with UBC's Paul Evans, and hope to continue doing so as long as he will join me in the ring of policy debate.

In China, I benefitted enormously from the thinking of Michael Pettis, David Shambaugh and James Fallows. And I have since followed their China work with great interest and pleasure. Bill Bishop's *Sinocism* blog continues to open my eyes to a world of highly relevant China reporting. Among the friendly guides in Beijing's diplomatic community, none were more amusing, engaging and generous than Mexico's then ambassador Jorge Guajardo and his wife, Paolo Sada. And no organization could have been kinder to Janet and me than the Beijing Center for Chinese Studies, which is associated with Loyola University Chicago.

Careers are nurtured and shaped by mentors, colleagues and friends. Don Campbell has been a thirty-year source of inspiration and good influence, and I owe a great deal to my more recent apprenticeships with people such as Jack Austin, John Manley, David Emerson and Kevin Lynch. Cathy Hesson, Sanjeev Chowdhury, Isabelle Savard, Owen Teo and Anne-Marie Regimbal taught me everything about loyalty, and, with Arif Lalani, Ron Hoffmann and Cindy Termorshuizen, reminded me of what the foreign service can be at its best. Two generations of wise Flannery women, Maria and Nereida, regularly encouraged me to look for the good in China. Tien Qing, a tireless educator of young women, and two courageous Vincentians, Tom Sendlein and Joe Loftus, helped me to find it.

My agent, Chris Bucci of Anne McDermid and Associates, helped bring this book to life over countless cups of coffee on Bloor Street. Diane Turbide and her team (with special thanks to Sandra Tooze and Justin Stoller) at Penguin Random House Canada and freelance editor Tara Tovell offered a rare blend of professionalism and kindness as they guided this neophyte through the many steps required to produce a manuscript worthy of their distinguished house.

And, finally, no words can convey the debt I owe to my patient and hugely supportive family. Janet, who opened up the world to me, continues to serve as my most trusted guide, and editor, in it. Aidan fed me constantly with a stream of articles that were timely, contentious or, much to my delight, just plain quirky. Kate's own writing set the bar for meticulous scholarship and absolute clarity. And although I entirely failed to meet her standard, I did at least manage to benefit from her introduction to the world of social media. Hong Kong–born Sean kept me focused on the situation in his hometown, something that encouraged me to remember what Canada owes to it. And Sherpa, happy in his new Canadian home, slept at my feet and kept me company through long and otherwise lonely hours of labour.

Index